W9-BYN-125

THE MEDIA ELITE

THE MEDIA ELITE

S. Robert Lichter
Stanley Rothman
Linda S. Lichter

ADLER&ADLER

The Media Elite is part of a larger study of social and political leadership in the United States of which Stanley Rothman is the director and S. Robert Lichter is the associate director. It is sponsored by the Center for the Study of Social and Political Change at Smith College, the Center for Media and Public Affairs, the Research Institute on International Change at Columbia University, and George Washington University.

Published in the United States in 1986 by
Adler & Adler, Publishers, Inc.
4550 Montgomery Avenue
Bethesda, Maryland 20814

Library of Congress Cataloging-in-Publication Data
Lichter, S. Robert.
  The media elite.
  Includes index.
  1. Mass media—United States. 2. Journalism—United States. I. Rothman,
Stanley, 1927–   . II. Lichter, Linda S. III. Title.
P92.U5L46 1986   001.51'0973   85-28747
ISBN 0-917561-11-2

First Edition

Printed in the United States of America

To Renatus Hartogs, Eleanor Rothman,
and Rose Batstone

CONTENTS

PREFACE

THIS BOOK looks at the social, psychological, and political milieu of the national media, and the relationship between this milieu and news coverage of controversial social issues. Our findings are the outcome of a lengthy and multifaceted empirical study that combined public opinion polling, psychological testing, and scientific content analysis. At the same time, this is the first installment of a series of books that will examine how social change in contemporary America is shaped by competition among elite groups. While the present volume is self-contained, its argument can best be understood in this broader context.

In 1956, C. Wright Mills described a self-perpetuating establishment of corporate, military, legal, and political leaders he called the power elite.[1] His notion that a few people with common social backgrounds and political outlooks made the key decisions that determined America's destiny was always overdrawn. Thirty years later, it has been completely overtaken by rapid change at the top. Today, the traditional elites are challenged by new opinion leaders and institutions that have gained immensely in influence since the 1960s. Among the emerging elites are the public interest movement, a vastly expanded federal bureaucracy, and a national media network that serves as watchdog over other social institutions.

The ultimate goal of our research is to illuminate the conflicts among these strategic elites and trace their impact on American life. Thus, this book is part of a larger study of leadership and social change in America, of which Stanley Rothman is director and S. Robert Lichter is associate director. This project was inaugurated by Rothman in 1977 to test his hypotheses about the role the new elites play in producing social and cultural change.

ix

He initially chose to compare business leaders, the archetypal elite of bourgeois industrial society, with the national media, a key elite of America's emerging post-industrial society. Later the project was expanded into a full-scale study of a dozen contemporary elite groups ranging from leaders in the military and religion to public interest groups and the entertainment industry.

In 1978, Robert Lichter joined the project with primary responsibility for the news media study and direction of the data collection and analysis. In 1979, Linda S. Lichter completed the research team as a specialist in content analysis and director of a study of television entertainment. This is the first of three volumes describing our findings, which will appear during the next two years. Robert Lichter is primary author of the current work on the news media; Linda Lichter will be primary author of a book on television entertainment; and Stanley Rothman will be primary author of a broader account of elite conflict and contemporary social change. That volume will present the findings of our entire range of elite surveys in the context of his theoretical framework.

This work focuses on the national media as an emerging elite whose role is central to understanding changing patterns of influence in American society. To a degree that was hardly envisaged a generation ago, the major media stand at the center of the struggle for social influence. They act as gatekeepers for the messages contending groups and individuals wish to send to each other and to the general public. As a result, considerable attention has been focused on the perspectives of those who staff national media organizations, as well as their coverage of controversial issues. Yet no previous empirical study has systematically examined both the life situations of these newspeople and the nature of their product, to determine whether or how the two are linked. This was the goal of our research. The studies in this book combine two distinct elements: a survey of the backgrounds, attitudes, and psychological traits of journalists at national media outlets, and content analyses of how these outlets covered some of the major social controversies of the past fifteen years.

The core of the book contains results from a survey of a random sample of journalists at America's leading national media:

the *New York Times, Washington Post, Wall Street Journal, Time, Newsweek, U.S. News and World Report,* the three major commercial television networks, ABC, CBS, and NBC, and public television. We examine their social backgrounds, political opinions, motivations, and orientations toward the news.

The book also presents the results of in-depth content analyses of three major public issues covered by the national media during the 1970s and early 1980s: busing to achieve integration, the safety of nuclear power, and the oil industry's role in the energy crisis.

There are unusual features to both the survey and the content analyses. In addition to standard attitude questions, the survey instrument contains tests designed to tap the manner in which journalists view news situations, and includes a set of ambiguous pictures, the Thematic Apperception Test (TAT), which those being interviewed were asked to interpret. The TAT is used widely by psychologists to study personality needs and motivational structures.

The content analyses are unusual both for their breadth and depth and for their attempt to establish norms against which news coverage is judged. For example, in order to check the accuracy with which journalists have reported the views of the scientific community on nuclear energy, we polled that community and compared their actual views with journalists' descriptions of them.

To minimize the possibility that we might affect responses through our participation, we hired Response Analysis, Inc., a commercial survey research firm, to administer the questionnaires and collate the data. Moreover, the psychological material was scored by professionals who knew nothing about either the nature of the study or the persons interviewed. The content analysis involved the development of empirical coding categories, which can be reviewed and replicated by other scholars. The computer tapes have been placed on file at the Roper Survey Center at the University of Connecticut for this purpose.

Our methods and instruments are explained in general, nontechnical terms in various chapters of this book. Additional details are provided in an appendix.[2]

The book consists of nine chapters. The first describes both the unique and lasting features of the American media and the rapid changes they have undergone during the past two decades. Chapter Two outlines our findings on journalists' backgrounds and attitudes and develops the argument that the national media have become a new elite. We also compare today's leading journalists with a recent class from the Columbia University Graduate School of Journalism, for a glimpse at some of tomorrow's potential media leaders.

Chapter Three goes beyond surface attitudes to examine the orientations and preconceptions journalists bring with them in covering the news. We consider their choice of reliable sources, their selective perceptions of newsworthy events, and the ways they interpret ambiguous social situations in light of their preexisting worldviews. The purpose is to show how social and psychological factors can structure journalists' interpretations and descriptions of reality in ways that are powerful, if subtle. The underlying theme of this chapter is that much of the debate over media bias is misguided. Addressing only the crudest overt instances of how journalists' preconceptions shape their view of the news distracts attention from the far more prevalent and subtle psychological processes that can operate beneath the level of conscious awareness.

Chapter Four takes us deeper still into the psychology of leading journalists. By analyzing motivational material from the Thematic Apperception Tests, we create a profile of the national media based on their scores on social psychological dimensions, such as the needs for power and achievement. After presenting the findings, we speculate as to how these inner forces might help explain some features of contemporary journalistic behavior, ranging from a focus on scoops to an adversarial stance toward politicians.

With Chapter Five our focus shifts from the newspeople to their product. We discuss the role subjective or personal elements play in all news coverage. If the news is something more than a mirror of reality, how can one take its measure, since all reality is mediated in one way or another? We describe a technique for judging news content by the procedures of scientific content analysis in conjunction with reviews of expert or scholarly opinion. We then proceed to our three examples of content analysis, which contrast expert opinion with news coverage of social issues that combine technical and political elements.

Chapter Six begins with our most thorough content study, that of nuclear safety. We trace the path of information leading from scientific and technical opinion through journalistic attitudes and practices and, finally, news coverage. As a norm against which to gauge media coverage of this issue, we surveyed large samples of scientists, engineers, and decision makers, as well as journalists, on their attitudes toward nuclear power.

We asked Dr. Robert Rycroft to serve as project director for this study. Dr. Rycroft, a political scientist who is associate director of the Graduate Program in Science, Technology, and Public Policy at George Washington University, first surveyed the technical literature on nuclear safety. On the basis of his survey, we developed a content analysis system to determine how major media covered the significant issues in this field from 1970 through 1983. Finally, we compared the results of our polls and literature review with the content analysis to compare news coverage with the views of scientists and other experts.

The other content analyses followed this approach of comparing expert knowledge with media coverage, though we lacked the resources to actually poll the experts on busing and the economics of petroleum. Chapter Seven presents findings on media coverage of busing for racial integration from 1971 through 1979. The project director for this study was Dr. Donald Jensen, who is a research associate of Stanford University's Institute for Research on Educational Finance and Governance. He reviewed the literature on the social scientific evidence on controversies ranging from white flight to minority achievement. The research team then developed coding categories and analyzed coverage of the significant issues in this debate.

The last content analysis, presented in Chapter Eight, concerns the role of the oil industry in the energy crisis of the 1970s. The research team for this project consisted of several individuals with advanced training and/or professional experience in international economics. The literature review was conducted by Eileen McColgan (M.B.A., Graduate School of Business, Columbia University). The coding was supervised by Karen Grip (M.A., School of International Affairs, Columbia University) and Joseph Hakin (M.A., School of Foreign Service, Georgetown University). The data analysis was conducted by Leslie Moushey (M.A., international relations, Goddard College).

We chose to study the long-range coverage of complex and ambiguous social issues, because underlying assumptions that affect the ways journalists view reality are more likely to show up there than in the coverage of relatively short-term and highly structured events, such as legislative debates or election campaigns.[3]

Finally, Chapter Nine reviews our findings and recapitulates the overall argument about the relationship between journalists and their work. This conclusion is also an introduction to the next phase of our ongoing research, which will consider the role journalists and other strategic elites play in the current transformation of American society.

Many people and several institutions assisted in the various phases of the research. The project was made possible by grants from the following foundations: Earhart, Harry Frank Guggenheim, Institute for Educational Affairs, John M. Olin, and Sarah Scaife. Institutional support was provided by Smith College, the Research Institute on International Change at Columbia University, and the Graduate Program in Science, Technology, and Public Policy at George Washington University. The surveys of journalists and businessmen were conducted by Response Analysis, Inc., under the supervision of Al Vogel. Other phases of the project were administered with the assistance of Dan Amundson, Barbara Benham, Robert Cohen, Jessica Fowler, Karen Grip, Rosemary Hollis, Janice and Carol Mason, and Sharon Shambra. Abigail Stewart and David Winter helped us to obtain TAT coders. John Williams and Alan McArdle brought welcome order to the chaos of the computer analysis. We also wish to thank collectively the many student coders and research assistants who contributed their time and skills. We are grateful for William C. Adams' close reading of the draft manuscript, which prompted substantial revision and, we hope, improvement of the final product. Finally, Audrey Wolf, our agent, and George Walsh, our editor at Adler & Adler, brought fresh perspectives to the work that helped shape a more readable manuscript.

THE MEDIA ELITE

THE RISE OF THE NATIONAL MEDIA

"This has been the best generation of all in which to have lived as a journalist in this country."

—Eric Severeid, CBS

SOME YEARS AGO, a reporter told the president, then late in his second term, that he hoped the press hadn't made the president's job too difficult. The puzzled occupant of the White House responded, "What could *you* do to *me?*" It is difficult to imagine those words coming from Richard Nixon or Lyndon Johnson. As economist Herbert Stein comments in recounting this anecdote, "No president since Eisenhower would or could have said that."[1]

In this era of the celebrity journalist and allegedly imperial media, it is important to remember how far the profession has progressed in recent years. Journalism's rapid rise to social prominence is bound up with a host of changes that have transformed American life during the past quarter century. The emergence of national networks in higher education, communications, and transportation have ensured that residents of Manhattan, Kansas, have access to much the same social images as their New York City namesakes. In today's information-hungry society, the media increasingly play a crucial role in linking social and political elites to one another and to the general public.

This expanded role, and the social changes underlying it, are responsible for the new elite status that the national media now enjoy. It is also responsible for the rising number of media critics. Indeed, the increased scrutiny of news reports may be the supreme compliment to the media's perceived importance. Unfortunately, much current media criticism is confined to short-term instant analysis. It is criticism of the moment at the moment, no less than news itself, and it is similarly limited by the ephemeral nature of the material. If we are to understand the media's changing role as society's mythmaker, transmitter of our shared sense of social reality, we must begin by taking a longer view.

Media Made in America

It is no accident that America, despite its relatively short history, took the lead in establishing a relatively free press. The rapid democratization of American life, under the aegis of the classical liberal ideology that defined the nation, is certainly responsible for that development.[2]

Ideologically, America has been the quintessential bourgeois capitalist nation. Classical liberalism, with its commitment to individualism, freedom, equality, private property, and democracy, provided the common philosophical groundwork for both the liberal and conservative camps in American politics.[3] This liberal-capitalist ideology emerged in England from a secularized version of Calvinism. There and in Europe, however, liberal-capitalism developed in the midst of societies emerging from feudalism—societies containing aristocracies, peasantries, and long historical traditions.

In Europe, liberal-capitalism was part of a complex whole; in America it was everything. As America lacked a peasantry, so it lacked a genuine aristocracy, except for remnants from British rule. And as it lacked a feudal heritage, so it lacked a history with which to compare itself. For these reasons America developed neither a class-conscious middle class, nor a class-conscious working class.

2

This heritage is also partly responsible for the fact that journalism for the masses first developed in the United States, followed closely by England and other Western European countries. The absence of sharp class prejudices and divisions in America made it easier to envisage a mass press. Further, the United States pioneered the technology of the mass press, just as it was to lead the world in the development of the automobile and television for the masses.[4]

While both America and Western Europe have been the home of a free press, the American media (both newspapers and television) have always differed from the European media for reasons having to do with cultural, economic, and political factors as well as with the sheer size of the United States.[5]

First, the mass media in the United States have been primarily privately owned businesses, even though radio and television operate within the framework of public regulation of a sort. Yet in most European countries, both radio and television have been primarily public enterprises. Even where private enterprise has recently come to play a more significant role, it is far less important than in this country.

Second, while newspapers in the United States and Western Europe are privately owned enterprises, the historical tradition in the United States has been quite different. In Europe, many newspapers and magazines began as the organs of political parties and remained closely affiliated with them. Others began as organs of the Catholic church, especially in countries such as Germany, where Catholics considered themselves an embattled minority, or France, where the church felt that it was crucial to protect its flock from the secularizing and anticlerical tendencies of the political Left's presses.

The American pattern was quite different. To be sure, some newspapers were party affiliated, and the Catholic press in this country (as well as papers produced by other religious groups) played some role. Since the mid-nineteenth century, however, few publishers have emphasized such group attachments. That left them free to concentrate on making profits, expressing their views, and reporting the news. Even before the ideal of objective

3

reporting began to take hold in the United States in the late nineteenth century, editors and reporters were not intellectuals. They also had little sense of the clash of ideological positions so characteristic of European countries.[6]

The differences between the European and American press tell us a good deal about the American heritage. The United States was characterized by a broad ideological consensus during the nineteenth and early twentieth centuries. It was assumed that both liberalism (i.e., a democratic republic) and capitalism had been handed down from on high. America did not develop a mass socialist party; nor did it develop a traditional conservative party. For some of the same reasons, the country lacked explicitly ethnic or religious parties. To become an American meant to see oneself primarily as a free individual, not as the member of some corporate group. One could join, indeed was encouraged to join, various ethnic or religious groups, but one did not form political parties based on them. To do so would have violated the underlying American compact.[7]

It is no accident that the notion of objective news reportage was first fully institutionalized in the United States at a time when most European newspapers still emphasized interpretive commentary. Living within the framework of a broad ideological consensus, American newsmen, like most other Americans, found it difficult to recognize that their view of the world might be shaped by a particular set of premises, a paradigm or *Weltanschauung,* which strongly influenced their views of social causation and hence their view of what the facts were. Under such circumstances the facts were merely the facts. As Michael Schudson notes,

> Before the 1920's, journalists did not think much about the subjectivity of perception. They had relatively little incentive to doubt the firmness of the "reality" by which they lived. American society . . . remained buoyant with hope and promise. Democracy was a value unquestioned in politics; free enterprise was still widely worshipped in economic life; the novels of Horatio Alger sold well. Few people doubted the inevitability of progress.[8]

4

Even in the 1920s and 1930s, as awareness of the inevitable elements of subjectivity in news reporting began to grow in this country, the response was to place greater emphasis on scientific understanding and training in order to approximate as closely as possible an objective reporting of the facts.[9]

On the other hand, the best European journalists, writing in societies rent by more severe social conflicts and political parties and ideologies based upon them, were far more aware that perceptions of social action flowed partly from the assumptions people brought to them. These historical differences still influence the manner in which American and European journalists approach the news. Despite their greater sophistication today, those in America still seem to find it difficult to recognize that the facts are not merely given, but rather are, to some extent, determined by the perspective one brings to them.

The American propensity for (and enjoyment of) exposing and denouncing political leaders stems from a powerful populist strain in the classical liberal tradition. Americans may have felt a strong attachment to their socio-political system, but they were wary of those to whom they delegated political power. As de Tocqueville noted, Americans have always been more than willing to criticize, expose, and denounce "political malefactors," though less likely to develop fundamental criticisms of the political system than their European counterparts.[10]

This difference is also partly cultural in origin. The European establishment has always considered the maintenance of order problematic. Their view derives from a classical conservative worldview. Since the mid-nineteenth century, Americans have generally assumed that order is relatively easy to maintain if the people are properly informed. To them the great danger lies in the possible tyranny of those chosen to govern.

One other unique quality of the American media deserves mention. Unlike most Western European countries, America has historically lacked a national press. To be sure, there were magazines with national circulations, growing newspaper chains, and, even before World War II, a very few prestigious newspapers such as the *New York Times*, which boasted a national influence.

5

However, localism was the dominant theme. The twenties may have roared in New York and Chicago, but Babbitt dominated Main Street in most cities around the country, including the ethnic enclaves of metropolitan areas. In the short run, at least, most Americans remained relatively unaffected by the middle- and upper-class culture of the few cosmopolitan centers.

All these features of the American media predominated until after World War II. Even in the midst of the great depression, most Americans were not especially conscious of New York or even Washington. Most also accepted the basic cultural and social parameters of their society as good and right and thought that those who wished to change them radically were either odd or evil. This view was reinforced by the images obtained from the newspapers, radio, and Hollywood. Newspaper publishers were relatively conservative, as were those who controlled the airwaves and motion pictures.[11]

The working press was probably more liberal than were publishers, and some newsmen were even radicals. But the reins of authority were in the hands of the publishers, and reporters who wanted to keep their jobs stayed in line. Publishers and network officials also actively catered to the preferences of their advertisers.

For the most part, however, the threat of economic pressure was not the major force behind the media's conservatism. News and entertainment took the hue they did largely because publishers and most reporters believed that was the way it was and should be. Key elites in American society accepted the broad framework of the American ideological consensus, and most did not even realize that there might be other ways to look at the world. Walter Lippmann, criticizing the *New York Times'* hostile coverage of the Bolshevik regime in the 1920s, correctly pointed out that the issue was not the control of publishers or advertisers:

> The news as a whole is dominated by the hopes of men who composed the news organization. . . . In the large, news about Russia is a case of seeing not what was, but what men wished

to see. . . . The chief censor and the chief propagandist were hope
and fear in the minds of reporters and editors.[12]

There were surely, in New York and a few other places, small
groups of radicals publishing journals, organizing workers, and,
with the onset of the New Deal, even entering government. For
the most part, however, their influence on the broader social,
cultural, and political underpinnings of society was marginal.
Even when some of these people rose to positions in the culture
where they might have an impact, a sense of limits (and fear) held
them back.

Television and the New Sensibility

Meanwhile, the nature of the American mass media was changing.
The changes were a function of both technology and affluence.
Improvements in communication led to the development of journals with large national audiences, while the development of the
jet airplane, universal automobile ownership, and a national high-
way system contributed to the breakdown of regional differences
and isolation.

Radio had also developed national audiences, and by the 1930s,
newspaper chains were forming, and national magazines, led by
Time and *Life*, were changing the consciousness of Americans.

Thus, the United States was beginning to develop a national
media network; that is, a relatively small group of media outlets
was increasingly determining the manner in which the world was
being presented to Americans. And these outlets were largely
centered in New York and, for political news, Washington.

The development of a national media network did not really
come to fruition until the late 1950s and early 1960s. This was due,
in part, to the emergence of television. By 1958, the number of
television sets almost equalled the number of American homes,
and the age of television began, dominated immediately by the
three major networks centered in New York. Given the expense
of producing programs, local stations came to depend on the
networks for both entertainment and news programs. At the same

7

time, the rapid growth of newspaper chains, and the death of major newspapers like the *Washington Star*, reduced diversity within the daily press. By 1976, media scholars Thomas Patterson and Ronald Abeles worried that, "Decisions about what the public will know rest increasingly upon the beliefs of the small elite which determines what they should know."[13]

By its very nature television added new dimensions to the communication of information, and radically changed the rules of the game.[14] By the middle 1960s, television was already transforming America. Most Americans owned television sets, and adults and children were watching television programs six to seven hours a day. Television had become an integral part of American life.

Television is a major business in a competitive capitalist society. Whatever the social and political views of those who make decisions, the bottom line was, and is, capturing audience attention and increasing the size of audiences. This is what produces profits and ensures solvency.

Given network television's need for mass audiences, and the visual and experiential information it conveys, its emphasis is bound to be on the personal and dramatic rather than the abstract and discursive.

It is difficult to distinguish the effects of television as an instrument of communication from its character as a commercial enterprise, but television clearly provides its audience with a sense that what it views is true and real far more than newspapers, radio, or movies. The audience sees events taking place in its living room. Stories, documentaries, even drama assume a reality with which other media cannot compete. Events are seen "as they happen." The written word can be discounted, but pictures seen in the privacy of one's home are more compelling.

Television has also broken down class and regional boundaries to a far greater extent than other media. Newspapers and books are segregated by area of distribution and readership. Few but the well educated read books on serious subjects, and the style of the *New York Times* appeals mainly to those with higher levels of education and affluence. Thus, newspapers and books encourage the segregation of knowledge. Radio begins to break down that

8

segregation. Television goes much further. The news is watched by millions of Americans of all educational and social backgrounds, and they see the same pictures and receive the same information.

Television breaks down regional boundaries in information retrieval as well. The same voices, the same accents, and the same lifestyles reach rural areas in Arkansas as readily as the upper East Side of New York. Insofar as those who live on New York's upper East Side or in Los Angeles help create the reality America sees, so they help change the expectations and outlooks of Americans.

At one time a young person from a rural background or a small town experienced a genuine culture shock upon enrolling in an eastern elite college or even a major state university. He or she experienced new and different lifestyles for the first time. The cultural gap between rural America, the main streets of small-town America, and urban metropolitan areas has been considerably narrowed, and the influence of new metropolitan styles created in New York or Los Angeles spreads far more rapidly than it once did.

This narrowing cultural gap has played an important role in weakening traditional ties of church, ethnic group, and neighborhood. It has contributed to American social and geographic mobility as much as the revolution in transportation, in part because it has enabled Americans to feel almost equally at home in Oshkosh, New York, or Dallas. It has homogenized American culture and nationalized it.

It is impossible to understand the revolution that took place in American values and attitudes during the 1960s and 1970s without taking into account the influence of television on the fabric of American life. For the first time metropolitan America was becoming all of America.

America has become, as Richard Merelman points out in *Making Something of Ourselves,* a "loose bounded culture."[15] Americans' primordial ties to family, locality, church, and what is considered appropriate behavior have eroded, and Americans have lost their sense of place. They are not alone in this: their experience is shared increasingly by Europeans and Japanese, and

9

certainly mass television is not the only factor at work. The revolution is real, however, and the epoch we live in is quite new. As Merelman puts it:

> The contemporary weakness of the Puritan, democratic and class visions of America has released large numbers of Americans from comprehensive group identifications and from firm social moorings. The liberated individual, not the social group must therefore become the basic cultural unit. . . . Group membership . . . becomes voluntary, contingent and fluid, not "given," fixed, and rigid.[16]

Working-class parochials may continue to identify with their co-workers, acquaintances, and neighbors, but public reality is now such that we also know and develop intimate and intense relationships with public figures of all kinds to a far greater extent than we once did. The stars of television, from anchormen, to rock performers, to politicians, have become pseudo-intimate acquaintances.

The impact of television on the substance of politics has been at least as great as it has been on our personal life. When viewing political events, the facial expressions and hand or eye gestures employed by political figures during an interview add a concrete dimension to these people. Politicians who perspire on television lose points with the public. The camera can make a political figure look as if he or she is evading a question or is stammering and confused, and situations that might never appear in print, or at least would not have the same impact, routinely appear on television.

Politicians and other newsmakers are caught exhibiting behavior on stage that in other epochs would have occurred only off stage, thus breaking down the barrier between the two realms. In print, for example, politicians and others can set their thoughts down carefully. They conceal their doubts, their boredom, their prejudices when they present public statements. In the age of television, however, this is far more difficult, especially in time of crisis. As television becomes more and more ubiquitous, we all have increasing access to backstage behavior.

The television revolution has also affected the approach of newspapers and newsmagazines. In part, it has forced them to turn to in-depth reportage of the kind television handles much less effectively. It has also encouraged them, partly for competitive reasons, and partly because television has created a new atmosphere, to seek out the same dramatic offstage exposés that television can achieve. However much Vietnam and Watergate later contributed to the development of an adversary press, so did the changing assumptions of media personnel as to what constitutes news and how one deals with political figures.

Paradoxically, the advent of television increased the influence of a few East Coast newspapers and magazines. What television had done, of course, was to nationalize and standardize communication to an extent never before achieved in the United States. New York and Washington styles and modes now became national styles and modes. The *New York Times* was read by the New York and the Washington elites, and by those who produced the news for the television networks. Thanks to their amplification via television, the issues the *Times* considered important and the approach it took to them would become national currency.[17]

Most studies agree that the key national news media today consist of national television, the *New York Times,* the *Washington Post,* the *Wall Street Journal, Time, Newsweek,* and possibly *U.S. News and World Report.*[18]

Since the early 1960s, television has been the main source of news for the greatest number of Americans. Moreover, the public consistently rates it above the print media and radio in terms of credibility and fairness.[19] Despite recent competition from Cable News Network and elsewhere, ABC, CBS, and NBC continue to hold the lion's share of the audience. On the average, approximately 50 million people per night watch one of these three evening newscasts. The Public Broadcasting Service is also important for its upscale audience and the high prestige of its news division.[20]

Among print media, the newspapers and magazines listed above outpace all others in their ability to reach decision-makers and opinion leaders, as several studies show. For example, Columbia University's Bureau of Applied Social Research examined the reading habits of top leaders of American institutions, ranging from senators and cabinet members to presidents of large labor unions and chief executive officers of major corporations.[21] Among newspapers, the *Times* was most widely read, but the *Post* was preeminent among Washington officialdom, and the *Journal* won out in the business community. The three major newsmagazines were just as dominant among periodicals. *U.S. News* usually finished behind *Time* and *Newsweek*, but it was competitive in official Washington, placing first on Capitol Hill.

No other magazine or newspapers came close to these six outlets in their access to America's leaders. These media are read by various leadership groups because they are perceived as influential and important, and they are influential and important because they are read by such groups.

The Sixties and Beyond

Even as the influence of the media grew, the nature of the journalistic community was changing. In the old days, most journalists, like most Americans, went to work with high school diplomas at best. While some journalists and executives on leading papers were from upper-middle-class backgrounds, journalism most often was a source of social mobility for working-class and lower-middle-class youth. The generally Democratic sympathies of working reporters in the 1930s were partly a function of their class background.

After World War II the pattern changed. Increasingly young people from upper-middle-class backgrounds began to seek jobs in newspapers and television as an exciting and creative career that would also have an impact on society. By 1961, a survey of the Washington press corps found that four out of five members were college graduates and one in five possessed a graduate degree.[22]

The professionalization of journalism reflected broader social changes. Although enrollment at American universities had been growing since the turn of the century, the post–World War II period saw a quantum jump in college attendance. In 1940, only 5 percent of Americans over twenty-five years old held college degrees. Thirty years later their number had tripled, surpassing the ten million mark. Between 1950 and 1974 the number of professionals in the work force also tripled, jumping from four to over twelve million.[23]

This boom in education was bound up with America's economic growth and our movement toward a post-industrial society fueled more by information than smokestacks. The number of college faculty reached a half million by the mid-1960s, and social policy increasingly came to depend on trained professionals whose ideas were formed in universities. By the 1960s, the number of these "metro-Americans," in Eric Goldman's phrase, had reached a critical mass capable of setting the tone of intellectual life.[24]

The combination of unprecedented affluence and intellectual and cultural sophistication produced a cosmopolitan sensibility that clashed sharply with the verities of small-town America. Skeptical toward received truths and civic myths, critical of traditional norms and the authorities who upheld them, the new strata of intellectuals and skilled professionals fanned out from the universities into government, think tanks, consulting firms, and other elements of the public arena.

Subtly but inexorably the national press shifted its focus to accommodate the upsurge of new opinion leaders and trendsetters. Coverage of the social and behavioral sciences increased, and with it the need for more sophisticated and highly educated reporters who could keep up with intellectual developments and their social and political consequences. Inevitably, this meant that many top journalists would go to the same elite schools and study the same material as the sociologists, psychologists, and economists whose work percolated down into the public arena. In order to keep the average American informed about these developments, the traditionally anti-intellectual working press was becoming an adjunct to the intelligentsia. The days were numbered for the self-educated newspaperman whose only degree was from the school of hard knocks. In his place a new generation of educated professionals began to bring the milieu of upper-status cosmopolitanism into the newsroom.

Then, in the 1960s, a changing journalistic profession suddenly collided with a series of political conflicts. The result would prove

13

fateful for both the media and society. In its broad contours this is a familiar story, and we need only recall it briefly here. During the early 1960s many young reporters, just out of college, cut their teeth on the civil rights revolution. A then-novel scenario of protest, repression, outrage, and renewed protest was played out in small towns and big cities across the South. This drama was carried to a national audience by television crews and by print reporters. The historic 1964 Civil Rights Act owed much to the newfound power of television to mobilize a new consensus on a political hot potato. In one study, almost two-thirds of the network correspondents interviewed credited network news for the passage of civil rights legislation. According to one NBC correspondent, "We showed [the American public] what was happening: the brutality, the police dogs, the miserable conditions [blacks] were forced to live in. We made it impossible for Congress not to act."[25]

In covering this struggle journalists could experience the exhilaration of acting as patrons of the oppressed.[26] To present this story from a racist's viewpoint, rather than a Martin Luther King's, would have been unthinkable. Good reporting seemed to permit or even require a point of view and a choice of one side against another.

Hard on the heels of the civil rights drama came another story that pitted the press against political authority, but in far more problematic and polarizing circumstances. The current era of more adversarial media-government relations probably dates from 1965, the year American advisors were replaced by regular forces in Vietnam. That summer CBS correspondent Morley Safer accompanied a Marine unit on a search-and-destroy mission in the village of Cam Ne. Safer sent back a dramatic report showing the Marines using their cigarette lighters to ignite the huts of the villagers. His story stressed the futility of the operation and the Marines' apparent casual cruelty. In his "closer" he asserted, "to a Vietnamese peasant whose home means a lifetime of back-breaking labor, it will take more than presidential promises to convince him that we are on his side."[27]

The immediate effect of this broadcast was to sour the relationship between CBS and the Johnson administration, a portent of future conflict. The Cam Ne story also became the prototype for the battlefield vignette, a genre of reportage that presaged a new style of television coverage. For it was not simply Safer's critical perspective that distinguished his report. It was the entire style of the story, which was far more emotional and interpretive than that of traditional journalism.[28]

Most importantly, the media were thrust into the middle of the Vietnam debate, which divided newsrooms as well as homes and offices. For the next eight years, the tenor of Vietnam coverage itself became the focus of heated debate and recurring acrimony during the Johnson and Nixon administrations. Television was most often the lightning rod. But the prestige press was also thrust into the spotlight, most prominently when the *New York Times* and *Washington Post,* along with the *Boston Globe,* published the Pentagon Papers.

Tensions reached a crescendo during and after the 1968 Tet offensive, when journalistic criticism of Vietnam policy was capped by Walter Cronkite's on-air call for peace negotiations. Press critics, most prominently former Saigon correspondent Peter Braestrup, later charged that the media had misrepresented the outcome and significance of Tet.[29] The resulting mistrust between the media and military has not yet abated.

In the early 1970s, even as America's Vietnam involvement wound down, a third front appeared in the now ongoing media-government conflict. Watergate became the next major long-running story in a decade to pit the national media against political authority. This time the *Washington Post* took the lead, though the *New York Times* and television also played major roles. In fact, the public image of a more adversarial media probably owes less to Bob Woodward and Carl Bernstein's investigations than to the celebrated confrontation between President Nixon and CBS White House correspondent Dan Rather.

In the years that followed Watergate, the national media rode a wave of popularity and perceived power. They appeared to have chosen the "right" side in the critical conflicts of a turbulent decade. Moreover, they had consistently picked the winning side.

They prevailed in conflicts with such seemingly entrenched forces as southern segregationists, Vietnam hawks, and two once-popular presidents. They were courted by politicians and revered on college campuses. Investigative journalism inherited the cachet young activists had earlier conferred on the Peace Corps and Nader's raiders. Bright and idealistic young people flocked to the profession, lured by the prospect of exercising both personal creativity and social influence, not to mention the chance for fame and fortune.

Inevitably, this wave of popularity crested and broke. By the early 1980s, public confidence in the press had dropped sharply from its Watergate high point.[30] Public criticism of media negativism and lack of fairness also began to emerge.[31] A series of scandals and libel suits also seemed to cast doubt on the credibility of several major media outlets. At one point three of the most important and prestigious news organizations simultaneously faced embarrassing and financially threatening lawsuits—CBS from General William Westmoreland, *Time* from Israeli Defense Minister Ariel Sharon, and the *Washington Post* from Mobil Oil's chief executive officer.

Public disenchantment with the media may simply reflect changes in the social agenda. After Watergate, the great issues of the day offered less opportunity for the media to play the role of public tribune. Issues like inflation and energy could neither be explained nor solved by public morality plays. Television played a major role in the Iranian hostage crisis, but the cameras proved impotent in resolving the events they conveyed. Then, in the 1980s, an upsurge of national pride, almost in reaction against a decade of bad news, seemed to catch the media by surprise. For the first time in two decades, the critical and reformist strain of national journalism seemed to go against the grain of a changing *Zeitgeist.*

A profusion of conferences and columnists have debated the significance of the public's apparent loss of confidence in the media. In actuality, though, they may not have risen so high nor fallen so low as the conventional wisdom holds. Sociologists Gladys and Kurt Lang recently deflated the popular myth of two unknown reporters bringing down a president during Watergate.[32]

Even in that time of triumph, the Langs show that the media were less initiators than translators of elite conflicts to the general public. As for their fall from grace, journalist and opinion analyst David Gergen has shown that the public continues to hold very mixed feelings about the media.[33] Indeed the criticism to some degree reflects a more general loss of confidence in social institutions (for which the media, ironically, are often blamed).[34] And a 1985 Gallup–*Times Mirror* survey concluded that the public supports a free press and gives it high marks for credibility, but is quite critical of journalists' day-to-day performances.[35] Gallup president Andrew Kohut summarized the findings, "We believe and value what [journalists] tell us, even while we also believe they can be rude, biased, subject to outside influence and prone to other sins as well."[36]

Even if their rising power and falling popularity are sometimes overestimated, the national media have unquestionably become a major force in American life and a lightning rod for political activists and social critics. It may be hyperbole that "one correspondent with one cameraman [can] become as important as . . . twenty senators," as David Halberstam wrote of Safer's Cam Ne report.[37] It may be apocryphal that Lyndon Johnson decided his Vietnam policies were doomed after he watched Walter Cronkite reject them. It may be an overstatement that Woodward and Bernstein toppled Richard Nixon. Yet all these instances of media impact are not only plausible but widely believed. This in itself illustrates the enormous strides in social influence the national media have taken in the past quarter century. Once only a William Randolph Hearst or a Henry Luce might have been credited with starting or stopping a war, electing or defeating a president. Now the focus of acclaim and blame alike has passed from the press lords to working journalists themselves.

This newfound prominence has its price. Even as journalists are courted by politicians and fêted as celebrities, they are regularly attacked for biased or one-sided coverage. Interest groups at every point on the political spectrum are well aware that they need the major media to get their point of view across. So it is not surprising that they should use sticks as well as carrots in their efforts to secure a good press. Thus the media (especially television) have been criticized as unfair to both business and labor,[38] to Israel and the Arab states alike,[39] and as tools of capitalist domination and communist disinformation.[40] Many of the darts are thrown by the political Right, whether in the form of Accuracy in Media's bimonthly barbs[41] or Senator Jesse Helms' dream for conservatives to take over CBS. Less publicized but equally entrenched is a leftist school of academic criticism that treats the media as a tool of establishment hegemony. In this view, journalists' reformist instincts merely provide a safety valve that protects the system from the most serious consequences of its internal contradictions.[42]

As critics to the left and right of them volley and thunder, some journalists don the traditional armor of objectivity. Others admit that total objectivity is impossible but insist that fairness is their goal. Still others wage a counterattack, asserting that, in a *Wall Street Journal* columnist's phrase, "media bias is in [the] eye of the beholder."[43] There is some truth in all three responses. As noted earlier, the American media have long aspired to an ideal of objective journalism. As interpretive reporting has increased in recent years, fairness has become the current incarnation of the striving for nonpartisan reportage. Finally, some press criticism undoubtedly reflects a belief that the media have deviated from a correct political "line."

The problem with these responses from the media is that they do not go deep enough. It is not only press critics but also journalists whose perspectives may influence their judgment of the news. Striving for fairness or objectivity cannot eliminate this problem. At best it narrows the parameters within which personal perspectives operate. Thus the author of *Time*'s "Newswatch" column recently rejected a critic's suggestion that the press pay more attention to viewpoints at *both* ends of the ideological spectrum. He asked rhetorically, "But how?" By playing up fears and suspicions that the *press itself* believes to be exaggerated?" (emphasis added).[44]

This comment cuts to the heart of the issue. What do journalists believe, how do they come by their beliefs, and how do these beliefs influence the news? These questions will be the focus of inquiry throughout this work. Our approach is that of the sociology of knowledge.[45] We seek to know whether journalists' perspectives on social reality are guided by their backgrounds, their beliefs, and their inner needs.

This approach, like any other, is only as good as its results. It is not enough to assume that the news reflects certain perspectives. One must demonstrate this by examining both newspeople and their product. That is what this book is all about. Moreover, there are many other factors at work, among them professional norms, the culture of the newsroom, and the dictates of the marketplace. For all this, there is always a place for nuance and perspective in the news, an opportunity to fill in the blanks. It is just this opportunity that draws many creative people to the media and exerts a pull toward more interpretive news formats that let them express their creativity.

It is unfortunate and misleading that such issues are usually raised as questions of bias, which suggest calculated unfairness. We regard them instead as questions of necessarily partial views of social reality. Our goal is not to expose biases but to identify the perspectives that inform journalists' understanding. A side effect of the debate over ideological bias is that it leads journalists to oppose any examination of how their attitudes may influence their work. Hence a *Wall Street Journal* reporter writes that "one needn't rely on studies here; simple common sense suffices."[46]

On the contrary, serious scientific studies are precisely what we need either to validate "common sense" or to expose it as unreliable conventional wisdom. Since individual perspective, unlike bias, is both unavoidable and infinitely adaptable, no one book can complete this task. We can only begin to specify the conditions of journalists' changing social and psychological situations and their relation to the news product. This must be an ongoing effort, one that is too important to be left to partisans.

GROUP PORTRAIT

"This business of us being a bunch of parlor pinks, limousine liberals and Harvard-educated pink-tea types who look down our noses at anybody who was born west of the Hudson River is a lot of baloney."

—James Deakin, White House Correspondent

ARE THE MEDIA BIASED? One premise of this book is that the question is wrongly phrased. Between overt bias and pristine objectivity exist infinite shadings, subtle colorations, and elective affinities between personal outlook and news product. The trail that leads from journalists' perspectives to the news they report is often poorly marked. It winds through conscious attitudes, unquestioned assumptions, and inner motivations. This chapter examines the first factor in this complex progression, the actual backgrounds and outlooks of leading journalists.

Who Are the Media Elite?

During 1979 and 1980, we directed hour-long interviews with 238 journalists at America's most influential media outlets: the *New York Times,* the *Washington Post,* the *Wall Street Journal, Time, Newsweek, U.S. News and World Report,* and the news organizations at CBS, NBC, ABC, and PBS.[1] Within each organization, in-

20

dividuals were selected randomly from the news staffs. From print media, we sampled reporters, columnists, department heads, bureau chiefs, editors, and executives. From television, we selected correspondents, anchors, producers, film editors, and news executives. The result is a systematic sample of the men and women who put together the news at America's most important media outlets —the media elite.[2]

To provide comparisons with a more traditional leadership group, we also surveyed 216 executives at six *Fortune*-listed corporations, ranging from a multinational oil company and a major bank to a public utility and a nationwide retail chain. They were chosen randomly from upper and middle management at each company.[3] The focus of our inquiry is the media elite. At appropriate points, however, we will compare their responses to those of the corporate executives.

Origins and Destinations. In some respects, the journalists we interviewed appear typical of leadership groups throughout society (see Table 1). The media elite is composed mainly of white males in their thirties and forties. Only one in twenty is nonwhite, and one in five is female. They are highly educated, well-paid professionals. Ninety-three percent have college degrees, and a

---

Table 1—Backgrounds of the Media Elite

White	95%
Male	79
From northeast or north central states	68
From metropolitan area	42
Father graduated college	40
Father's occupation "professional"	40
College graduate	93
Postgraduate study	55
Individual income $30,000+	78
Family income $50,000+	46
Political liberal	54
Political conservative	17
Religion "none"	50

---

majority attended graduate school as well. These figures reveal them to be one of the best-educated groups in America.

Geographically, they are drawn primarily from northern industrial states, especially from the northeast corridor. Forty percent come from three states: New York, New Jersey, and Pennsylvania. Another 10 percent hail from New England, and almost 20 percent were raised in the big industrial states just to the west—Illinois, Indiana, Michigan, and Ohio. Thus, 68 percent of the media elite come from these three clusters of states. By contrast only 3 percent are drawn from the entire Pacific Coast, including California, the nation's most populous state.

Journalism is a profession associated with rapid upward mobility. Yet we found few Horatio Alger stories in the newsroom. On the contrary, many among the media elite enjoyed socially privileged upbringings. Most were raised in upper-middle-class homes. Almost half their fathers were college graduates, and one in four held a graduate degree. Two in five are the children of professionals—doctors, lawyers, teachers, and so on. In fact, one in twelve is following in his or her father's footsteps as a second-generation journalist. Another 40 percent describe their fathers as businessmen. That leaves only one in five whose father was employed in a low-status job. Given these upper-status positions, it is not surprising that their families were relatively well off. Nearly half rate their family's income as above average while they were growing up, compared to one in four who view their early economic status as below average.

A distinctive characteristic of the media elite is its secular outlook. Exactly half eschew any religious affiliation. Another 14 percent are Jewish, and almost one in four (23 percent) was raised in a Jewish household. Only one in five identify as Protestant, and one in eight as Catholic. Very few are regular churchgoers. Only 8 percent go to church or synagogue weekly, and 86 percent seldom or never attend religious services.

In sum, substantial numbers of the media elite grew up at a distance from the social and cultural traditions of small-town middle America. Instead, they came from big cities in the northeast and north central states. Their parents were mostly well off, highly educated members of the upper middle class, especially the educated professions. In short, they are a highly cosmopolitan group, with differentially eastern, urban, ethnic, upper-status, and secular roots.

As in any such group, there are many exceptions to these general tendencies. On the whole, though, they are rather homogeneous. For example, we could find few systematic differences among media outlets or job functions. Even television and print journalists differ mainly in their salaries. The proportions of men and women, whites and blacks, Jews and Gentiles, religious observers and abstainers are all roughly equal at the networks and the major print media. Moreover, the family backgrounds of print and broadcast journalists are similar in terms of national and ethnic heritage, financial status, parents' educational levels, and political preferences.

A New Elite. What do journalists' backgrounds have to do with their work? In general, the way we were brought up and the way we live shape our view of the world. And journalists' perspectives on society have obvious relevance to their work. Indeed, this book is devoted to exploring systematically this basic point.

Of particular concern is the impact of leading journalists' rising social and economic status. At the time of our survey, one in three had personal incomes above $50,000, and nearly half (46 percent) said their family incomes exceeded that amount. As salaries continue to rise, these data understate their current income levels. By 1982, the *National Journal* found that well-established reporters at the *Washington Post* and the Washington bureaus of the *New York Times, Newsweek,* and *Time* earned from $55,000 to $60,000.[4] Reporters and editors at the *Washington Post* are now required to file financial disclosure statements detailing holdings in stocks, bonds, and real estate. According to a financial department editor, "it used to be rare that staffers had such investments, but now that annual salaries average in the mid-forties and two-worker families have incomes of $100,000 or more, they are more common."[5]

Moreover, there is sometimes a considerable difference between salaries and overall incomes. Columnists, investigative reporters, and television correspondents are all in demand on the lecture circuit, where they command four- and even five-figure fees. In a 1986 article entitled "The Buckrakers," *The New Republic* reported that television anchors command up to $25,000 for a speech, well-known columnists charge from $12,000 to $18,000, and *Time*'s Washington bureau chief recently raised his fee from $3,000 to $5,000.[6] Thus columnist Jody Powell recently castigated his colleagues for potential conflict of interest over speakers' fees:

> Washington correspondents, anchors, bureau chiefs, columnists and editors are frequent travellers in the lecture circuit too. We speak to groups that have a definite interest in how we make the subjective judgments that are an inherent part of our job. And most of us get paid a good bit more than senators and congressmen who are limited by law to $2,000 for a speech.[7]

This is not to suggest that these journalists do not earn or deserve such incomes. By way of comparison, newly minted law school graduates may earn over $50,000 annually in major New York firms and over $40,000 per year in Washington firms. As this comparison suggests, the figures merely demonstrate that leading journalists are now solidly ensconced in the upper middle class.

Print personnel are still at the bottom of the media income ladder. It is television that can make millionaires of journalists. Anchors at all three major networks now make over $1 million annually, and six-figure salaries are common among reporters and correspondents.[8] Even public television can pay enough to attract some network stars willing to trade top dollar for increased creative freedom. For example, correspondent Judy Woodruff joined PBS's "MacNeil/Lehrer NewsHour" for $150,000 a year, half her former salary at NBC.[9] As James Deakin comments, "Over the years, newspapers and magazines have written breathlessly about the incomes of entrepreneurs and entertainers: John D. Rockefeller, Andrew Mellon, the Hunts of Texas, Clark Gable, John Wayne, Elizabeth Taylor. Now it is the anchorpersons and superstars of television news."[10]

The journalist as millionaire celebrity, star of the lecture circuit, filer of financial disclosure forms—it is enough to make Hildy Johnson turn over in his grave. It also makes many current journalists uneasy. David Broder, a highly regarded columnist and *Washington Post* reporter, recently wrote, "The fact is that reporters are by no means any kind of cross-section. We are over-educated, we are overpaid in terms of the median, and we have a higher socio-economic stratification than the people for whom we are writing . . . . There is clearly a danger of elitism creeping in."[11]

Note that Broder's concern goes beyond income level to encompass journalists' new social and educational status as well. Ironically, not so long ago media critics complained instead of the profession's low-status insularity. As journalist turned media critic Ben Bagdikian writes:

> Before World War II newspapering was one of those occupations that afforded working-class families . . . middle class status or better. College educations were seldom required and were often a disadvantage . . . [this] produced a majority of journalists whose only perceptions of the outside world after they left junior or high school were what they saw and heard in the newsrooms. . . . It also provided a simplistic view of society and . . . the strong strain of anti-intellectualism that characterized American newsrooms for generations.[12]

Now the worry is that urbanity and cosmopolitanism bring their own distortions, or at least limitations, of perspective. Thus, the *Post*'s White House correspondent, Lou Cannon, complains, "As reporters climb up the income scale, their social values change. . . . The gulf is growing between reporters and working-class Americans."[13] Columnist Henry Fairlie gives this line of thought more bite:

> The most certain avenue to celebrity and considerable wealth [in Washington] is not now in the institution of government . . . . It is through the intricate networks of the media . . . the people of the media are today the wheelers and dealers. Point to any others so skillful at using the machinery of Washington, and so

protected from any public challenge or scrutiny . . . . The media
have removed themselves from all contact in their daily lives
with the ordinary middle-class life and tastes of the community.[14]

For a modest example of the perspective that worries some
journalists, consider a recent magazine article by syndicated
columnists Jack Germond and Jules Witcover. The subject is how
reporters survive the rigors of the campaign trail. But the underlying theme is the upper-status cosmopolitan's scorn for parochial
middle America. The authors' advice: "If you're in some enclave
of civilized conduct such as New York . . . have a few belts in the
Oak Room at the Plaza . . . if you're in some backwater town like
Columbia, South Carolina, your choice is to eat early . . . and then
find a decent bar. . . ." They offer survival tips on various "uncivil-
ized" cities. Cleveland: "If you're going to be in a plane crash in
Cleveland, it's preferable that it happen going in." Indianapolis:
"Pray you don't have to go here. . . ." Birmingham: "Never go
there, certainly not overnight. . . ."[15] Such patronizing attitudes
can be viewed as following in the great "boobseoisie"-baiting tradition of H.L. Mencken. But it's difficult to imagine many of
today's high-flying columnists choosing to live out their lives in
Baltimore, like the Sage of Menlo Park, far from the civilized
surroundings of the Plaza's Oak Room.

Another alleged result of wealth and celebrity is a sense of
self-importance that redefines the role of journalists as newsmakers themselves. For example, the naming of a network anchor is
now front-page news in the major dailies. When Roger Mudd was
demoted at NBC, the *Wall Street Journal* informed its readers that
his "abrupt removal" was one of "two big stories in the national
news this week," along with a presidential press conference. The
Washington Post's ombudsman responded tartly, "With highest
regard for Mr. Mudd . . . it is respectfully suggested that people
paid to convey the news have no business becoming front-page
news themselves." He noted, however, a colleague's rationale for
the contrary position: "They come into your living room. They set
out the complexities of life, like the clergy used to do."[16]

26

More serious is the question of how journalists' enhanced status has affected their relations with the newsmakers they cover. Some critics maintain that journalists' elite status has undermined their independence or compromised their proper role as public tribune. In Fairlie's words, "The very profession that should be the acid, relentless critic of the affluence and cynicism of Washington is now the most ostentatiously affluent and cynical profession in the city."[17]

Others argue the opposite, that the formerly low status of journalists led them too often to revel in vicarious participation in the halls of power. Bagdikian criticizes old-school journalists for their "habit of close association with formal power which came to be seen as a natural reward of their occupation."[18] By contrast, today's leading journalists may be better paid and better educated than the politicians and bureaucrats they deal with. They may also be even more in demand socially. A publicist for Gray and Company, the influential Washington public relations firm, says matter-of-factly, "When we're putting together a guest list, including a journalist is just as important as including a diplomat or a Cabinet member."[19]

It would not be surprising if many of his colleagues agree with Jack Nelson of the *Los Angeles Times,* "I don't see any reason why we shouldn't consider ourselves on equal footing with those we cover."[20] The extent to which the tables have turned is illustrated by an encounter between Senator (and presidential candidate) Alan Cranston and CBS's Dan Rather during the 1984 New Hampshire primary. The two were having lunch when a CBS aide approached Cranston to say, "Senator, Mr. Rather will only have time for one more question."[21]

If society treats newscasters as more important than senators, it is unrealistic to expect the newscasters to reject society's opinion for long. Nor should we be surprised if journalists make use of their rising status to wrest control of the flow of information from politicians and other newsmakers. In keeping with their newfound status, leading journalists are increasingly likely to see themselves as professionals who translate the news rather than craftsmen who merely transmit it.[22]

Thus, the much-debated adversary relationship between media and government may be partly a function of reporters' changing lifestyles as well as their outlooks. They no longer need defer to the newsmakers they cover. As the late columnist Joseph Kraft wrote in 1981, "those of us in the media enjoyed an enormous surge of status and power in recent years. That surge coincided with the decline of various other groups, to the point where we could perceive ourselves as the only institutional force left on a well-nigh devastated plain . . . increasingly the media are an unrepresentative group—a group that is better educated, more highly paid, more sure of itself and more hostile to the system than the average."[23]

Kraft's analysis concludes that increases in the social, economic, and educational status of journalists are linked to liberal or anti-establishment attitudes. This is an issue our survey addresses in depth. So let us turn from the demography to the outlook of the media elite.

The View from the Newsroom

Politics and Perspectives. How do the leading journalists describe their own political leanings? A majority see themselves as liberals. Fifty-four percent place themselves to the left of center, compared to only 17 percent who choose the right side of the spectrum. (The remainder pick "middle of the road.") When they rate their fellow workers, an even greater difference emerges. Fifty-six percent say the people they work with are mostly on the Left, and only 8 percent place their co-workers on the Right—a margin of seven to one.

These subjective ratings are consistent with their voting records in presidential elections from 1964 through 1976. Of those who say they voted for major party candidates, the proportion of leading journalists who supported the Democratic candidate never drops below 80 percent.[24] In 1972, when more than 60 percent of all voters chose Nixon, over 80 percent among the media elite voted for McGovern. This does not appear to reflect any unique aversion to Nixon. Despite the well-publicized tensions between the press and his administration, leading journalists in

1976 preferred Carter over Ford by the same margin. In fact, in the Democratic landslide of 1964, journalists picked Johnson over Goldwater by a sixteen-to-one margin, or 94 to 6 percent.

More significant, though, is the long-term trend. Over the entire sixteen-year period, less than 20 percent of the media elite supported any Republican presidential candidate. Across four elections, the Democratic margin among elite journalists was 30 to 50 percent greater than among the entire electorate.

Also consistent with their self-descriptions are the media elite's views on a wide range of social and political issues (see Table 2).

Table 2—Media Elite Attitudes and Voting Records

	Agree
Economics	
Big corporations should be publicly owned	13%
People with more ability should earn more	86
Private enterprise is fair to workers	70
Less regulation of business is good for U.S.	63
Government should reduce income gap	68
Government should guarantee jobs	48
Political Alienation	
Structure of society causes alienation	49
Institutions need overhaul	28
All political systems are repressive	28
Social-Cultural	
Environmental problems are overstated	19
Strong affirmative action for blacks	80
Government should not regulate sex	97
Woman has right to decide on abortion	90
Homosexuality is wrong	25
Homosexuals shouldn't teach in public schools	15
Adultery is wrong	47
Foreign Policy	
U.S. exploits Third World, causes poverty	56
U.S. use of resources immoral	57
Goal of foreign policy is to protect U.S. businesses	50
CIA should sometimes undermine hostile governments	45

Table 2 *(Continued)*

	Agree
*Presidential Elections**	
1964	
Goldwater	6%
Johnson	94
1968	
Nixon	13
Humphrey	87
1972	
Nixon	19
McGovern	81
1976	
Ford	19
Carter	81

*Electoral percentages based on those who reported voting for major party candidates. Third party vote never exceeded 2 percent.

In the economic realm, over two-thirds agree that the government should reduce substantially the income gap between the rich and the poor. They are more evenly divided over the issue of guaranteed employment, with a slight majority opposing the entitlement issue. Most are anything but socialists. For example, they overwhelmingly reject the proposition that major corporations should be publicly owned. Only one in eight would agree to public ownership of corporations, and two-thirds declare themselves strongly opposed. Moreover, they overwhelmingly support the idea that people with greater ability should earn higher wages than those with less ability. Most also believe that free enterprise gives workers a fair shake, and that some deregulation of business would serve the national interest.

There is no contradiction between such praise for private enterprise and support for government action to aid the poor and jobless. These attitudes mirror the traditional perspective of American liberals who (unlike many European social democrats) accept an essentially capitalistic economic framework, even as they endorse the welfare state.

In contrast to their acceptance of the economic order, many leading journalists voice discontent with the social system. Almost half agree that "the very structure of our society causes people to feel alienated," and five out of six believe our legal system mainly favors the wealthy. Nonetheless, most would reject calls for a "complete restructuring" of our "basic institutions," and few agree that "all political systems are repressive." But they are united in rejecting social conservatism and traditional norms. Indeed, it is today's divisive "social issues" that bring their liberalism to the fore. Leading journalists emerge from the survey as strong supporters of environmental protection, affirmative action, women's rights, homosexual rights, and sexual freedom in general.

Fewer than one in five agrees that "our environmental problems are not as serious as people have been led to believe." Only 1 percent strongly agree that environmental problems are exaggerated, while a majority of 54 percent strongly disagree. They are nearly as united in supporting affirmative action for minorities. Despite both the heated controversy over this issue and their own predominantly white racial composition, four out of five media leaders endorse the use of strong affirmative action measures to ensure black representation in the workplace.

In their attitudes toward sex and sex roles, members of the media elite are virtually unanimous in opposing both governmental and traditional constraints. A large majority opposes government regulation of sexual activities, upholds a pro-choice position on abortion, and rejects the notion that homosexuality is wrong. In fact, a slight majority would not characterize adultery as wrong.

They overwhelmingly oppose traditional gender-based restrictions. Ninety percent agree that a woman has the right to decide for herself whether to have an abortion; 79 percent agree strongly with this pro-choice position. Only 18 percent believe that working wives whose husbands have jobs should be laid off first, and even fewer, 10 percent, agree that men are emotionally better suited for politics than women.

Only 4 percent agree that government should regulate sexual practices, and 84 percent strongly oppose state control over sexual activities. Seventy-five percent disagree that homosexuality is wrong, and an even larger proportion, 85 percent, uphold the right of homosexuals to teach in public schools. Finally, 54 percent do not regard adultery as wrong, and only 15 percent strongly agree that extramarital affairs are immoral. Thus, members of the media elite emerge as strong supporters of sexual freedom, and as natural opponents of groups like the Moral Majority.

We also inquired about international affairs, focusing on America's relations with Third World countries. The majority agrees that American economic exploitation has contributed to Third World poverty and that America's heavy use of natural resources is "immoral." Precisely half agree that the main goal of our foreign policy has been to protect American business interests.

Two issues dealing more directly with American foreign policy also elicit a nearly even division of opinion. A majority would prohibit the CIA from undermining hostile governments to protect U.S. interests. Just under half would ban foreign arms sales altogether or restrict them to democratic countries. About the same proportion would supply arms to any "friendly" country, regardless of the regime. Only 4 percent would be willing to sell arms to all comers. Thus, in several controversial areas of international relations, the media elite is deeply divided.

In sum, the media elite's perspective is predominantly cosmopolitan and liberal. Their outlook reflects the social (rather than economic) emphasis of what political scientist Everett Ladd calls the "new liberalism"[25] of upper-status groups. Leading journalists criticize traditional social norms and establishment groups; they are very liberal on social issues such as abortion, homosexual rights, affirmative action, and environmental protection. Many endorse an expanded welfare state, but they also emerge as strong supporters of the free enterprise system. Most describe themselves as liberals and most support Democratic presidential candidates.

Not surprisingly, these attitudes place them to the left of business executives, a traditional conservative elite, on virtually every issue the survey addresses.[26] On issues ranging from homosexuality and abortion to income redistribution, the gap between the two groups nears 40 percentage points. For example, 60 percent of the executives agree that homosexuality is wrong, 76 percent call adultery morally wrong, and only 29 percent favor government action to close the income gap between rich and poor. Even journalists' substantial support for free enterprise pales somewhat before businessmen's overwhelming endorsement. For example, 90 percent regard private enterprise as fair to workers, and 86 percent favor less government regulation of business. These figures exceed journalists' support levels by 20 and 25 percent, respectively.

It may seem obvious that corporate executives would be more conservative than leading journalists. The differences are documented here in order to establish that the businessmen are indeed an appropriate comparison group for the journalists. In Chapter Three we will ask whether these overt ideological differences are reflected in divergent perceptions and predispositions toward social reality. (The question of whether journalists are also more liberal than the general public was answered by a 1985 *Los Angeles Times* poll; see page 40).

Journalists on the Media. Some years back, columnist Joseph Kraft criticized his colleagues for holding such liberal perspectives. He argued that the major media had adopted an elitist and adversarial perspective on American society that made them combatants rather than observers of the political wars. Kraft wrote:

> We no longer represent a wide diversity of views. We have ceased to be neutral in reporting events . . . . The media have been taken in tow by the adversary culture . . . . We are skeptical about established authority . . . . We are sympathetic to the claims of those with grievances—whether black or brown or Indian or senior citizens. We tend to favor helping them, even though the benefits—integrated neighborhoods, school busing, affirmative action—tend to be paid for by middle America. As for middle America's complaints—about gun control, anti-abortion rulings, abolishing the death penalty, yielding Panama

33

—we tend to write them off as disconnected single issues. Not only are we not representative, we are aligned on one side in the hottest class contention now dividing America.[27]

Such criticisms are not new, but rarely have they issued from such a prominent member of the journalistic profession. Our survey also asked journalists to evaluate some of these and other commonly voiced criticisms about themselves: Can journalists be unbiased when they are emotionally involved with an issue on which they are reporting? Do they have a liberal bias? Are they too attentive to minority groups and too critical of the establishment? Alternatively, are they too easily co-opted by the establishment? Should the media play a central role in promoting social reform?

A surprising number of leading journalists are willing to admit to problems of bias, at least in principle. At the same time, they strongly reject more specific criticisms of their practices and product. They are almost evenly divided over their role in promoting social reform; a slight majority agrees that the media should play a major role. At the same time, a majority agrees that the media have a liberal bias, and almost one-third believe that journalists cannot be impartial when they feel strongly about issues on which they report.

These findings suggest division within the media elite over their role in American society. In acting as the public's tribune against the powerful, journalists may seek to combine personal satisfaction with social service. But involvement in social issues may mean a loss of impartiality. This tension between professional objectivity and personal involvement in the newsroom will prove a leitmotif of this study.

However, specific criticisms about news coverage seem to produce a closing of ranks. Over four out of five reject the allegation that the media are too attentive to minorities, and an even greater proportion deny that they are too critical of United States institutions. Only 1 percent agrees strongly with either of these criticisms, while the proportions disagreeing strongly are 48 and 60 percent, respectively. Nor do many give credence to the notion that journalists are easily co-opted by government officials. Once again, fewer than one in four agrees, and about half disagree strongly. Overall, then, concerns about the media's political role seem more likely to be expressed in general terms than on specific issues.

The Big Picture. Thus far we have examined elite journalists' opinions on the great and small issues of the day. By charting their responses to numerous social issues, we try to understand their general perspectives on society and politics. The results, though, may be deceptive. They create the impression of a broad ideological portrait of the media elite without ever asking journalists to deal with the "big picture." Their attitudes toward issues like abortion, affirmative action, and arms sales provide benchmarks for understanding their outlook, since most people have opinions on such pressing and hotly debated questions. But they do not address some of the most basic underlying issues of political life: What directions should American society take? What groups exert the most influence over social goals and political processes? How much influence should be wielded by such forces as business, labor, minorities, and the media?

These issues are as old as political philosophy. But it is not only philosophers who grapple with questions like "who should rule?" and "what is the good society?" Most people have answers to these questions, even if they haven't consciously arrived at them. Their answers express basic values that underlie their transient opinions on current social issues.

The interviews we conducted tried to tap these fundamental predispositions of political thought. First, journalists were asked about the goals America should pursue during the next decade. From a list of eight choices, they selected the most important, second most important, and least important goal. The list, created by political scientist Ronald Inglehart, includes:

1. Maintaining a high rate of economic growth
2. Making sure that this country has strong defense forces
3. Seeing that the people have more say in how things get decided at work and in their communities
4. Trying to make our cities and countryside more beautiful

35

5. Maintaining a stable economy
6. Progressing toward a less impersonal, more humane society
7. The fight against crime
8. Progressing toward a society where ideas are more important than money.

Inglehart classifies these choices as "instrumental" and "acquisitive" values, on one hand, vs. "expressive" and "post-bourgeois" values, on the other.[28] In this list, the post-bourgeois choices are those dealing with participation, a humane society, a beautiful environment, and placing ideas above money. Unlike standard polling items, these choices are not presented periodically to cross-sections of the American public. So the sample of business leaders functions here as a comparison group. As archetypal representatives of a bourgeois society, they should be oriented toward more conservative "acquisitive" values.

Substantial segments (though still a minority) of the media elite endorse the post-bourgeois value orientation that Inglehart calls a "silent revolution" transforming the political culture of advanced industrial society. One in three journalists (33 percent) deems citizen participation, a humane society, or a society less oriented toward money as our most important goal—more important than either economic well-being or national defense. By contrast, only one in eight (12 percent) business leaders picks any of the "expressive" values as America's most pressing concern.

Even among the journalists, a majority (52 percent) favors economic stability as the most important value. However, almost half the media elite (49 percent) pick post-bourgeois values as their second choice, compared to 30 percent of the business elite. Forty percent of these leading journalists select a humane society as either their first or second priority, more than double the proportion among business leaders. Conversely, the businessmen list national defense more than twice as often as the newsmen. Finally, the journalists are almost twice as likely as the executives (by 39 to 21 percent) to choose acquisitive values as the *least* important for America to pursue. Overall, the media elite show a substantially greater preference for post-bourgeois goals than the business elite.

For many leading journalists, liberal views on contemporary political issues apparently reflect a commitment to social change in pursuit of the good society, as they visualize it. Such a commitment would align them with emerging forces of social liberalism who are pitted against more established leadership groups. Therefore, the survey also examined the media elite's evaluation of its competitors for social influence.

Beyond inquiring about the direction our society should take, we asked a more pointed question: Who should direct it? Specifically, journalists were asked to rate seven leadership groups in terms of the influence each wields over American life. Then they were asked to rate the same groups according to the amount of influence they *should* have. They assigned each group a rating from "1," meaning very little influence, to "7," representing a great deal of influence.

The seven groups represent a cross-section of major competitors for social power in contemporary America. They include black leaders, feminists, consumer groups, intellectuals, labor unions, business leaders, and the news media. Media leaders see four of the groups as relatively disadvantaged in the competition for social power. They rate feminists as weakest, just behind black leaders, intellectuals, and consumer groups. All four are clustered tightly together in their ratings, well below the "big three" of labor, business, and the media. The unions rank third, leaving the media close on the heels of business leaders, whom they perceive as the most powerful social group.

When the journalists were asked about their preferences, this picture changed drastically. They would strip both business and labor of their current influence, while raising the status of all the other groups. In the media elite's preferred social hierarchy, business leaders fall from first to fifth position, and unions drop to the very bottom of the ladder. Feminists move up only slightly, but blacks, intellectuals, and consumer groups would all have more influence than either business or labor. Emerging at the top of the heap, as the group most favored to influence American society, is the media.

There is a certain irony in the media elite's choice of itself as preeminent in the race for influence. The press is traditionally ambivalent about its power, and journalists often either deny or decry the notion of a powerful media elite. In a 1976 study of elites conducted by the *Washington Post* and Harvard University, the media leaders were the only group to claim they want less influence than they already have.[29] In fact, one could say the same of the subjects in our survey, but it would be a deceptive interpretation. In absolute terms, leading journalists would assign themselves a lower influence rating than they now have. Yet they would assign even lower ratings to other groups, thereby leapfrogging themselves from second position to the top spot.

The business leaders, by the way, return the compliment. They perceive the media as far and away the most powerful influence on American society, with labor a distant second and business only third, followed by the four emergent groups. Not surprisingly, they would also prefer to sit atop the influence hierarchy, while burying the media well back in the pack in fifth position (precisely where the media elite would place business). Indeed, the antipathy these two elites seem to feel toward each other is noteworthy. Business leaders regard the media as the most influential group listed and would reduce the influence of journalists more than any other group. Media leaders perceive business leaders as the most influential group and would likewise strip away most of their influence. One might speculate that these elites view one another with such mistrust precisely because each attributes great influence to the other. In the ongoing struggle over social influence, each appears wary of the other as its strongest competitor.

The media elite is also homogeneous in its politics. We found only slight ideological differences across media outlets or job functions. To illustrate this, we compared self-described liberals and conservatives across various subgroups. The Left-Right split is quite similar among print and television journalists. Fifty-three percent of those in the print media call themselves liberal, compared to 19 percent of those who choose the conservative label;

among broadcast journalists, liberals predominate by 56 to 14 percent. Within the press, moreover, reporters and editors hold nearly identical political self-images. The liberal-to-conservative margin is 52 to 16 percent among reporters, 51 to 20 percent among editors. The gap narrows somewhat at the top of the newsroom hierarchy. Among senior print editors and executives, the margin closes to 41 vs. 24 percent; among senior television producers and executives, however, it remains more than two to one (44 vs. 16 percent).

Thus, ideological diversity among leading journalists seems confined to a relatively narrow band of the political spectrum. By contrast, no more than 22 percent of the general public have ever placed themselves to the left of center in Gallup polls conducted over the past decade. Nor has this group ever equalled the proportion of those who place themselves on the political right. At the time our survey was conducted, conservatives outnumbered liberals by 31 to 17 percent nationwide.[30]

Old Attitudes, New Freedoms

Surveying the Surveys. There is considerable evidence from other sources to corroborate our portrait of liberal leading journalists. No other studies have focused on precisely those journalists we term the media elite. But a group that overlaps ours in membership and influence, the Washington press corps, has been surveyed repeatedly. In 1976, a *Washington Post*-Harvard University survey of accredited Washington reporters found that 59 percent called themselves liberal and 18 percent conservative.[31] This is strikingly close to the 54 to 17 margin we found among the media elite four years later. Moreover, these self-descriptions were reflected in Washington reporters' voting preference in the 1972 election. Of those who voted, 70 percent chose McGovern and only 25 percent picked Nixon.

The *Post*-Harvard study also found, as we did, that management is less liberal than working reporters but not nearly as conservative as the general public. Their companion survey of newspaper managing editors and TV and radio news directors around the country revealed a liberal-conservative split of 40 to 17 percent.

Thus, there were fewer self-styled liberals, more moderates, but no more conservatives in management than among the Washington reporters. This group was also less Democratic in its voting preferences, but a slight majority still supported McGovern over Nixon (51 to 45 percent).

In 1978, the Washington press corps was again surveyed by Stephen Hess of the Brookings Institution. He found fewer reporters willing to call themselves liberal (42 percent) but virtually no rise in the proportion of conservatives (19 percent).[32] Thus, the liberal vs. conservative ratio remained greater than two to one, though less than the three to one margins found elsewhere. (The difference may be accounted for either by a slightly different wording of the questions or by the low response rate, under 25 percent.) Hess also found, as we did, that a slight majority of journalists themselves found a political bias in their ranks. Of those who considered the Washington news corps biased, 96 percent felt it was liberal. By contrast, only one percent complained of conservative bias.

Another well-known study, conducted in 1971, reported self-descriptions of journalists at "prominent" news organizations, including the networks, newsmagazines, and major newspapers. Among executives, 73 percent placed themselves on the Left and 10 percent on the Right. Among staffers, the comparable figures were 53 and 17 percent, respectively.[33]

A more recent study of the politics of journalists was conducted in 1982 by scholars at the State University of California at Los Angeles. This survey of journalists at America's fifty largest newspapers found 50 percent self-described liberals and 21 percent conservatives.[34] The voting breakdown of this group during the 1972 election was McGovern 77 percent, Nixon 21 percent. This study also reports results for the 1980 election. The newspeople interviewed gave a slight majority to Carter (51 percent), with the remainder split almost evenly between Reagan (25 percent) and Anderson (24 percent). At about the same time, a group of scholars at Indiana University interviewed a random sample of 1,001 journalists around the country. Among those in "prominent" news organizations, 32 percent claimed a Left orientation and 12 percent a Right orientation.[35]

The most recent, most thorough, and perhaps most remarkable survey of journalists was conducted in 1985 by the *Los Angeles Times*.[36] Almost 3,000 newspaper reporters and editors, randomly selected at over 600 papers around the country, were polled on over 100 questions, including some of the same ones we asked. Equally important, the same questions were asked of a national random sample of about 3,300 adults. This makes possible direct comparisons between press and public attitudes.

The results document a wide disparity between the attitudes of journalists and the general public, with the former consistently to the left of the latter. On the average, for all questions, the *Times* reports a gap of 25 percent between the attitudes of journalists and their audience. For example, as table 3 shows news staffers are over twice as likely as their audience to favor government regulation of business and American disinvestment from South Africa, to oppose prayer in public schools and increased defense spending, and to disapprove of Ronald Reagan's performance. (The precise figures are presented in the Appendix on page 293.)

On several issues we asked about, this massive survey replicates our findings while also demonstrating a gulf between news producers and news readers. Thus, 82 percent of journalists are pro-choice on abortion, vs. 51 percent of the public; 81 percent support affirmative action for minorities, vs. 57 percent of the national sample; and 89 percent uphold homosexual rights in hiring, vs. 56 percent of the public. Only 26 percent of the journalists voted for Reagan in 1984, a figure that resembles our findings from previous elections, as well as the Cal State 1980 results.

Economic issues constitute a partial exception to the overall pattern. Here the poll finds that journalists are "slightly, but not markedly more liberal" than the public.[37] They are much more likely to favor government regulation of business, by 49 to 22 percent. But they are slightly less likely (by 50 to 55 percent) to favor government action to reduce the income gap between the rich and poor. The leading journalists we surveyed are more

41

liberal on this issue, with 68 percent agreeing that government should close the gap. Still, journalists around the country seem to echo the media elite's strong support for private enterprise and low opinion of business and labor alike. The pollsters conclude, "It appears that on questions that affect their interest, as opposed to purely ideological matters, journalists behave like other high-status elites."[38]

To return to the ideological self-description we have used as a benchmark, 55 percent of these journalists call themselves liberal and 17 percent conservative, a difference of one percent from our own finding. On the other hand, 24 percent of the general public term themselves liberal, a figure 31 percent lower than among journalists. In fact, the pollsters report that newspaper journalists are also "markedly more liberal than others of similar educational and professional standing."[39] Thirty-seven percent of other college-educated professionals say that they are liberal, an 18 percent drop from the press percentage. And 57 percent of other professional people give Reagan a positive rating, compared to 30 percent of the journalists.

Finally, the pollsters took on the Herculean task of questioning *every* news and editorial staff member of the *New York Times, Washington Post,* and *Los Angeles Times.* Despite a low response rate at the *Post,* they completed about 500 interviews at these three major newspapers. They found that, "The combined staffs of the two *Times*es and the *Post* would seem, if anything, slightly more liberal than journalists on other papers."[40]

These results from numerous independent surveys are uniformly consistent with our own. Although the number of self-described liberals varies somewhat, the conservative population among major media journalists ranges only from 10 to 21 percent across the various surveys. Thus the liberal to conservative ratio always exceeds two to one. Similarly, the proportion of Nixon voters in 1972 ranges from 19 to 25 percent (except among news managers), about 35-40 percentage points below the level of Nixon's support among the electorate that year.

The *Los Angeles Times* findings on journalists' issue stands are also in line with our findings, despite the more elite status of our subjects. Indeed, the final portrait etched by the *Times* pollsters bears strong resemblance to the media elite: "They are emphatically liberal on social issues and foreign affairs, distrustful of establishment institutions (government, business, labor) and protective of their own economic interests."[41]

The New Professionals. Liberal and Democratic sympathies among journalists are not new. What may have changed more over the years is the relevance of journalists' social attitudes to their news product. When Leo Rosten conducted the first systematic survey of the Washington press corps in 1936, he found reporters to be mostly Democrats but very much under the thumb of their superiors. At a time when most newspapers were controlled by Republican publishers, 64 percent of the reporters favored Roosevelt in the coming election, and 6 percent favored Socialist or Communist candidates. Rosten compared these results to a contemporary Gallup poll showing that only 50 percent of the public favored Roosevelt, while 2 percent chose left-wing third parties.[42] At the same time, over 60 percent of reporters agreed with the statement, "My orders are to be objective, but I know how my paper wants stories played." Even more telling, a majority admitted having their stories "played down, cut, or killed for 'policy' reasons."[43]

By 1960, this situation had changed dramatically. In 1961, journalism professor William Rivers again surveyed the Washington press corps. He found that Democrats still outnumbered Republicans among newspaper and broadcast correspondents, by margins exceeding three to one.[44] However, only 7 percent recounted ideological tampering with their work. In fact, Rivers concludes, "of all the changes in the Washington press corps during the past twenty-five years, none is more significant than a new sense of freedom from the prejudices of the home office."[45] He cites one longtime correspondent who recalled the difference from the old days: "the publishers didn't just disagree with the New Deal. They hated it. And the reporters, who liked it, had to write as though they hated it, too."[46]

Seventeen years after Rivers' study, Hess concludes from his own survey that "writing to fit the editorial positions of publishers

[has] simply disappeared as an issue of contention. . . . The near absence of disagreements over political slant is a by-product of higher professional standards as well as the passing of the press 'lords' . . . who view their publications as outlets for their own views."[47] Hess notes further that today's Washington reporters initiate most of their own stories, which usually receive little or no editing. Journalism has come a long way from the days when Henry Luce could defend *Time*'s partisan coverage of the 1952 election with the comment, "it was *Time*'s duty to explain why the country needs Ike. Any other form of journalism would have been unfair and uninvolved."[48]

Our study corroborates the notion of a new era for reporters. We asked subjects how much influence they generally have over the content of news stories with which they are involved. They marked a scale ranging from "very little" to "a great deal" of influence. By far the lowest or least influential scores were recorded by executives of both print and broadcast outlets. So it is not only the press watchers who argue that the influence of reporters has increased relative to that of their bosses. This perception is shared by the journalists themselves.

The new authority structures influence media content only insofar as they permit different values to shape the news product. There is little doubt, however, that this has happened. In 1974, Ben Bagdikian summarized this dramatic shift of journalistic standards:

> There has been a rapid change within news institutions in the last decade. The received conventions that decade after decade automatically conditioned each novice journalist to comply with traditional values are being rejected and reformed. Standards of "legitimacy" are being questioned. The primacy of direction from above is being challenged from below. A different kind of novice professional has entered the field.[49]

The Once and Future Media Elite

How did journalists come to their liberal views? Are they liberal and cosmopolitan in outlook because their profession makes them

so, or do the media attract people with ready-made liberal leanings? Many journalists argue that their professional milieu is a
natural source of liberalism. As an Atlanta *Constitution* columnist
recently wrote, "Experience impacts attitudes, and journalists
have more of the kinds of experiences that would challenge cozy
conservative assumptions than most folks do. . . . It is far easier
to harrumph in a country-club bar about welfare than it is . . . in
a tenement listening to a welfare mother who can't pay her winter
heating bill."[50]

This so-called nature vs. nurture question could be answered
with certainty only by going back in time to determine what
today's top journalists thought and felt at the beginnings of their
careers. Despite the impossibility of securing such information,
there are other ways of gaining insight into this question. First, we
sought to determine whether liberalism related to age among leading journalists. If their experience in the profession is a liberalizing
factor, one would expect older journalists to be more liberal than
younger ones, who lack experience.

Yet just the opposite occurs within the media elite. We divided
journalists into the old guard (over fifty years old), the mid-career
group (between thirty-five and fifty), and the post-Watergate generation (under thirty-five). Among the old guard, 43 percent place
themselves left of center, not quite double the 23 percent who pick
the right side of the spectrum, with the rest choosing the middle
of the road. In the mid-career group, the proportion of liberals
rises to 52 percent and that of conservatives drops to 16 percent,
about a three to one ratio. Among the rising generation who joined
the profession in the wake of Watergate, 70 percent are liberals
and only 13 percent conservatives, a ratio exceeding five to one. So
younger journalists, by their own descriptions, are substantially
more liberal than older ones.

Another approach is to look not to today's journalists but
tomorrow's. If students at an elite journalism school are already
liberal, it would support the position that liberal journalists are
born into their profession, not made by it. If, on the contrary,
those about to enter the profession are more conservative than
working journalists, it would support those who see the work itself

45

as the primary agent of journalists' liberalism. Interviewing today's journalism school students also provides a glimpse at the future of the profession. By comparing today's media elite with a select group of young people poised to enter the field, one may gain some sense of what to expect from tomorrow's leading journalists. **The Next Generation.** Among journalism schools, one graduate program stands out as particularly prestigious. The cream of the crop among aspiring journalists attend Columbia University's Graduate School of Journalism. Columbia offers not only excellent academic credentials, but also valuable contacts with the major New York–based media outlets.

We surveyed a random sample of the school's 1982 degree candidates, excluding foreign students (see Table 3). Twenty-eight students were interviewed, representing one-sixth of the entire class.[51] They answered the same questions asked of the media elite, as well as a few new ones. The results provide a striking portrait of some of tomorrow's potential leading journalists.

The student group is less dominated by white males than today's leading journalists. Nearly half are female, more than twice the proportion of women among the media elite. One in five of the students comes from minority groups, four times the percentage of those already at the top.

In most other respects, though, the students are even more homogeneous than their elders. They are drawn even more heavily from the northeast. They are also almost twice as likely to come from metropolitan areas. Fewer than one in five were raised in small-town or rural America.

Seventy percent of the journalism students have college-educated fathers, up from 40 percent of the media elite. A majority rate their family's income as above average, and only one out of nine say they were raised in homes with below-average incomes. Thus, while the media elite are products of a comfortable background, the students hail from an even more select and privileged stratum of society. Like today's leading journalists, most of the students are not religiously observant. Nearly half claim no religious affiliation, and only one in twelve say they attend religious services regularly.

46

Table 3—Backgrounds and Attitudes of Columbia University Journalism Students

Backgrounds

White	79%
Male	54
From northeast states	71
From metropolitan area	82
Father graduated college	70
Father's occupation "professional"	29
Political liberal	85
Political conservative	11
Religion "none"	46

Attitudes

Economics

Big corporations should be publicly owned	39
People with more ability should earn more	77
Private enterprise is fair to workers	32
Less regulation of business is good for U.S.	39
Government should reduce income gap	82
Government should guarantee jobs	63

Political Alienation

Structure of society causes alienation	71
Institutions need overhaul	50
All political systems are repressive	36

Social-Cultural

Environmental problems are overstated	14
Strong affirmative action for blacks	67
Government should not regulate sex	93
Woman has right to decide on abortion	96
Homosexuality is wrong	18
Homosexuals shouldn't teach in public schools	7
Adultery is wrong	78

Foreign Policy

U.S. exploits Third World, causes poverty	75
U.S. use of resources immoral	74
Goal of foreign policy is to protect U.S. businesses	89
CIA should sometimes undermine hostile governments	33

On the eve of their entry into the profession, what do these young people believe about politics and society? First, an overwhelming majority place themselves to the left of center. Eighty-five percent describe themselves as political liberals, while only 11 percent consider themselves conservatives. So the journalism students see themselves as substantially more liberal than today's media elite, and over three times as liberal as the general public. Moreover, their self-assessment translates into political behavior. In 1980, only 4 percent voted for Ronald Reagan, compared to 59 percent who backed Jimmy Carter and 29 percent who cast their ballots for John Anderson.

The students' presidential choices and self-descriptions are consistent with their views on a wide range of social and political issues. They are more critical than today's media elite toward business and private enterprise, more alienated from the political system, and about as liberal as their future colleagues on social and cultural issues. On economic issues the students are stronger supporters of an expanded welfare state and much more severe critics of the capitalist system. A large majority views the government as responsible for both guaranteeing jobs (63 percent) and reducing income disparities (82 percent). Only one in three students believes that private enterprise is fair to workers, compared to over two-thirds of their elders. While almost two of three elite journalists believe that less regulation of business would be good for the country, nearly the same percentage of Columbia journalism school students rejects this idea. Finally, the students are over three times more likely than the current journalists to advocate public ownership of corporations. Almost two in five subscribe to this notion.

The students' dissatisfaction with the economic order is accompanied by pronounced political alienation. While just under half the media elite view the structure of our society as causing alienation, over seven out of ten students endorse this criticism. Similarly, half the students believe that our social institutions need to be overhauled completely. Although the students far surpass the media elite in their unhappiness with the economic and political order, the two groups are united in their rejection of traditional

48

morality and their support for social liberalism. They are almost equally strong supporters of environmental protection, affirmative action, women's rights, homosexual rights, and sexual freedom in general. The students are more unified than their elders, however, in criticizing American policies abroad. For example, three out of four believe the U.S. exploits Third World nations, and almost 90 percent believe the main goal of our foreign policy has been to protect business.

In sum, these elite journalism school students are at least as critical of traditional social and cultural mores as today's leading journalists. They express greater hostility toward business, heightened political alienation, and a more critical view of America's role in world affairs. In light of these attitudes, it is not surprising that they choose post-bourgeois goals for our society in greater numbers than their elders. A majority of the students, compared to only one-third of the media elite, selected the post-bourgeois choices in the survey over instrumental ones. In particular, they are more likely to favor the goals of community participation and an idea-oriented society. Of those students who focus on acquisitive goals, most are concerned with economic growth. Finally, the students rank national defense below all other goals. None considers it most important, and over two out of five consider national defense the least important of all goals listed.

To gain a sense of how their views might affect their perceptions of the current political scene, we solicited the students' opinions of several prominent national and international newsmakers. They could indicate strong or mild approval or disapproval, or feelings of neutrality toward each. The results show that their perspectives on leading newsmakers accord with their broader social outlooks. The most positive ratings all go to prominent liberal figures. The most popular is consumer advocate Ralph Nader, followed by feminist Gloria Steinem, Senator Edward Kennedy, Atlanta Mayor Andrew Young, and economist John Kenneth Galbraith.

The students' strongest disapproval is reserved for conservative groups and individuals. Seventy-eight percent disapprove of Ronald Reagan, a negative rating exceeded only by their rating of the Moral Majority. By margins greater than three to one, the students also reject two Reagan allies, then United Nations Ambassador Jeanne Kirkpatrick and British Prime Minister Margaret Thatcher. In fact, they rate Cuban Premier Fidel Castro almost as highly as Thatcher, and considerably more positively than Ronald Reagan. Two out of three strongly disapprove of Reagan, compared to only one in four who feel as negatively about Castro. Nicaragua's Sandinistas, a bête noire of the Reagan administration, are viewed more positively than any of the conservative figures listed. Forty-one percent approve of the Sandinistas and only 26 percent disapprove.

Finally, we wanted to know where tomorrow's news gatherers get their perspectives on the news. So the students were asked to rate the reliability of a dozen organs of fact and opinion, including liberal and conservative journals, as well as avowedly nonpartisan outlets. They rate the *New York Times* and the *Washington Post* as highly reliable, along with public television. But they also rate a journal of the intellectual Left, the *New York Review of Books,* as highly reliable. *Time, Newsweek,* and *U.S. News* all weigh in as moderately reliable. Yet they rate the *New Republic* and the *Nation,* longtime representatives of liberal and left opinion, respectively, as no less trustworthy than *Time,* a major newsweekly. They reserve their lowest ratings for two more conservative journals of opinion, *Commentary* and *National Review,* along with TV network news.

More liberal and cosmopolitan than today's leading journalists, more alienated from both our economic and political institutions, sympathetic to liberal newsmakers and hostile toward conservatives, Columbia "J-School" students may be on the cutting edge of a new wave in American journalism. However, we cannot be certain of how their political or professional values may evolve as they become integrated into their chosen profession. Theirs may be the "progressivism" and skepticism of youth, yet to be tempered by the experiences or responsibilities of age. Of course, this would mean that integration into the news business is a conservatizing experience. We began by considering the opposite hypothesis, which presents journalism as a liberalizing force. So this possibility would challenge the notion that today's media elite became more liberal over time.[52]

For the most part, though, one could not expect so liberal a group as these students to turn very far to the right. Thus, Senator Daniel P. Moynihan's prediction some years back may yet come to pass:

> . . . the political consequence of the rising social status of journalism is that the press grows more and more influenced by attitudes genuinely hostile to American society and American government. This trend seems bound to continue into the future . . . the young people now leaving the Harvard *Crimson* and the Columbia *Spectator* for journalistic jobs in Washington will resort to the [Lincoln] Steffens [muckraking] style at ever-escalating levels of moral implication.[53]

Conclusion: An Ambivalent Elite

Many leading journalists are uncomfortable with both their newly proclaimed elite status and any liberal "do-gooder" self-image. Thus *Washington Post* editor Richard Harwood defends his colleagues against Moynihan's charges of elitism with the hypothesis that they are part of the working class: "An alternative hypotheses . . . might be that newspapermen are Democrats and liberals because they see themselves as part of [the] working class . . . . They are not, after all, 'professionals' in any classical or reasonable sense of the word. They pursue a 'trade' or a 'craft' for which there are no entrance requirements. Most of them are members of . . . a 'working class' union . . . ."[54]

This argument against media elitism might not be appreciated in other contexts. One need only refer to the *New York Times'* outrage over a state court decision refusing "professional" status to journalists. In opposing the judicial opinion that "a journalist is not, legally speaking, a professional," the *Times* printed a stinging editorial that concluded, "There is no byline on the court's opinion, suggesting that it didn't deem it worthy of more than boilerplate. The modesty is appropriate."[55]

In fact, the rapid rise to elite status has produced a deep

ambivalence in many leading journalists. Few people in any profession are so embarrassed by newfound prominence that they give back their paychecks and renounce their influence. On the other hand, the loss of identification with the hoi polloi is a genuine problem for those who pride themselves on representing the little guy against the powerful, and standing up for individuality and idiosyncracy against the gray flannel suit crowd.

In his account of life on the press bus during the 1972 election campaign, Timothy Crouse quotes Dan Rather as giving voice to the old and cherished image of the journalist as outsider: "The average journalist, including myself, is a whiskey-breathed, nicotine-stained, stubble-bearded guy. . . ."[56] Crouse suggests that this represents a triumph of self-image over reality: "Rather was wearing a beautifully tailored blue suit and he gave off the healthy glow of a man who has just emerged from a hotel barber shop. I had never seen him smoke and I doubt whether, on a typical day, his strongest exhalation could budge the needle on a breathalyzer."

Torn between an emotional commitment to an older professional image and the obvious advantages of a newer one, today's leading journalists would not be the first to try to have it both ways. A similar kind of denial often operates when journalists have to choose between the self-images of Menckenesque cynic and committed social reformer. Our survey found that a majority of leading journalists do see social reform as a major role of the media. On some level, many probably identify with David Halberstam's recollection of his youthful motives in becoming a journalist: "I believed deeply that . . . journalism had a crucial role as the societal conscience of last resort."[57]

Yet this image conflicts with another powerful persona—the journalist as the cynical outsider, the man in the trenchcoat, Bogart in the first reel. As James Deakin recounts,

> Most journalists do not like to talk about [their] public-service motive. They are hard-boiled, realistic, worldly. It does not fit their self-image. In some strange way, they think it makes them vulnerable. Reporters tend to regard their idealism as sex was formerly regarded. It is embarrassing. The subject comes up

only rarely. When it does, someone usually introduces a distraction. Another drink is suggested.[58]

Despite disclaimers and inner conflicts, the basic sociological profile of journalists at national news outlets is clear. They are a largely homogeneous group that is cosmopolitan in background and liberal in outlook. And they are an elite in terms of economic status, public perception, and social influence. As Stephen Hess writes, "Being described as an elite disturbs many reporters. But, of course, they are.[59]

Yesteryear's ragtag muckrakers, who tirelessly championed the little guy against powerful insiders, have become insiders themselves. Newsmen have long cherished the vantage point of the outsiders who keep the insiders straight. But now, leading journalists are courted by politicians, studied by scholars, and known to millions through their bylines and televised images. In short, the needs of a post-industrial society increasingly hungry for information have contributed to the rise of a national news network. These journalists are anything but the low-lifes and ambulance chasers mythologized in *The Front Page*. Instead, they constitute an elite that competes for influence alongside more traditional leadership groups representing business, labor, government, and other sectors of society.

Their rise to prominence has hardly gone unnoticed. Some hail them as the public's tribunes against the powerful, as indispensable champions of the underdog and the oppressed. Others decry them for allegiance to an adversary culture that is chiseling away at traditional values. The crucial task that remains is to discover what relationship, if any, exists between how these individuals view the world and how they present that world to the public.

WHOSE NEWS?

"We shall give a correct picture of the world."
—James Gordon Bennett, *New York Herald*

THERE ARE FEW ideologues in major media newsrooms. The American press has a longstanding tradition of fairness and nonpartisanship, and journalists whose news judgments stem blatantly from their politics are unlikely to survive long in mainstream news organizations. They may have productive careers as columnists or at journals of opinion from the *National Review* to the *Nation.* Or they may move into positions that combine journalistic skills with partisan temperaments, as press secretaries, speechwriters, or public relations executives. Those who remain in the mainstream usually accept the necessity to overcome one's biases as the hallmark of the journalistic profession.

Yet this cannot be the whole story, because news judgments are no more "value free" than social science judgments. A majority of the journalists surveyed believe their work should be a force for social reform. It is hardly surprising that people in this profession should hope that their work might, in some way, help bring about a better world. But the kind of world one desires, and how to attain it, underlie all ideological divisions.

The media uphold two conflicting ideals that cannot always be reconciled. The reformer's social commitment coexists uneasily with the cool nonpartisanship of the objective observer. This is a dilemma that even the best journalists rarely face head-on. For example, Walter Cronkite was once asked whether journalists were "liberals," biased against established institutions. He replied that this was not the case; they merely tend "to side with humanity rather than authority."[1] This statement cuts to the heart of the issue; it is not a matter of conscious bias but rather of the necessarily partial perspectives through which social reality is filtered. If the world is divided into authority and humanity, then naturally one sides with humanity. But is the world always divided that way? Who is assigned to each side? In what circumstances does one take a stand for one side and against the other? Such judgments are anything but self-evident.

We all reconstruct reality for ourselves, but journalists are especially important because they help depict reality for the rest of society. They do so through the everyday decisions of their craft: What story is worth covering? How much play should it get? What angle should it be given? What sources are trustworthy and informative? The unavoidable preconceptions journalists bring to such decisions help determine what images of society are available to their audience.

Searching for Sources

Thus the problem is not simply to subjugate bias to ideals of objectivity and professionalism. More broadly, it is to recognize the inevitable role that values and perspectives play in shaping news judgment. To probe these matters, which are infinitely more subtle than ideological bias, our interviews included some hypothetical questions and psychological tests. The most straightforward of these concerns the use of sources. We asked journalists where they would turn for reliable information on four different topics. These were broad topics that had been both controversial and newsworthy for several years—welfare reform, consumer issues, pollution and the environment, and nuclear energy.

For each topic, subjects could mention as many sources as they wished. The key question is whether these journalists' thoughts turn spontaneously to sources whose perspectives accord with their own. Or alternatively, do their professional instincts lead them to balance liberal and conservative sources on each topic? Of course, it might be argued that the most reliable sources on a particular topic line up on one side of the political spectrum. In this case, an ideologically balanced listing might be artificial. But this, too, is a matter of judgment that may be influenced by one's own perspective. To provide a baseline for comparison, therefore, the business leaders produced their own lists of reliable sources. Thus, journalists' responses can be gauged against those of a more conservative and traditional leadership group. The responses of both groups are shown in Table 4.

Welfare Reform. Since welfare reform has received attention and legislative proposals from liberals and conservatives alike, we questioned whether leading journalists would turn equally to both camps for sources. The individuals and groups they mention range across the entire ideological spectrum. After excluding government agencies and officials, however, a large number of sources can be reliably assigned to either the political left or right.

Liberal sources cited include such journals of opinion as the *New Republic* and *Mother Jones;* organizations like the National Welfare Rights Association, the Urban League, and Reverend Jesse Jackson's PUSH; and individual activists, such as former congresswomen Barbara Jordan and Bella Abzug. On the conservative side are such organizations as the American Conservative Union, the Hoover Institution, and the U.S. Chamber of Commerce, and individuals like William F. Buckley. After some deliberation, we also included Senator Daniel Patrick Moynihan in this group. At the time, Moynihan was viewed widely as a neo-conservative critic of the welfare system who had promoted a welfare overhaul as a member of the Nixon administration. In addition to these liberal and conservative groupings, other sources mentioned frequently include federal executive agencies, individual federal officials, state and local agencies, and nonpartisan media sources like *National Journal, Congressional Quarterly,* and *Facts on File.*

How do journalists regard the sources at either end of the ideological spectrum? Their choices are weighted heavily toward the liberal end. Three out of four journalists mention at least one liberal source. In sharp contrast, fewer than one in four cites a

Table 4—Types of Sources Cited as Reliable		
	Media	Business
Welfare Reform		
Liberals	75%	17%
Federal Regulatory Agencies	51	25
Federal Officials	38	25
Conservatives	22	22
State and Local Agencies	16	30
Consumer Protection		
Ralph Nader/Nader Groups	63	33
Federal Regulatory Agencies	46	28
Consumers Union	44	30
Other Activist Groups	41	26
State and Local Agencies	36	40
Business Groups	22	49
Pollution and Environment		
Environmental Activists	69	25
Activist Federal Agencies	68	56
Business Groups	27	34
Liberal Activists and Officials	24	8
Other Federal Agencies	19	11
Nuclear Energy		
Anti-Nuclear	55	—
Technical Magazines	40	—
Federal Regulatory Agencies	39	—
Other Government	37	—
Pro-Nuclear	32	—

Note: Excludes nonpartisan media sources and categories mentioned by fewer than 15 percent of all subjects.

conservative source. In fact, avowedly liberal individuals, groups, and journals constitute by far the largest sources of information on which these journalists would rely. The disparity between liberal and conservative sources would be even greater if Moynihan weren't classified as a conservative in this context. He alone is mentioned by 12 percent of all journalists, the largest total for any individual on this topic.

How do these results compare with the responses of business leaders? The business group gives the more ideologically balanced response, with conservative sources outweighing the liberal ones, but only by a five percent margin (22 to 17 percent). Among the media elite, liberal sources predominate by 53 percent (75 to 22 percent), better than a three to one margin.

Consumer Protection. On consumer issues, there is no clear-cut split between a conservative and liberal approach. But we were interested to see whether journalists would attempt to balance their reliance on consumer advocacy groups with business-related sources. Another question was whether greater attention would be given to an organization of relatively narrow focus, such as Consumers Union, which publishes *Consumer Reports,* or to activist groups with broad social reform agendas, such as the various Nader groups. Third, would journalists look more to government regulatory agencies or to nonprofit organizations, such as those in the public interest movement?

One finding stands out. When the media elite deal with consumer protection, their thoughts turn to Ralph Nader. Nearly two out of three mention Nader or one of his allied organizations, such as Congress Watch or Public Citizen. One out of five cites Nader himself, the most mentions given to an individual on any of the four topics. No other category garners a majority of mentions, but three are clustered just above 40 percent. One is federal regulatory agencies, particularly the more activist agencies like the Occupational Safety and Health Administration.[2] The other two categories are nonprofit groups, ranging from the Consumer Federation of America and Common Cause to social activist groups like the American Civil Liberties Union and Americans for Democratic Action.

The paucity of business-oriented sources is also notable. Some journalists try to balance their reliance on Nader groups and liberal activists with such sources as the Better Business Bureau, Chamber of Commerce, and industry trade associations. One would even turn to "lobbyists for big industries." Overall, though, only 22 percent cite some such business-related source of information.

Once again, there is a great gulf between journalists and businessmen. Almost half the business leaders mention a business-related source. Only one in three cites the Nader network, making them only about half as likely as journalists to rely on Nader. They are also substantially less likely to cite other activist groups. Of course one could hardly expect the business community to flock to Ralph Nader, an adversary of long standing. But neither is it self-evident that Nader still epitomizes the now far-flung consumer movement to the extent that journalists' responses might suggest. Nor would one automatically associate consumer protection with such groups as the American Civil Liberties Union and Americans for Democratic Action. So these very different patterns of responses illustrate how these different occupational groups, with their different perspectives on society, diverge drastically in their search for reliable information.

The fact that businessmen would turn to different sources does not mean their sources are necessarily better or worse than those of journalists. It is just a reminder that news stories are not chosen randomly. They reflect the inevitable choices that journalists continually make as they put their stories together. Journalists' reliance on Nader groups is also a reminder of the rapid ascendance of public interest groups as sources of information about social issues. Twenty years ago such groups existed only as isolated organizations, promoting particular causes. Today they constitute an influential network, dispensing information and providing litigation on a variety of causes ranging from consumerism to civil rights to environmentalism. That their names now rest on the tips of journalists' tongues attests to their success in helping reshape the news agenda.

Environmental Issues. In light of leading journalists' preferences for information on consumer issues, their preferred sources on pollution and the environment come as no surprise. The largest number, over two out of three, select environmental activist groups and individuals. These groups include the Environmental Defense Fund, Friends of the Earth, Sierra Club, and Natural Resources Defense Council, as well as local organizations like Pete Seeger's Clearwater anti-nuclear group. Individual activists range from Robert Redford to Barry Commoner. Nearly as many mention the activist (at the time) federal regulatory agencies, such as the Council on Environmental Quality (CEQ) and Occupational Health and Safety Administration. These activist public and private-sector groups eclipse all others as favored sources of information.

Again the question arises: Are these the "obvious" choices that anyone would make? It helps to note potential sources that receive short shrift. For example, fewer than one in five among the media elite mention any other federal bodies with responsibilities in this area, such as the Energy Department, National Academy of Sciences, and National Institute for Occupational Safety and Health. Similarly, only one in fourteen mentions non-activist groups (again, at the time), such as the National Wildlife Federation and the Wilderness Society. Even fewer would rely on scientific or technical journals, such as *Science, Nature,* or *Scientific American.*

All these subsidiary information sources were overshadowed by a category called liberal activists and officials. One in four journalists cites groups or individuals not primarily associated with environmental issues. These include Jane Fonda, Ralph Nader, and Tom Hayden, and such elected officials as senators Edward Kennedy and Gary Hart, and then-Governor Jerry Brown of California.

The number of these liberal sources is roughly equalled by the totality of all business-related sources, including organizations like the Edison Electric Institute and Business Roundtable and publications ranging from *Business Week* and *Nation's Business* to *Forbes* and *Fortune.* It may be that some journalists seek to balance liberal sources with business-oriented perspectives on the environment. But this does not include the great preponderance of activist environmental groups cited, most of which have often locked horns with industry over pollution and related issues.

Businessmen are far less likely to view the latter groups as reliable sources. Only one in four selects any of them, compared to two out of three journalists. Just as predictably, businessmen are only one-third as likely as journalists to mention liberal acti-

vists or officials, and most who do so focus on nationally prominent politicians. Names like Tom Hayden and Jane Fonda do not
spring to mind among the business elite. On the other hand, a
majority of business leaders also cite activist federal agencies like
the Environmental Protection Agency (EPA) and CEQ. The key
difference between the two groups lies in journalists' willingness
to accept the reliability of environmental activists in the public
interest movement.[3]

Nuclear Power. Finally, in a follow-up mailing soon thereafter, we
asked journalists to write down any sources of information on
nuclear energy that they considered reliable.[4] Then we compared
the number of responses citing pro-nuclear and anti-nuclear
sources, along with sources that didn't fall into either camp. Pro-
nuclear sources cited include industry trade associations and public utilities, such as the Atomic Industrial Forum, Babcock and
Wilson (a reactor supply .firm), and Con Edison; utility trade
publications; and a few pro-nuclear scientists, including Edward
Teller and Hans Bethe. The anti-nuclear sources are much more
diverse. They include anti-nuclear groups like the Union of Concerned Scientists, Environmental Action, and the Clamshell Alliance, along with such publications as *Critical Mass Journal* and
the *Progressive*. Also included are many individual activists, such
as Ralph Nader and Jane Fonda, in addition to those with scientific credentials, among them John Goffman, Henry Kendall,
Barry Commoner, and Helen Caldicott. There are also many
sources not clearly aligned with either the pro- or anti-nuclear
side.

There is no contest; anti-nuclear sources far outstrip their
pro-nuclear opponents, who finish behind the pack. A majority of
those listing reliable sources mention an anti-nuclear group or
individual. No more than 40 percent would turn to a scientific
journal, a federal agency, or other government body. Even fewer,
less than one in three, select any pro-nuclear source. This leaves
a 23 percent margin of difference between anti- and pro-nuclear
sources cited (55 vs. 32 percent).

To summarize, journalists' responses to all four issues fall into
the same general pattern. Where do the media elite turn for

reliable information? On welfare reform, liberal sources predominate over conservative ones. On consumer issues they look to Ralph Nader, the public interest movement, and liberal activist groups. On pollution and the environment, they select activist environmental groups and, once again, liberal leaders. On nuclear energy, anti-nuclear sources are the most popular. In short, their responses tend to coincide with the perspectives catalogued in Chapter Two.

To be sure, the business executives predictably select more conservative, business-oriented sources. That is precisely the point. People gravitate toward sources whose perspectives accord with their own. Differences between the two groups are statistically significant at .001 for each of the topics.* The extent of this tilt should not be overstated. Journalists by no means depend exclusively on liberal viewpoints. They cite a mixture of public and private, partisan and non-partisan, liberal and conservative sources. But the liberal side consistently outweighs the conservative.

This does not imply a conspiracy to exclude conservative voices, but merely reflects the human tendency to turn more often to those you trust, and to trust most those who think most like you do. This presents a special problem for journalists. A large portion of their craft rests on the ability to sift through various sources and viewpoints and pass them on to their audience. As columnist Joseph Kraft wrote, "The occupational weakness of those of us in the news media should be obvious. . . . We are not

---

*For readers unfamiliar with the concept of statistical significance, it expresses the probability that a given difference could result from sheer chance or sampling error. The lower the significance level, the greater our confidence that differences found among random samples express true differences between the populations from which the samples are drawn. Thus a significance level of .001, or $p = .001$ (read: probability equals .001) expresses a difference that would occur by chance only one time in a thousand. By convention a significance level of .05 is normally the highest acceptable, although levels below .10 may be said to "approach" an adequate level of significance. Unless otherwise noted, the significance levels cited are based on the chi-square statistic.

scholars or even experts. We cannot, accordingly, be original sources of light. We depend heavily, if not entirely, on what other people tell us. Our professional skill is in judging sources, and in fitting bits and pieces of evidence into coherent patterns."[5]

Reconstructing Reality

The difficulty in judging sources extends to a broader issue. Social perspectives may unconsciously color the very way journalists perceive the news itself. This might strike psychologists as a very mild hypothesis, almost an axiomatic principle.[6] Why should journalists be any less prone to selective perception than anyone else? Yet the way they perceive the news is tremendously important, because it determines the kind of stories they transmit to the rest of us.

In addition, we have argued that the major obstacle to objectivity in contemporary American journalism is not unyielding partisanship but unavoidable preconceptions. Therefore we would expect the media elite to process information mostly in a straightforward fashion, but with occasional evidence of selective recall. When such slippage occurs, however, it should tend to be consistent with their overt attitudes, which can act as perceptual filters.

To examine the estimations of reality that underlie news judgments, we created several news stories. The stories deal with controversial current issues ranging from offshore oil drilling to affirmative action. They variously contain primarily liberal or conservative cues or balance opposing perspectives. During the interview, each subject looked briefly at the stories, handed them back to the interviewer, and then attempted to summarize each story in a single sentence. We were interested not in whether a summary contained the "correct" interpretation, but whether the media and business groups would give somewhat different readings of the same material, corresponding to their different perspectives on society.

After the interviews were completed, each summary was examined separately by two scorers, neither of whom knew the study's purposes or the identities of the participants. The scorers simply grouped anonymous summaries into the categories described below. (This method of "blind" scoring was a standard procedure for the psychological tests.) The fact that the scorers agreed over 90 percent of the time suggests that their classifications are quite reliable. Finally, we compared the response patterns of the two groups. Each story is reprinted here in its entirety, so that readers can judge its content for themselves.

Affirmative Action. The first example concerns the heated debate over affirmative action measures and their impact:

> In the wake of the Bakke decision, a growing number of white males are fighting back against affirmative action programs that favor women and minorities in employment and university admissions. Steelworkers in Louisiana, firemen in Pittsburgh, and teachers in Detroit are all raising their voices in protest.
>
> The chairman of the Equal Employment Opportunities Commission says that this backlash places affirmative actions programs in "severe jeopardy." Conservative forces, he warns, are trying to exploit this reaction against "reverse discrimination" and throttle all efforts to bring women and racial minorities into the economic mainstream.
>
> A white male teacher recently rejected for tenure in favor of a female colleague disputed this, saying, "It's all right to talk about eliminating discrimination, until your ox is gored. Then it brings the issue into focus."

Majorities of both groups (62 percent overall) summarize this story either in straightforward, neutral language (e.g., "it's about the controversy over affirmative action"), or in balanced terms, mentioning both sides in the debate. Typical of the latter is an NBC producer's recollection:

> "Blacks tend to feel that if affirmative action is to make up for many decades of disadvantage, it must include specific goals, something akin to quotas, but a good many whites are now challenging this on the basis that disadvantaged whites should not be forced to make all the concessions."

The remaining responses are divided almost equally between those mentioning only the pro–affirmative action argument (18 percent) and those confined to the reverse discrimination side (20 percent). But the answers of journalists and businessmen are not evenly distributed among those two groups. Among those remembering only the affirmative action side, journalists outnumber businessmen by 62 to 38 percent. Conversely, businessmen predominate on the reverse discrimination side by 58 to 42 percent. These differences are significant at the .01 level.

Most pro–affirmative action responses focus on the danger that anti-discrimination measures might be undermined. A *New York Times* reporter's summary is typical: "The decision in the Bakke case appears to be resulting in further discrimination on minorities." Likewise, a *Time* correspondent states, "the Bakke decision has had a backlash effect that is jeopardizing affirmative action programs for women [and] minorities." A *Washington Post* reporter concurs, "The Bakke decision has set off a wave of reverse discrimination cases that threaten the advances made in earlier equal opportunity decisions." Among the smaller number of journalists who stress the other side of the argument is an NBC producer who writes, ". . . given a choice of an 'A' student or a 'C' student let into school to prove a point, I'd rather let in the 'A' student."

Business Bribery. The next story focuses on businessmen themselves. It concerns a law prohibiting American businesses from bribing foreign officials to secure overseas clients. This time the story leads with the business viewpoint, while including some opposing material:

> Not long ago Congress passed a tough law that prohibits bribery of government officials in foreign business dealings. Many American executives are now complaining that, as a result, they have lost sales worth millions of dollars to competitors. In their view, the new morality has compounded America's balance of payments deficits and raised the cost of goods to consumers.
>
> The president of a major company complained, "American businessmen are operating with both hands tied behind their backs. What's business all about, anyway?—to make money. You pay a commission to make a deal, you make a profit, everyone's happy."

Government spokesmen counter that Americans will not stand for a double standard in business ethics at home and abroad. Nevertheless, a widespread feeling persists that American business is being hurt.

This time 69 percent of responses could be classified as neutral or balanced. Of the remainder, those criticizing business tactics almost double those defending them, by 20 to 11 percent. Once again, the two groups gather on opposite sides, to a statistically significant degree ($p < .01$). Journalists account for 68 percent of those recalling only criticisms of business ethics, while businessmen make up 64 percent of those recalling the necessity for bribery to compete abroad.

Journalists in the first group often come down hard on business for double standards and unethical behavior. For example, an ABC executive accuses American businessmen of ". . . trying to rationalize unethical means to do business." A *U.S. News* reporter asserts: "There is no possible legitimate reason for American businessmen to operate under double standards of business ethics . . ." And one ABC producer seizes the opportunity to pass judgment on domestic business practices: "Who said bribery wasn't always the way in American business to begin with . . . under the table deals have always been the way of life in America."

Journalists who recall the other side of the argument tend to be more straightforward, often carefully attributing it to the "complaints" of businessmen. For example, in a *U.S. News* reporter's summary, "American industry is complaining that it's hard to do business overseas under U.S. regulations which prohibit bribery of foreign officials." This contrasts with the much more pointed comments of businessmen in this group, who tend to employ phrases like "fighting a battle with one hand tied behind you."

Race and Income. A story on the economic gap between blacks and whites produces another split between media and business leaders. This story leads with the view that racial discrimination continues to hinder black achievement. However, it also presents an affirmative view that black economic achievement is rising.

> The economic gap between blacks and whites is widening, according to a report released by a major civil rights organization. According to the report, the black-to-white family income ratio has fallen sharply, while black unemployment has increased more rapidly than that of whites.
>
> These findings challenge recent studies claiming that economic achievement by blacks is on the upswing, and that the current plight of blacks is better accounted for by class differences than by racial discrimination. Proponents of this view argue that increased and improved education has made blacks more competitive in the job market, while government-mandated minority hiring programs have had little effect.
>
> A spokesman for the civil rights groups calls this a "dangerous misconception" that increases white resistance toward efforts to bring about racial equality. He warned that a slackening of such efforts would produce renewed urban unrest.

This story elicits some of the strongest sentiments recorded. The cue of the civil rights report proved strong enough to outweigh even the neutral and balanced responses. They account for only 42 percent of all subjects. A majority of 52 percent recalls only the argument that the racial economic gap is widening. That leaves only 7 percent who refer solely to the contradictory claims from the story's second paragraph. Nonetheless, a familiar division of perceptions appears along occupational lines. Journalists account for two-thirds (66 percent) of those reciting summaries about an increasing income gap, while businessmen represent an even greater portion (69 percent) of those who reject this notion or attribute it to class rather than racial factors. This pattern of differences is significant at the .001 level.

Some journalists not only affirm the notion of a widening gap, but also debunk the contradictory position. Thus, an ABC correspondent castigates whites for unsupportable optimism: "the white perception that blacks are making major progress in achieving an equal economic status with whites is simply untrue or incorrect." Others stress the warning that any slackening of efforts to decrease the gap would engender unrest. A *New York Times* reporter puts this view in stark terms: "The notion that blacks are better off is an illusion which whites had better take note of or run the risk of seeing more racial disturbances in the big cities." Still others attribute the faltering economic condition of blacks to pervasive racial discrimination. In the words of a *Post* reporter, "The problem of class distinction within the black race is being used to overshadow the continuing racial discrimination problems of the day."

A few journalists reaffirm a declining income gap or attribute economic differences to class rather than racial factors. A public broadcasting administrator even asserts, "the annual income of blacks has increased and is beginning to surpass that of the average white income." And an ABC executive offers a rebuke: "Just a continuing offense on the part of the civil rights groups. Positive strides have been made in the past 20 years—sometimes a great deal of paranoia tends to exist among civil rights groups. . . ." Such responses, however, are the exception. More typical is an independent producer's contention that, "There's always been and will always be a broad gulf between black and white due to racial discrimination."

The Politics of Energy. The last story deals with a struggle between consumers' groups and the oil industry over offshore drilling:

> The House Rules Committee will vote today on a bill designed to provide a more orderly development of offshore oil and natural gas reserves.
>
> The bill has been passed by the Senate, and supporters had thought House passage was secure. But under intense lobbying pressures from the oil industry, which contends that the measure would slow development of offshore energy, several committee members have withdrawn earlier expressions of support.
>
> The director of a consumer group said, "The bottling up of this bill would be an unconscionable power play by the oil industry to prevent urgently needed reforms."

Whose News?

Industry lobbyists, however, tried to play down their part in today's vote. The head of a local lobbying group said, "We've played a very minor role. We are just trying to point out that the bill hurts the little companies."

A slight majority (52 percent) of the summaries are neutral or balanced. Most of the remainder (40 percent) criticize the oil industry or lobbyists in general. Only 8 percent support the industry's position that the bill would not be in the public interest. These one-sided responses fit a familiar pattern, but to a lesser degree. Journalists make up 58 percent of the anti-industry comments, and businessmen recall 57 percent of the pro-industry summaries. For the first time, however, the magnitude of these differences isn't great enough to attain statistical significance. This apparently reflects a widespread distaste for lobbyists that is shared by journalists and businessmen alike. A network film editor's comment is typically succinct: "Lobbyists are sleazy and that's the crux of it." This is not so different from an oil company executive's more prosaic lament that, "Lobbying often has a detrimental effect upon legislation designed for the common good."

Surely, many journalists dispute the coupling of corporate and national interest. As a *Post* reporter puts it, ". . . [the] oil industry has influenced [Congress] to take action that would benefit the major oil companies to the detriment of the country." But others, like a CBS producer, remember just the opposite message: "The bill . . . would badly affect the industry and the country."

Although the differences in the responses on this final story are slight, the dominant pattern remains clear. For stories dealing with racial income disparities, affirmative action, and bribery in business practices, the media and business summaries differ to a statistically significant degree. After reading the same stories, the media group is more likely to recall a rising racial income gap and the business group to remember a declining one; the journalists differentially tend to see threats to affirmative action where the businessmen observe reverse discrimination; members of the press more often perceive a lack of business ethics where the industrialists find unfair standards. Finally, the media subjects are slightly

69

(but not significantly) more critical of the industry position on offshore drilling.

The magnitude of these differences should not be overstated. The percentage differences between the two groups on individual categories were often small, reaching a maximum of 22 percent on the racial income gap story (where 62 percent of journalists gave a "liberal" response, compared to 40 percent of businessmen). Indeed, one might regard the findings as testimony to the professionalism of leading journalists, since the majority of all responses fell into the neutral or balanced categories. This may also reflect more general patterns of perception, since the businessmen were slightly more likely than the journalists to produce such responses.

Still, the overall pattern of responses should not be underestimated. This was an artificial and highly structured situation in which participants knew they were being tested in some way. Nonetheless, statistically significant differences appeared on three of the four test items (i.e., the stories). And in every case the direction of slippage was consistent with the differences in the two groups' social attitudes.

Moreover, when the responses are summed across all four stories, the group differences stand out more sharply. To create an overall index, we treated the first response in the dichotomies summarized above (pro-affirmative action, criticism of business ethics, etc.) as a "liberal" perception, and the second (reverse discrimination, unfair standards hurt industry, etc.) as its "conservative" counterpart. Neutral and balanced responses were considered nonpartisan. By this measure, 56 percent of the journalists produced at least one liberal response, while only 38 percent provided a conservative answer. By contrast, only 44 percent of the businessmen gave one or more liberal summaries, but 62 percent produced conservative perceptions. These group differences become sharper if we take into account the total of each individual's liberal or conservative responses across all four stories. For example, nearly half the sample produced two or more summaries tilted in either the liberal or conservative direction. Of this subgroup, journalists account for two-thirds (66 percent) of those with two or more liberal responses, while businessmen make up three out of four subjects (74 percent) with at least two conservative summaries.

Finally, we created an overall index of selective recall by subtracting the conservative responses from the liberal ones. Thus, the higher an individual's score, the more his or her liberal responses outweigh the conservative ones. The net results, shown in Table 5, demonstrate a consistent and statistically significant ($p < .001$) relationship between occupation and perception. The businessmen make up two-thirds of the group with the most conservative perception; the journalists account for nearly three-quarters of those with the most liberal perceptions.

Thus, when leading journalists confront new information, they usually manage to process it without interjecting their own viewpoints. At the same time, some selective recall seems inevitable. When this does occur, the net result is to push their perceptions of the news somewhat in the liberal direction. In sum, these findings suggest that journalists are neither strangers to selective perception nor its prisoners. How could it be otherwise? This confirms that they are not ideologues, but also that they are only human. It recalls one newspaper ombudsman's response to our survey: "They are professionals, but there is bound to be slippage. The problem is that the slippage may be mostly in one direction."

Pictures in Our Heads

Thus far the psychological probes have been rather straightforward and closely related to journalists' daily work. What sources do they trust? What angle do they spontaneously give to a story?

Table 5—Liberal Perceptions of News Stories			
	Low	Medium	High
Media	34	51	73
Business	66	49	27
	100%	100%	100%

Their own responses to these questions suggest that their social perspectives cannot be divorced entirely from their news judgments.

We sought to probe more deeply still into the media's collective mentality—to uncover the underlying personality tendencies that guide perceptions and judgments. To measure these, the interview included a personality test called the Thematic Apperception Test (TAT). The TAT consists of several pictures of social situations that can be interpreted in many different ways. For example, one picture shows an older man talking to a younger man in an office. The older man could be comforting the younger man, giving him advice, or criticizing him. The "test" is to write a fictional story about the people in the picture.

The TAT's underlying assumption is like that of the Rorschach "ink-blot" test. When people use their imaginations to structure an ambiguous situation, they inadvertently reveal what is on their minds. Such stories reveal a good deal about inner needs and motivations that people may not even realize they possess. Thus, the TAT is intended to tap imagination and creativity and, with it, one's fantasies and projections. It allows access to the underlying fantasy life that helps shape our understanding and expectation of social reality. If dreams are the royal road to the unconscious, the TAT at least provides a poor man's path.

Initially we chose this test to measure basic psychological dispositions, such as the need for power, the need for achievement, and the capacity for intimacy. There is a long history of social psychological research on such key personality traits. The findings in these areas are presented in Chapter Four. However, many of the themes and images also had a social or political cast. So, we also employed a system, devised by Eileen McColgan of Columbia University, to score TAT stories for social and political imagery.

Each subject was shown five pictures and asked to write a story about the characters depicted. Because the pictures were originally chosen to measure personality traits rather than politically relevant fantasies, the majority of stories did not convey such concerns. Of those that did, however, we asked once again whether the responses of the media and business groups differed significantly in ways corresponding to their differing social perspectives.

Four of the pictures produced socially relevant themes. We will discuss each in turn with examples to convey the flavor of the responses. The examples are reproduced verbatim from the questionnaires. Our underlying goal is to show which aspects of ambiguous situations journalists pay the greatest attention to, and how they structure social reality for themselves.

Men in Uniform. The first picture (see fig. 1) shows two uniformed men flanking a third, who wears a different uniform. Their positioning and expressions suggest to many subjects that the man in the middle is subordinate to the others or even at their mercy. As a result, this picture sometimes produces stories about authority relations. However, such stories are coded as socially relevant only if the characters' individual behavior is connected to that of a larger institution or organization, such as the police or military.

In these cases, a story's portrayal of institutional authority is scored as positive if the authority figures or the institutions they represent are portrayed as helping an individual or otherwise producing beneficial outcomes. Stories are scored as negative when authority figures, acting as representatives of their institution, are portrayed as punitive or arbitrary, or otherwise produce detrimental outcomes.

How do the two groups differ in the fantasies they create about authority and its effect on the individual? About one story in five (19 percent) could be coded for such themes. Journalists make up two-thirds (65 percent) of those who create anti-authority tales, while businessmen account for 58 percent of the pro-authority plots, a statistically significant difference (p < .05).

About one in five journalists sees the two authority figures as policemen and the man in the center as their prisoner. A recurring theme is that of the innocent victim facing his captors. Thus he is variously described by a *Time* reporter as "unfairly put in jail for robbery," and by a *Newsweek* reporter as "the quite innocent victim of some Kafkaesque persecution." This theme is sometimes overlaid with visions of social oppression. A PBS staff member portrays a farmer who "has been involved in activities that are

73

Figure 1

considered subversive. He is a socialist in the 1950's and his way of thinking is very unpopular. . . . He is concerned about what will happen to his family and farm if he doesn't sign the loyalty oath the policemen want." In a *Washington Post* editor's story, the young man is a "farm labor organizer" about to be arrested because he "is engaged in a campaign against agricultural producers . . . to establish minimum wages and working conditions. . . ."

Such prisoners often face a rough ride from the authorities. An independent producer tells of an innocent man who "hasn't a chance . . . with no money for proper legal defense. . . . They will try to get him to confess to a crime he didn't commit." A PBS administrator uses the first person technique to convey the prisoner's plight. "After the escape from prison, I ran into a field where I spent the night. . . . When I awoke two authorities were

74

standing over me with guns pointed at my face. . . . They began to beat me."

So for some journalists this picture provides an opportunity to identify with the prisoner as the often innocent victim of intimidation or police brutality. More often, though, their complaints are against a different institution—the armed forces. Three out of four depict a military setting, and their descriptions of military life are shot through with sarcasm and depictions of punitive behavior. Several journalists portray the man in the middle as a scared recruit at the mercy of two superiors. A *Washington Post* reporter writes, "This young man was inducted, probably against his will. He may abhor military life and the regimentation it entails, but he has little choice." A more concrete version of this theme, by a PBS staffer, has two sergeants tell a recruit, "There are eighteen tons of horseshit out in that field, son, and you've got one week to pick it all up." Faced with this unpleasant task, he goes AWOL and escapes to Canada. Eventually he takes a journalist's revenge: "He later writes a tough honest novel about army life and wins a Pulitzer prize."

In addition to identifying with the victim, these journalists often express anger against those who abuse power. Thus a PBS production staffer describes the two authority figures as "faceless brutes . . . smugly complacent in their authority," while an ABC reporter complains of their "arrogance that comes with power over the powerless." A *Newsweek* reporter speculates that "the commanding officer . . . may even enjoy inflicting punishment," and a *Time* reporter alludes to "the sadism of army non-coms." A CBS correspondent even provides a psychological sketch of the compensatory function of bullying. His career Marine officer is ". . . a real son of a bitch. He's a man who's grown frustrated with his lack of progress. He takes out his aggression on recruits, enjoys the fear he can see on their young faces just by raising a fist."

The threat of sadistic aggression occasionally becomes an actuality. According to one *Wall Street Journal* reporter, two Marine drill instructors "are trying to figure out a way to shit-can the recruit, to drum him out of the corps. . . . After repeated punches to the stomach his Adam's apple will be squeezed, he will be gouged. . . . He will crack up . . ." Even this graphic description falls short of a *New York Times* reporter's story, which carries the theme of authoritarian brutality to its grisly conclusion: "The guard with the gun will shoot the young man in the head and the other will kick his body."

Several stories are peppered with derogatory comments about the armed services. A good example of how anti-military and anti-authority themes are interwoven is a *Washington Post* reporter's story, which begins, "Once again—the military. America never escapes it . . . never escapes the faces of the military which —incidentally—never change . . . an ordinary soldier . . . has gone AWOL. . . . He is captured by two officers. They are predictably the stereotypical bully types . . . relishing their task." Another *Post* reporter expresses resentment more succinctly: "the superior officers are enjoying the authority they can exert, just because they are in the military," while a *New York Times* reporter asserts that "the [military's] goal is order not justice."

The pro-authority stories invert most of the themes stressed above, upholding military authority and its institutional ethos. For example, an NBC producer justifies the rigors of Marine Corps boot camp: "Certain people can use this type of experience [for] its help in molding character." A *Post* editor legitimizes military authority relations by introducing that stock character, the outwardly tough sergeant with a tender heart: "Sgt. Breitenback would like to see the recruit make good . . . deep down he sympathizes with the recruit's difficulties, and he feels committed to the Marine ethic 'the Marine Corps builds men'. . . the tough MP Sgt. will help him in quiet ways to get over his fear of the military." Overall, however, journalists create over four times as many anti-authority themes (by 17 to 4 percent), with stories of the "little guy" being badgered, beaten down, or brutalized by malevolent authorities.

Boxers. This picture of two boxers (see fig. 2) might seem an unlikely candidate to produce social imagery. It shows one man in the foreground with another silhouetted in the background. The man in the foreground apparently is staring into space; the other seems to be training or sparring.

Figure 2

Just as some journalists treat the first picture as a cue to criticize authority, they differentially use this opportunity to write about boxers as social underdogs. The journalists are significantly more likely than the businessmen to identify one of the boxers as black, to see them as fighting against poverty, or to portray them

77

as exploited by higher-ups such as crooked managers. Moreover, contrasting subplots often emerge in the stories about underdogs fighting against a hostile world. The businessmen tend to echo Horatio Alger themes, portraying the boxers as successful in their quest for victory, a championship, and fame and riches. The journalists tend to end their stories on a downbeat note, concluding that these underdogs will lose their struggle, both in the ring and in life.

One writer in three (33 percent) infuses his or her story with such social relevance. Among those who see the fighters as social underdogs, journalists predominate by 69 to 31 percent. Conversely, Horatio Alger themes are usually the province of businessmen, by 62 to 38 percent. These differences are significant at the .001 level.

Several journalists carry the theme of race or racism into their stories. A recurring theme pits a black boxer against a "great white hope." These stories deal with the effects of racism on the characters. An NBC correspondent tells a story about an aggressive young redneck from Mobile, Alabama, who is "gonna fight a black man no less from Detroit in his first fight for money. His first fight with a black man since [Viet]Nam." But the bout won't go well for him. "He's going to get the cockiness beaten out of him —and by a black man." The upshot? "Billy's going to do his fighting for the Klan."

Other subjects have their characters strike a blow against racism. An independent producer writes that boxing taught Tony, his protagonist, "the fundamentals of self-control and friendship. ... His feelings toward other minorities, once hardened by racism, have softened into respect." And a CBS producer spins a tale about the triumph of principle over ambition. His white fighter rejects the "great white hope" hype surrounding him. "He would like this fight to be fought strictly on its merits without any racial overtones. He makes up his mind that he will call off the fight until it can be held without stigma of racism. It means the end of his career but he feels he has indeed won a greater fight." Here it is irrelevant whether the background boxer is "actually" black or white. The ambiguity is itself the message. It allows some subjects to give rein to their concerns about racism in American society.

Other journalists' characters are poor and downtrodden, and likely to remain so. A *Wall Street Journal* reporter notes that "boxing has long been a road of advancement for the unskilled and uneducated young man in our society." His protagonist "is typical of these . . . the oldest brother of a large, poor New York family. His favorite movie is *Rocky* and he sees himself advancing to the top ranks of the pros." But the promise will likely prove false. "Already the pounding is starting to take its toll and . . . he may end up poor and punch drunk."

Journalists tend to forecast such failure and misery for their struggling young strivers. A CBS executive foresees that "both will continue to fight and in the end will wind up broke and unemployed." And in a *Time* reporter's forecast, "they will sustain more beatings in the ring. Eventually they will wind up on some skid row as punch-drunk has-beens." Sometimes failure is attributed to personal or social exploitation. In a *Washington Post* reporter's story, two poverty-stricken boxers aim at the title fight that will bring them money and "a reputation." But "they will not get it because they will be exploited." Who does the exploiting? Usually an avaricious manager, as in his *Post* colleague's story: "his manager asks him to take a dive and split the winnings of a big bout." A producer of PBS documentaries lays out the whole no-win scenario. His boxer "took a dive, got hurt and dumped by his promoters. Unable to work—started drinking—pulled himself together—trying to make a comeback. . . . He will fight and lose. He will have a final revelation . . . and realize he can't win."

For these journalists, then, the picture of two boxers does not bring to mind thoughts of Rocky triumphant, of overcoming the odds to win victories or championships. Instead, they ruminate on racism, poverty, exploitation, and the ultimate failure of the downtrodden. The controlling metaphor comes less from *Rocky* than *The Grapes of Wrath.*

Office Scene. This picture (see fig. 3) shows two men talking in an office. One man is middle-aged or older, the other much younger. The office is well appointed and the men are well dressed. These are the bare facts, the stage scenery. The rest is up to the viewer's imagination.

Stories are coded for social imagery only if the characters are portrayed in the context of an institutional role, such as businessmen making a deal or lawyers preparing a legal case. If the men are portrayed in a highly complimentary fashion or are shown

Figure 3

contributing to the good of society, they are coded as positive. If the characters intend or commit some illegal, unethical, or otherwise clearly objectionable act, they are coded as negative. Such stories must go beyond a passing positive or negative reference to make a strong judgment about the characters.

Most subjects see the figures as businessmen, while the remainder identify them mostly as lawyers or politicians. If the occupations portrayed are similar, though, the plots are sharply varied. One story in eight (13 percent) builds a plot around the two men's occupational functions. Journalists make up over three-quarters (78 percent) of those who portray the characters' behavior as corrupt or otherwise objectionable. However, journalists also constitute 62 percent of those who praise the characters' behavior. Nonetheless, the journalists' portrayals are significantly more negative ($p = .001$) than those of the business group.

How can this be so? The apparent paradox results from the small number of pro-authority stories—only 5 percent of all responses. So even though journalists account for the majority of this small group, they still produce twice as many negative as positive stories (13 vs. 6 percent of all journalists' stories, respectively). Businessmen write fewer codeable stories overall, and these are split evenly between positive and negative stories, with 4 percent in each category. Thus the media elite portray crooked or venal businessmen, deceitful lawyers, and self-serving politicians over three times as often as the business elite (13 vs. 4 percent).

A *Washington Post* editor creates a scenario that might have led to an airline crash: "The setting could be McDonald-Douglas [*sic*], the aircraft corporation, on the verge of deciding to go into production of the DC-10 transport. The older man has learned that the design tests show a serious, systemic flaw that will almost certainly cause crashes. . . . The younger associate is deciding that the arguments of his associate are not sufficiently compelling to risk the loss of status and prospects for advancement. He is on the verge of selling out."

Similarly, a *Newsweek* reporter tells of a hard-nosed chief executive pulling his faint-hearted subordinate into line: "Look at me, I personally kicked families out of houses for ten years before my dad brought me into the front office. Bill, you've got to go out there and foreclose on that [housing] project. You know the bundle we'll make when they put the office tower up on their place. Don't give me any crap about it not being really legal." And according to a senior editor at the *Washington Post,* "the older man is explaining to the younger why it is more important for the company to bribe an Iranian official to get a contract and keep the stockholders happy than it is for them to live up to the letter of the American law that prohibits foreign bribery."

Sometimes tales of corporate skullduggery spill over into more direct statements on the motives and mores of the business world. A high-level editor at *U.S. News and World Report* bypasses plot lines entirely in favor of an essay on business ethics: "Corporate greed and graft are a way of life to many who live in the Executive Suite. Sometimes it is a style passed from father to son, often to the disbelief of the younger person. Whatever happened to honesty, he may ask. But wealth prevails."

Businessmen are not the only target of the media elite's criticism. Lawyers are castigated for deceitfully protecting their clients, to the public's detriment. One editor portrays a young Washington lawyer who is reprimanded for being too "honest and straightforward" in representing "a big defense contractor" before a congressional committee. Eventually he learns "to play along and be a member of the team" in order to "make money with a big law office, with a big house in the suburbs."

Politicians fare even worse. A *Post* reporter's story holds the State Department responsible for Uganda's notorious Idi Amin: "The younger man by the window is the U.S. ambassador to Uganda in 1970. The older man is the department chief for Africa at the State Department. A decision has been made to mount a coup to bring Idi Amin to power. The older authority figure is convincing the younger and more honest-looking figure that the U.S. should not oppose the coup. He prevails, Idi Amin comes to power, but the policy backfires as Amin runs amok. . . . The older man retires, becomes a combatant for South Africa, and the struggle for influence continues."

In sharp contrast are stories that portray positive authority figures or actually praise the business community. These are invariably blander than the more sharply etched negative stories. Typical is an NBC producer's scenario: "A senior executive at a large corporation is addressing a bright, ambitious young executive. He's explaining why it's necessary to make an unpopular decision. The young man feels it's important to avoid the decision. . . . The unpopular decision is made, the young executive eventually discerns that it was the correct and proper thing to do." Rarely does the theme of business having social benefits become an integral part of a journalist's story. Thus, an ABC producer sees the two businessmen as benefiting the larger community: "In private industry an opportunity to grow and refine one's theories is to compare them with those of others . . . the body of common business knowledge will expand. As business refines itself the consumer and economy will prosper."

More often, though, journalists portray these establishment figures as slavishly pursuing personal profit or narrow self-interest at the public's expense. One NBC producer even offers a preferred alternative in his story about a father "trying to get [his son] to consider a 'proper' business career." The son "wants to do his own thing, doesn't consider the family business all that exciting and doesn't give a damn whether he winds up a millionaire." The denouement? "He's going to tell his father no thanks, he would rather be . . . a public interest lawyer working with Ralph Nader."

Adult and Child. The picture of a black male adult and child (see fig. 4) summons up many of the same themes as the boxer picture, with some intriguing variations. Almost one-third (31 percent) of all stories contain socially relevant themes. Although nothing in the picture suggests they are poor, poverty is a fairly common theme. Racial themes also appear in many guises, including stories about discrimination, racial pride, and minority advancement in white society. Journalists are significantly more likely than businessmen to apply themes of racial or social disadvantage. They comprise 62 percent of such stories, with the businessmen furnishing only 38 percent, a difference significant at the .01 level.

Figure 4

One recurring motif is the effort to overcome racial discrimination. Some stories concern past discrimination. A reporter for
Time writes, "He was 40, a black from Atlanta, and all the old
crimes of the past stayed with him. He remembered the time his
daddy tried to take his family to a Holiday Inn, only to be turned

away by the old we're-all-filled-up routine and being forced to
spend the night in the tacky Blue Midnight down the road, the
only motel around that slept blacks. He felt obligated to tell his
young son of his travails, travails that the boy would never experience because of the roads paved by his father."

Other stories deal with the lingering residue of racism. In a
Post reporter's version, a father tells his son that "despite recent
gains in human relations and equal opportunity . . . he must
always remember that he is black, which carries with it a special
burden and a special heritage." And a *Newsweek* reporter's story
raises the issue of current racial images in mass culture. Here a
teacher tries to explain why the comic books "always show Super-
man as a white dude." The boy complains, "But he's so powerful
. . . why can't he be black once in a while?" The teacher replies,
"I know, and the whites are always seeming too strong too. But
that's the heritage of 400 years of slavery and segregation in this
country. We got blacks coming on strong now too. It's going to
take time."

Occasionally such racial pride is equated with "black power"
and opposition to white society. One editor tells about a son
rejecting his father's advice: "the father wants him to do better so
he can 'succeed' and become an 'Uncle Tom.' The boy will rebel at
being forced to enter a middle-class, white, achievement-oriented
society. He will join his own people and work for black power."
And a reporter ridicules the adult character as "a black teacher
teaching a black boy in a white man's school" and complains, "I do
not associate black men sitting down with their youngsters—being
as I am a believer in the black matriachal society."

For most journalists who write socially relevant themes,
though, this picture evokes a less polarized message. Blacks can
"make it" if only they are afforded freedom from discrimination,
access to positive role models, and the opportunity for educational advancement. Thus a CBS producer imagines that this "father and son had heard Jesse Jackson speak . . . . Jackson had
urged both the parents and their children to work hard in school
stressing education is the key. . . . The Jackson speech had made
a tremendous impact on both father and son. Both had decided

that if the boy wanted to go to college, he'd better start working now."

In sum, journalists are consistently more likely than businessmen to uphold social underdogs and criticize authorities. Figures of authority differentially evoke journalists' fantasies about the abuse of power, whether by greedy businessmen, conniving politicians, intimidating policemen, or bullying military superiors. Conversely, they more often portray the average man as a victim of malevolent higher-ups or an uncaring or unjust social system. These differences are only relative. There is no correct response to this test, and no one theme or image is more proper than another. Moreover, the differences only represent group tendencies, which certainly do not hold for every journalist interviewed. Only a minority responded to each TAT picture with a socially relevant story that fit our scoring categories.

On the other hand, the group differences on all four pictures are statistically significant. The consistency of these findings suggests that occupational differences do exist in the fantasies the TAT pictures evoke about social relations. Moreover, when media and business responses are totaled across all four pictures (following the procedures used for the news stories, some sharper overall) distinctions appear. To make this comparison, we classified anti-authority and social underdog themes as liberal and pro-authority and Horatio Alger themes as conservative. To create a single continuum, we then added together each subject's liberal themes and subtracted his or her conservative themes from the total.

The net results, shown in Table 6, confirm that journalists make up nearly three-quarters (73 percent) of those with the most

Table 6—Liberal Themes In TAT Stories			
	Low	Medium	High
Media	37	56	73
Business	63	44	27
	100%	100%	100%

liberal TAT imagery, while businessmen account for the bulk (63 percent) of the most conservative themes.[7] These results are within a few percentage points of the earlier index of liberal and conservative story summaries (see Table 5). So the different outlooks of these two groups are reflected almost equally in both their perceptions and their apperceptions—the distinctive mindsets through which they experience the world.

The crucial point is quite simple. Journalists' source selections, summaries of news stories, and TAT themes tend to be consistent with the social attitudes they express. This suggests that their conscious opinions are reflected to some degree in the ways they subconsciously structure reality. It also suggests that total objectivity is impossible to attain, since the conscious effort to be objective takes place within a mental picture of the world already conditioned by one's beliefs about it. This is a truism to social psychologists, but one that journalists are understandably not eager to endorse. After all, it implies that dealing with the effects of personal perspective on news coverage may call for more than individual effort. It may require a heterogeneous newsroom where competing views of all stripes lessen the chance that any one perspective will be taken for granted.

It is probably impossible to deal with the world around us without some paradigm or worldview informing our approach to reality. On the basis of our upbringings and life experiences, we all make judgments about which facts are important and whom we can trust. Journalists and social scientists alike try to approach objectivity by developing self-awareness and by using techniques that minimize this natural and unavoidable partiality. But the pressure-packed environment of working journalists makes it especially difficult to attain a critical distance from the very news judgments on which they must depend.

New York Times editor Bill Kovach recently gave eloquent expression to this problem. In his words, "we are all prisoners within our own skins and there are values attached there that we are not even aware of . . . these values that we carry in our heads every day are the worst and most insidious because we don't recognize them."[8]

Whose Values? It is not only journalists, however, who tend to minimize the role their values play in news coverage. An important school of thought among social scientists holds that journalists' personal beliefs are unimportant, because their stories are shaped mainly by the needs of commercial news organizations. As Leon Sigal puts it, "The assumption . . . is that organizational pressures and bureaucratic politics account for much more of news content than, say, the political proclivities of individual newsmen."[9]

This organizational perspective encompasses two lines of argument. The first stresses the importance of constraints like those of time, money, and competition in shaping the news product. The second holds that editorial control overrides any bias by reporters, or that conservative editors, acting as agents of management, provide a check on liberal reporters.[10] Several influential books that appeared during the 1970s developed variations on these arguments as counterweights against charges of media bias by conservatives.[11] Indeed the authors sometimes invoked Spiro Agnew as representative of the perspective they rejected.[12]

By emphasizing the social context of newsmaking, organizational perspectives provide a needed corrective to crude conspiracy theories of the news. However, they also contain some limitations. First, social control in the newsroom is not what it used to be. Dramatic changes in the journalistic profession have significantly weakened the ability of senior management to reshape reportage, especially at national media outlets. Moreover, the political distance between reporters and editors is often overstated. We found little difference between the two groups, and a recent national survey of journalists found virtually identical ideological orientations among supervisors and news staffers.[13]

Second, organizational theorists lean heavily on the method of participant observation to prove their case. This method consists of visiting news organizations to observe journalists at work. The observation can last for months and include interviews with the newspeople under study. Such research may yield significant insights into journalists' behavior, but the insights will always reflect the impressions of the observer, and hence the perspective he or she brings to the research.

This does not invalidate such insights, but it does highlight their subjectivity. Participant observation can show how news values commonly attributed to personal perspective might instead reflect organizational imperatives. But it cannot preclude the impact of personal values, because it does not test for them in any reliable and systematic fashion.

Finally, after downgrading the direct effects of personal perspectives on the news, organizational theorists often bring them in through the back door. For example, Edward J. Epstein wrote *News from Nowhere* to show that "the news presented on network television is fixed to a large extent by organizational requirements."[14] But he notes that within these organizations,

> controls tend to be disregarded when executives, producers and correspondents all share the same view and further perceive it to be a view accepted by virtually all thoughtful persons. News reports about such subjects as pollution, hunger, health care, racial discrimination, and poverty fall in this category. On such consensus issues, correspondents are expected by executives openly to advocate the eradication of the presumed evil and even put it in terms of a "crusade."[15]

How such problems should be presented is not a "consensus issue," but a matter of heated debate all across the political spectrum. Inevitably, then, "crusading" news reports on these issues will generate controversy. Even if such crusades end once they become widely disputed, their cumulative effect will push the news in the direction of the media's conventional wisdom, i.e., the view of "all thoughtful persons."

This problem shifts attention to the intellectual milieu of the national media. To the degree that this milieu is distinctive and homogeneous, it will put its stamp on the news agenda, quite apart from the conscious intention (or even recognition) of individual journalists. To deal with this problem, theorists who stress the role of organizations introduce the notion of a consensual news judgment—the "latent news values" that are, in Bernard Roshco's phrase, "the relatively unrecognized, and often unintended, biases that shape news content."[16] But this "solution" admits that shared perspectives provide the tracks along which the news agenda runs. As Herbert Gans remarks, "Values enter the news most pervasively in the form of reality judgements, the assumptions about external reality associated with the concepts which the journalists use to grasp it."[17]

Thus, to maintain the primacy of organizational imperatives, it becomes necessary to claim that journalists' reality judgments are either nonpartisan or reflect the news audience's own values. Proceeding in this vein, Gans argues that,

> The beliefs that actually make it into the news . . . are neither liberal nor conservative but *reformist,* reflecting journalism's long adherence to good-government Progressivism. . . . Thus, when the news is about unusually high oil-company profits . . . the journalists are being neither liberal nor conservative in their news judgement but are expressing the reform values of their profession. . . . many [of these values] are shared by the rest of the audience. They are called motherhood values . . .[18]

This argument brings the debate full circle. Even in the organizational model, journalists' values turn out to be important in shaping the news. They allegedly have no partisan effect, because news judgments are rooted in popular or consensual values. The only problem with this conclusion is that there is no scientific evidence for it. Like the other theorists cited here, Gans relies on his own impressionistic participant observation. Thus, he qualifies his listing of "values in the news" by noting, "The methods by which I identified the values were impressionistic. . . . Since I undertook no quantitative analyses, [the list] does not suggest which values appear most frequently."[19] He concludes that journalists' personal value systems are those of progressivism, that these are the values that inform news coverage, and that they are also the values of most Americans. Yet none of these propositions is supported by systematic empirical evidence.

To cite some obvious counter-examples, neither turn-of-the-century progressive values nor contemporary national polls would predict the attitudes journalists expressed toward abortion, affirmative action, homosexuality, gun control, school prayer, or South African disinvestment, in the *Los Angeles Times'* survey. Nor do they account for the different ways journalists and the public evaluate news coverage. For example, a survey conducted for the Associated Press Managing Editors Association asked both newspaper journalists and the general public to evaluate coverage of various groups. Journalists who criticized current coverage tended to rate news about police as "too favorable," and news about blacks, hispanics and communists as "not favorable enough." None of these evaluations was shared by the public.[20]

On the other hand, these responses accord with what is variously called upper-status liberalism, the "new liberalism," or, in our own phrase, a liberal cosmopolitan perspective. Thus, where Gans sees the influence of "small-town pastoralism" in the news,[21] Pulitzer Prize–winning journalist Theodore H. White worries about the "breach in American culture" between the Manhattan-based national media and the heartland: "We came here, or were chosen to come here, because somehow we were ahead of the common thinking. . . . My point is, right now are we too far ahead?"[22]

More broadly, what journalists believe, what values their coverage reflects, and the relationship between the two are all questions of fact. In order to answer them, the impressions generated by participant observation or other qualitative research must be subjected to empirical tests that yield replicable results. The failure to do so leaves competing schools of interpretation in lieu of generally accepted explanations. The organizational approach has added greatly to our understanding of the news process. Nevertheless, the role that the personal element plays is still an open question.

Our finding that journalists' attitudes seem imbedded in their perceptions of social reality poses the question even more urgently. As Leo Rosten wrote in 1937, "Since absolute objectivity in journalism is an impossibility, the social heritage, the 'professional reflexes,' the individual temperament, and the economic status of reporters assume a fundamental significance."[23] This chapter has shown how journalists' reality judgments are consistent with their social and political perspectives. We turn now to the link between individual temperament and professional behavior.

INSIDE THE MEDIA MIND

"The relationship between personality and journalism may be the most promising field of study for explaining why news is as it is."
—Stephen Hess, *The Washington Correspondents*

"Why do I have this feeling? I don't know. Dr. Freud may know but he's not around to answer."
—Morton Mintz, *Washington Post* reporter

WHO KNOWS what newsmen want? This may seem a strange place to paraphrase Freud's famous query about women. Don't we all know what journalists want? They want to get the story. They want to "score a beat." They want to make the deadline. In the long run, they want to win a Pulitzer, see history in the making, right some wrongs, watch their memoirs make the bestseller list. Like most people, they would probably choose fame and fortune, but settle for the chance to do some good, have an interesting job, and earn the respect of their peers.

But is it really so simple? Are journalists' personalities interchangeable with those of accountants or lawyers? Or are the media elite in some ways a breed apart, driven by needs and motives distinctive to their demanding profession? The excitement of having a ringside seat at historic events, the never-ending chase for the story, the Damocles sword of the deadline—all these factors might tilt the profession toward a collective personality style, by weeding out the timid, the meek, and the self-conscious. Consider CBS producer Susan Zirinski's description of life "on the ragged edge of disaster": "When I first started working, I was panicked all the time. I even went to a psychiatrist. But then I thought, maybe it's better to be nervous. It gives you an edge."[1]

In the words of James Deakin, for many years White House correspondent for the *St. Louis Post-Dispatch:*

> It is the motivation that is important—because it determines the results. For the majority of journalists, the prime motivations remain sheer curiosity and the belief that communicating information and explanations is a public service. For others, the chief spur is reform. And for some, it is fame, power and $1 million a year. It is permitted to be in more than one category.[2]

If Deakin is correct that motivation determines results in journalism, how does the merely curious reporter differ from the reformer? In what ways does the ambitious reporter, the one who yearns for riches and fame, get different results from his colleague who is just performing a public service? Of course it is not so simple, as Deakin's teasing closer admits. Some reporters may want to satisfy their own curiosity, explain things to their readers, stir up reformers against injustice, and become wealthy and influential, all at once. Occasionally very good and very lucky reporters from Henry M. Stanley to Woodward and Bernstein may even succeed on all fronts.

But who is to say these are all the fronts? People continually outflank themselves, projecting their inner lives onto their daily struggles, carrying out agendas they hide from others and even from themselves. What are the inner drives that direct men and women toward the high-pressured, hectic, but often rewarding and glamorous life of the media elite? Let us rephrase our original question. How can we know what journalists want? How can we understand their underlying motivations in a way that is systematic, not impressionistic?

Probing the Psyche

The Thematic Apperception Test provides a tool for just such a scientific approach to understanding motivation. TAT results in Chapter Three showed how journalists perceive the world in ways consistent with their social and political outlooks. When they were shown ambiguous pictures, they filled in the blanks with plots and relationships that meshed with their own values.

The social world journalists created from the TAT pictures, peopled by brutal soldiers, corrupt businessmen, and struggling underdogs, tells us something about how they view the world around them. But it doesn't tell us much about their emotional worlds, the inner drives and conflicts that may express themselves in behavior. A person may see authority as corrupt, but whether he becomes a reformer, an anarchist, or a hermit will depend on many other factors, both within and without. It it is just such deeper emotional factors that the TAT was designed to explore. It is time we put this test to its earlier (and most powerful) use, to probe the collective psyche of the media elite.

The psychologists who created the TAT wanted to probe below the "social derm of personalities" to reach the "covert springs of fantasy and action."[3] They sought out the emotional wellsprings of such surface desires as social reform and personal influence. Their test provides a means to find out what makes journalists tick, what their underlying motivations really are, even those they may not recognize themselves. The basic rationale behind this method was stated by the test's creators in 1938: "the subject reveals some of his innermost fantasies without being aware that he is doing so."[4]

Psychologists have developed objective scoring systems for TATs, by isolating phrases and themes that indicate the presence of specific needs or motives. By applying these scoring systems, which are coded "blind" by trained professionals, researchers can prevent their own biases or expectations from coloring their interpretations of the test. David McClelland, the pioneer in scientific

95

TAT analysis, once used a TAT picture of a man at a drawing board to illustrate the kinds of stories produced by people with strong needs for power, on one hand, and for personal affiliation, on the other.[5] The latter story reads, "George is an engineer who is working late. He is worried that his wife will be annoyed with him for neglecting her . . . . He seems unable to satisfy both his boss and his wife, but he loves her very much and will do his best to finish up fast and get home to her."

Compare this overriding concern for human relationships with the power-oriented story: "This is Georgiadis, a famous architect, who wants to win a competition which will establish who is the best architect in the world. His chief rival, Bulakrovsky, has stolen his best ideas, and he is dreadfully afraid of the disgrace of losing. But he comes up with a great new idea, which absolutely bowls the judges over, and wins!" Here, of course, the emphasis is all on winning and losing, the rivalry for fame and fortune, the desire for prestige and victory. The other person in the story functions only as an impediment to the hero's advancement.

The different themes addressed by these two stories are readily intuited. But how do they reflect the different ways people live their lives? The answer is based on the accumulated evidence of experimental and social psychologists over the past thirty years. These researchers have discovered that people driven by a desire for power are likely to write stories in which one character seeks to control another, to impress others, or to build up his prestige or reputation. By contrast, people motivated by a need for friendship are more likely to write about needing people, to express concerns for friends or relatives, and to inject feelings of love or loneliness into their stories.

Equally important, this body of research shows that people who write certain types of TAT stories behave in ways that seem to reflect the concerns arising in their stories.[6] Consider the example of power motivation, which these psychologists refer to as "n Power" (i.e., the need for power). Experiments show that in day-to-day living, a high n Power TAT score successfully predicts patterns of self-assertiveness and instrumental behavior toward others. Such behavior includes participation in competitive and contact sports, impulsive aggressive activity (such as public arguments), sexual aggressiveness, and unstable dating and marital relationships. Power-oriented people are also attracted to symbols of prestige. With the effects of class differences taken into account, n Power predicts ownership of sports cars and a large number of credit cards.[7]

These findings are reinforced by experimental studies of small groups. They show that people who write power-oriented stories tend to be argumentative, manipulative, and competitive in dealing with others. Psychologist David Winter sums up the results of these studies:

> n Power is related to having smooth relationships with those who make up one's inner circle or power base, but having a competitive or hostile stance toward those of higher status or power who are outside the immediate group . . . high n Power people attack established leaders of high status.[8]

Such measures were developed and tested by psychologists who wanted to use the TAT material for the scientific study of social groups. They created scoring systems to identify statistical differences between *groups* of people. Their tests should not be used to probe the personalities of *particular* individuals. Likewise, we intend to explore psychological differences between groups of media and business leaders.

Journalists' and businessmen's TAT stories were scored for several key personality dimensions, including the need for power, fear of power, need for achievement (n Achievement), capacity for intimacy, and narcissism. How did the two groups compare? The journalists scored higher on the need for power, fear of power, and narcissism, while the businessmen scored higher on the need for achievement and the capacity for intimacy. All these differences except the last were statistically highly significant ($p \leq .001$). The group difference on the intimacy measure approached but did not attain a conventionally acceptable level of significance ($p < .10$).

How large were these differences? A more complex statistical analysis provides a more specific indication of their magnitude. A procedure called discriminant analysis allows researchers to predict from each person's TAT scores whether he or she belongs to the media or business group by knowing nothing about them except their levels of narcissism, power needs, and other psychological scores. The more the two groups differ, the easier it is to guess (from their test scores) each individual's true group. On this basis, one can correctly identify two out of three men (67 percent) and three out of four women (78 percent). So the TAT reveals that these journalists and businessmen have very different motivational profiles. But what do these scores really mean? What kinds of stories do the two groups write, and how do they differ? We will illustrate each motive in turn, beginning with the need for power.

Power motivation. This personality trait is scored when a character in a TAT story wants to control or influence others or is concerned about his reputation or prestige.[9] What kind of stories do typical "power-oriented" journalists write? The picture of two men in an office (see fig. 3) brought forth considerable power imagery, revolving around office politics. Thus a *Wall Street Journal* reporter describes an authority conflict between a worker and his boss:

> This appears to be an employee being lectured by his superior. He appears unhappy or resentful. . . . The man being lectured to has probably done something to draw his superior's anger. . . . Resentment by the employee; anger by the superior. The employee probably wants to argue back but will not. The superior wants an apology or a promise that the employee won't repeat his mistake. The employee will likely apologize or do what is requested of him.

Similarly, a PBS staffer stresses the interplay between decision-making and personal ambition:

> These are two men who work for the same company. The younger man is in power; the older man is trying to convince him on a point of action. The older man has usurped his responsibility. . . . The younger man is convinced that the older man is right, but that he mustn't jeopardize his own authority. The

older man wants to prove he knows what he's doing. The older man will continue, frustrated, as a has-been but capable underling.

Power relationships need not have negative consequences to be scored for *n* Power. The struggle for fame or influence can be presented in a positive or neutral light as well. The darker side of power themes is captured by the Fear of Power scoring system. **Fear of Power.** This is scored when someone reacts to power with feelings of doubt, conflict, irony, or deception. It is also scored when characters seek power for themselves ostensibly to benefit others. In effect, it measures the ambivalence of being drawn to power and repelled by it. Winter and Stewart call this response an "aversive attraction" to power:

> This aversive attraction involves an unusual sensitivity to power and awareness of power relationships in the world, coupled with a negative feeling about them. That is, an individual high in Fear of Power is interested in power in order to avoid the appearance of having power oneself . . . research evidence suggests that Fear of Power derives from the experience of powerlessness. . . . Power is experienced as both outside the self and inescapable.[10]

High scorers in Fear of Power behave in ways that suggest they are fearful of other people gaining power over them. They are suspicious of others, anxious, and very concerned to establish and defend their personal autonomy. Individuals strongly motivated by Fear of Power mistrust other people and institutional authority and are very concerned with protecting their own independence. Thus, they seem to desire power to protect themselves against other people, whom they perceive as seeking power over them. Ironically, their very fear of power generates a defensive need to feel powerful. These tendencies are reminiscent of a syndrome that psychoanalyst W.W. Meissner terms the "paranoid" style.[11]

Power relations are associated with conflict, fear, and punishment in a *New York Times* reporter's response to the picture of men in uniform (see fig. 1). He sets his story in World War II

Germany. An army recruit, Franz, gets fed up with the Nazis and tries to escape. He is caught by soldiers who suspect he is an American spy. The story concludes, "The future for Franz looked bleak. Whatever he did—confess the reality or contrive to deny the accusation—would lead to the same end—execution."

This story illustrates several facets of the fear of power. The authorities are real brutes—Nazis. The outcome of the power relationship will be the protagonist's death. And a sense of irony contributes to the despairing tone. Either the truth or a lie, for different reasons, will produce equally dreadful consequences. Remember, the author could have had Franz escape or lie his way out of the dilemma. His future needn't have been so bleak in a story less pervaded by Fear of Power imagery.

Even the picture of an adult and child (see fig. 4) stimulated some writers to produce Fear of Power motifs. Thus, a *Washington Post* reporter describes an apparent supportive relationship that is grounded in guilt rather than affection:

> The executive father is a busy man who worries about neglecting his family. He feels guilty enough to set aside a few hours each week to relax with his heir and attempt to motivate him. The executive-father wants his son to have the same drive as he did to raise himself up from his bootstraps and "make it". . . . The executive-father will have some of his guilt assuaged after spending a couple of hours lecturing his kid. The kid will feel oppressed and go about his lazy way.

This is a good example of an attempt to influence someone for one's own purposes (assuaging guilt) under the guise of altruism. Note too that the activity has a negative effect on its recipient. The child feels oppressed and is not motivated to change. On both counts the author characterizes ambivalence within the power relationship he describes.

Finally, one TAT picture provides some commentary on sexual politics (see fig. 5). The only picture not described in Chapter Three, it shows an apparently unclad woman lying in bed. Standing above her is a man burying his face in an upraised arm.

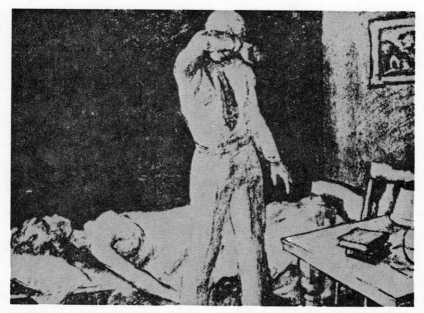

Figure 5

This picture sometimes brought out tabloid tales of assault, rape, murder, and suicide. Take an NBC executive's brief soap opera scene:

> "Oh my God, what have I done?" he cried as the limp form of the lovely woman lay lifeless on the bed. Hadn't she led him on, forcing him, yes forcing, to believe that she could be his for the asking? Then all hell had broken loose. She resisted to the end. And the end it surely was as he had crushed the life from the lovely body. All that remained was suicide. And that would surely follow.

The theme of a physical assault that brings pain and unhappiness is the darkest side of the power relationships scored for Fear of Power.

Need for Achievement. Power is only one of many themes that have been explored by psychologists using the TAT. In fact, the first and most thoroughly researched topic to attract attention was the need for achievement. This motive is scored when a character shows concern over performing well in relation to a self-defined standard of excellence. It stands in contrast to situations in which activity is structured by external rewards. Many studies have shown that high levels of achievement imagery predict moderate risk-taking and entrepreneurial or managerial success, even in noncapitalist societies.[12]

In *The Achieving Society,* David McClelland showed that achievement imagery in children's readers was related to national rates of economic growth. On the basis of this and other evidence, he argued that achievement motivation is central to a character structure suited to promoting industrial development. In fact, drawing on Max Weber's celebrated formulation, he suggested that it is the motivational link between the "Protestant" work ethic and the spirit of modern capitalism.[13]

Despite the relatively low scores of journalists, there are enough examples to convey the flavor of story lines scored for *n* Achievement. The boxer picture (see fig. 2) was a source of a few. An ABC producer writes of two fighters who train together:

> Two boxers who have trained together for three years practice daily, hoping to perfect their style. The boxers, although assigned to different weight classes, use each other as a measure of their own prowess. Naturally the aim of both men is to win fights. But to win, one must perfect the art of defense and offense. They are given the opportunity by training together and watching each other progress. The end result, hopefully, will be success for each.

These characters need not be Zen-like in their devotion to their craft. But the successful performance is paramount, not the external rewards that winning brings. The key is what a CBS correspondent calls his protagonist's "keen desire . . . to excel."

Intimacy. Thus far we have considered only motives that have little to do with concern for other people, except as objects of manipulation. To measure the need for close personal relationships, we turned to psychologist Daniel McAdams' method of scoring TATs for the capacity for intimacy. He defines this as a concern to create relationships characterized by openness, caring, and reciprocity. The coding scheme is related closely to Harry Stack Sullivan's "collaborative relationship" and Martin Buber's "I-Thou" encounter. McAdams' research shows that people scoring high in intimacy prefer egalitarian, nonmanipulative relationships characterized by reciprocal and noninstrumental dialogue, openness, and concern for the welfare of others. They perceive good interpersonal relationships as convivial and enjoyable in themselves.[14]

Most of the relatively few intimacy themes among journalists were written about the black adult and child. A typical example is by a public broadcasting executive, who portrays a student being helped by a volunteer teacher's assistant:

> Each is enjoying the other's company, and is pleased with a relationship which is pleasant, comfortable, and useful. Each feels a sense of fun and company from the other, and enjoys a quasi-familial relationship. The boy will go on, but stay in touch. The man will continue to volunteer, and build up a network of such "sons" for whom he will provide a life-long link to special caring.

Similarly, a *Wall Street Journal* reporter stresses reciprocal intimacy between father and son: "Jim appreciates his Dad's attention and willingness to listen. To his father, Saturdays are a chance to grow closer to his oldest son . . . [They] have a warm, easy relationship and enjoy doing things together."

Narcissism. At the opposite end of the emotional spectrum from the concern for intimacy lies narcissism. Adult narcissism is an ever-fluctuating reservoir of self-esteem that forms the basis of the individual's experience of oneself and the world. Healthy narcissism is an adequate basis of positive self-feeling, which enables the individual to weather life's ups and downs. But narcissism also has a dark side that is responsible for its popular association with selfishness and egotism. People who lack confidence in themselves, who suffer what psychologists call "narcissistic deficits," often rely on egocentric mechanisms to enhance their self-esteem and maintain a sense of identity. This leads to behavior that commonly is termed narcissistic.[15]

One such means of raising self-esteem is a distorted self-perception that produces a wishful or grandiose self-image. Typical narcissistic defenses include denying the presence of undesirable qualities in oneself and projecting these threatening traits onto others. This devaluation of other people also protects one against envy. In general, the narcissistic person uses others primarily to regulate his or her own self-esteem, rather than treating them as separate individuals with their own needs and identities.

The scoring system we used, developed by clinical psychologist Jennifer Cole, tests separately for self-centered imagery and devaluation of other individuals.[16] Journalists outscore businessmen on both measures, with each difference significant at .oo1.[17]

Self-centered orientation probably comes closest to the everyday meaning most people attach to the term "narcissistic." It measures a writer's use of the TAT story to gratify exhibitionistic needs rather than addressing interpersonal issues. This category is scored when the author seems to be showing off, calling attention to him- or herself, and ignoring interpersonal relations.[18]

The boxer picture evokes some exhibitionistic imagery, as in this composition by a public broadcasting executive:

> "Hell of a way to make a living," thought Joe—"boxing in a moving train for the entertainment of newly arrived zoo animals? Crazy bastards—just because those particular bears were used to being based next to an army camp in Djakarta doesn't necessarily mean that they can only be made happy by having more of the same here. Christ! Why not give them movies to watch? Or make them face the fact that they're in a new country now—too much pandering to their needs," he said, hoping against hope that someone would catch the pun.

This story touches all the bases. There is the unlikely setting (a moving train filled with animals), the use of some mild obscenities to catch the eye, and a totally internalized focus on Joe's reactions. Neither the second figure in the picture nor any other person is mentioned. In closing, the author urges readers to "catch the pun," for fear we might miss his humor and creativity if we weren't nudged. In short, this story ignores the opportunity to develop a plot line or characterization in favor of calling attention to the author as a witty and creative fellow.

A hallmark of self-centered imagery is a willingness to ignore the picture's obvious areas to explore more flamboyant possibilities. The picture of a man and woman, which offers perhaps the most titillating cues, attracts some of the most narcissistic imagery. A *Time* reporter is the most succinct writer to exploit its potential shock value: "Either boy has just banged his sister and it was no good. Or he finds himself impotent and doesn't like it." Themes of sex and violence are fairly common reactions to this picture. But incest qualifies as an eye-opener (presumably a calculated one) even in this context. Moreover, the themes of incest and impotence are introduced and dropped with equal abruptness. Once he has utilized their shock value, the author has no other use for them. They serve no function in terms of plot or character development. They just say, "look at me."

Narcissistic attribution concerns a writer's tendency to attribute narcissistic qualities to his or her characters. It is scored when characters are portrayed as exploitative, haughty, manipulative, grandiose, cold, ruthless, or hollow. This reflects the narcissistic individual's tendency to project a negative self-image onto other people, and to build oneself up by denigrating others as egotistical and Machiavellian.

Journalists' TAT stories are filled with such narcissistic people, especially those occasioned by the pictures of uniformed men (fig. 1) and the well-appointed office (fig. 3). A brief reprise should suffice: Various characters are described as "conniving," "notorious," "greedy," "smug," "complacent," "vacuous," "weak, "arrogant," and "sadistic." Where simple adjectives fail, nouns tell a similar tale. From the "no-account playboy" and the "stuffy imbecile" to the "faceless brutes" and the "sons of bitches," characters run the gamut from incompetence to malevolence. As if what they are weren't bad enough, what they do is worse yet. The least of them "mouth stuffy platitudes," "prefer confrontation," and "make asses of themselves." The really bad apples "sell out," "practice skullduggery," "operate by greed and graft," and even "destroy someone else's life."

A more extended version, from the boxer picture, is a *Post* reporter's portrayal of unhappy lovers:

> Two homosexuals are discussing their relationship. The fellow in the background . . . may be a heroin addict. . . . The more aggressive man in the foreground is thinking he can never hold onto a relationship for long. But that is his nature. The fellow in the background is feeling sorry for himself.

It is probably a moot point whether or not the author considers homosexuality to be a negative characteristic. More telling is the apparently gratuitous mention of possible heroin addiction, as well as the men's emotional incapacities. One is aggressive and incapable of long-term relationships; the other feels sorry for himself. Neither is concerned about anyone's interests other than his own. This is the emotional milieu of the narcissistic personality.

The picture of a man and a woman (fig. 5) is especially interesting in this regard, since it offers ample cases for both power-oriented and affiliative themes. A male producer offers the classic portrait of an unfeeling seducer who loses interest in his prey once he has succeeded.

> It has taken him six months to get Larry's wife into bed. Six months of cajoling, soft words, good wine, and, finally, words of love. Words unmeant but believed. Now it was all over. . . . And, he wondered, how the hell will I ever get rid of her.

Another example is notable for its emotionally flat tone and casual indictment of every character in a lovers' triangle. It belongs to a PBS staffer with a clipped prose style and a penchant for apostrophes:

> They are having an affair. Man and woman. The private police and the woman's husband enter. She's high on drug's. . . . The lover pay's off the private cop's. The wife become's a lesbian.

To summarize the patterns of personal motivation revealed by the Thematic Apperception Test, the media elite scores significantly higher than the business group in their power needs, fear of power, and narcissism. The businessmen have significantly stronger achievement needs and a slightly greater capacity for personal intimacy. In less formal terms, leading journalists appear more likely to want to be the center of attention and to feel important and influential. They seem more fearful that others may gain control over them. These concerns are more salient for them than for business executives. Conversely, the need to meet an internal standard of excellence or develop warm personal relationships seems somewhat less salient to the journalists than the businessmen.

To provide an independent check on our findings in these categories, random samples of thirty businessmen and thirty journalists were selected for further study. Dr. Jennifer Cole analyzed their TAT stories and wrote clinical portraits based on what she found. She knew nothing about either the nature of the study or the professions of the subjects. Nonetheless her clinical portraits mirrored the statistical findings. In general, she described the journalists as people with rich emotional lives who were, however, highly narcissistic and conflicted. In fact, she hazarded the guess that they were "artists" of some sort. By contrast, the businessmen seemed to her emotionally "flat" or self-controlled, but also more at ease with themselves.

This is not to say that all leading journalists are power-hungry and narcissistic, or that any journalists are motivated exclusively by such inner needs. We all share needs for power and achievement, intimacy and isolation, mutuality and dominance. Yet the balance of these fundamental and ubiquitous human needs differs from one individual to another. Indeed, this is in large part what makes us individuals. But such individual variations may also produce aggregate differences between groups of individuals. That is why we tried to probe the collective psyche of the media elite by comparing them to corporate executives.

Statistical differences between these two groups do not permit inferences about particular individuals. The test reveals achievement-oriented journalists, power-oriented businessmen, and others who go against the general trend. Nor do we know how either group stacks up against the general population. For example, the TAT literature suggests that both journalists and business managers tend to have higher power needs than other occupational groups, such as lawyers, doctors, teachers, and clergy.[19] In addition, the only study to compare journalists with a matched control group of educated professionals and managers found that the journalists scored significantly higher in both n Power and the "self-assertive" expression of power needs.[20]

The divergent motivational patterns of these two competitors for social influence may have significance for the future development of the American civic culture. We have seen that the national media represent a new elite with increasing impact on the public agenda. By contrast, corporate executives have been a linchpin of America's traditional network of elites. The widely noted antipathy between these groups partly reflects basic conflicts over America's intellectual and cultural milieu, which both seek to shape. Daniel Bell has argued that America's economic and cultural elites represent different sensibilities, with the former more oriented toward achievement and the latter toward self-expression.[21] Our findings suggest that such differences may extend to the level of personal motivation.[22]

Do Motives Matter?

What difference do leading journalists' unconscious needs and motivations make in their work? Can such information really help explain the news product? Or is this just engaging in the academic parlor game called psychiatric labeling? Does this study aid the enemies of a free press by tarring its practioners with tags like "power-hungry" and "narcissistic" to no good purpose? Such concerns are good arguments against "pop" psychology. But this is the first study to apply social scientific procedures and established psychological tests toward understanding the psychodynamics of the media elite. The real question is not whether such information might be used in the "wrong" way, but whether it might lead to new insights about the behavior of journalists and their social impact. These psychological findings could provide fertile ground for just such advances in understanding the news process and its relation to society.

We would like to begin this effort by considering some notable features of contemporary journalism in terms of the personality needs our survey identified. In the absence of clinical case histories and national statistical norms for TAT motive scores, this account is necessarily speculative. It may be likened to Weber's use of "ideal types" to reconstruct historical processes.[23] That is, if one assumes that the TAT results do identify a motivational syndrome distinctive to leading journalists, might this shed new light on the meaning and import of their behavior? What follows, then, is an inquiry into the role that personal style may play in contemporary journalistic practice.

In his 1981 study of the Washington press corps, Stephen Hess remarks, "There is a personality type in journalism."[24] Like other observers, however, he can only speculate about just what traits are involved at all but the surface level. The TAT findings focus attention on the effects of a heightened if ambivalent concern for power, strong narcissistic needs, and a relatively low need for achievement and concern for personal intimacy. These traits seem highly relevant to several aspects of contemporary major media coverage. They range from the emphasis on power, competition (including the electoral "horse race"), and the adversarial style increasingly adopted by journalists, to the negativism and resistance to criticism that many attribute to the profession.

Hyping the Horse Race. The media elite's power needs may underlie the tendency of many journalists to attribute great importance to power relationships. The news business is highly competitive in many ways. The journalist competes daily with colleagues to get the story and file it first, even as he competes with newsmakers to control the nature of the story. For example, a *Time* article on ABC White House correspondent Sam Donaldson concludes that his job of "jousting with Presidents" perfectly suits his aggressive temperament. In Donaldson's words, "I love this business. Every day it is victory or defeat, and you do not have to wait to see which."[25]

This heightened sensitivity to winning and losing, while functional for journalists, may find its way into their reportage. An obvious example is their tendency to concentrate on the "horse race" aspects of political campaigns. Academic and other press critics almost universally agree that coverage of the race itself drives out coverage of substantive issues and candidates' qualifications to a degree that poorly serves the public.

Television is a particular target of such criticism, since the nightly newscasts contain a fixed amount of time that cannot be expanded to accommodate both horse race and issue coverage. Yet the media continue to concentrate on the candidates' chances for victory, their relative position in the polls, and the success or failure of their strategies for victory. As Michael Robinson and Margaret Sheehan note in their book on the 1980 campaign, "no systematic study of any national medium has ever uncovered a campaign in which the modern press, during the course of an election year, emphasized anything more than it emphasized 'horse race'. . . . 'Horse race' permeates almost everything the press does in covering elections and candidates."[26]

The situation looks similar from the inside. Indeed, some journalists take a fatalistic view, as if the primacy of horse race coverage were a fact of nature. In the wake of campaign '84, *Washington Post* columnist Haynes Johnson admitted, "Try though we in the media did to rein in our 'who's ahead' reportorial instincts, they triumphed as always in the end." He noted a lengthy article that appeared in his newspaper on election day, headlined: "Hopefuls Hit the Road—for '88; Presidential Race Seen Wide Open in Both Major Parties." Johnson could only comment plaintively, "So much for a temporary respite from the horse race. Buckety-buck, away we go, galloping off again."[27]

The Primacy of Power. Of the many possible reasons for this nonideological bias in reportage, one may be that it is simply what journalists respond to most strongly. To the extent that their inner lives emphasize power themes, they will find it personally gratifying to concentrate on this aspect of the world around them. The inside dope on the latest shift in campaign strategy (particularly if it's an exclusive story) is simply more alluring than poring over a candidate's position papers.

Similarly, the candidates' standings on any given day seem more interesting than their thinking. Although journalists tend to attribute this to the quality of politicians' thought processes, it may reflect their own preferences as well. In Deakin's words, "Most reporters are simply intrigued by the human activity known as power; they like to observe it and describe its . . . effects."[28] So they focus on who has power, who is trying to get it, and what the prospects are for the various power seekers.

To take but one example from campaign coverage, consider the reporting of presidential debates. These events provide the voters with their only opportunity to compare directly the two main contenders for the presidency as each tries to set forth his campaign agenda and rebut that of his opponent. Presidential debates are heavy on substance, as the candidates seek to demonstrate their mastery of the issues and reveal the flaws in one another's positions. Yet the media's focus in reporting such debates is not on what we learn about the candidates' positions and abilities. Instead, the first question asked in headlines and telecasts is "who won?" The next question is, how will the outcome of this particular battle affect the overall campaign? The candidates' presentations are then assessed in terms of their contribution to victory or defeat.

As we have seen, it is a short step, though a crucial one, to move from focusing on certain elements of an event to creating those elements with a bit of poetic license. Thus, Clancey and Robinson argue that in 1984, with no horse race in sight, the networks actually tried to create one. They conclude that, "journalists did little things to *produce* a horse race when none seemed to exist [their emphasis]. Out of impishness, they played games with the news agenda, or even the spin, hoping to make the race tighten."[29]

The inclination to concentrate on power relations has many implications beyond campaign coverage. Indeed, the point might be extended to political reporting in general. Journalists internalize a definition of "news" that emphasizes conflicts among powerful people. This leads them to overlook underlying structural changes in society that may be related only indirectly if at all to the more portentous struggles among elites. David Paletz and Robert Entman note in *Media Power Politics,* "Prime news generally involves prominent, powerful people in action or, more desirable from the media's point of view, in conflict. . . . Stories emphasize the surface appearances, the furious sounds and furious sights of battle. . . . Underlying causes and actual impacts are little noted nor long remembered."[30] Of course, journalists might well argue that they cover the sound and fury precisely because it is the stuff of news. The drama of the battle, the tactics of the generals, the victory or defeat are newsworthy, even if the quieter long-term changes prove more historically significant.

There may be something to this argument, but it also begs an important issue. After all, how does anyone know what the news is? Journalists notoriously are resistant to systematic inquiry on this point. They prefer to trust their instinctive feel for news, which is informed by their experience in the news business. But where does this feel come from? It may have something to do with what the news audience wants, but playing to the audience is more characteristic of the tabloids than the prestige press. *Washington Post* reporter Robert Kaiser probably reflects the consensus of his peers when he writes, " 'giving them what they want' is an abdication of journalistic responsibility. . . . Journalism is not a passive exercise; human beings have to decide what they think is important, what readers or viewers ought to know or worry about."[31] For all their dependence on the Nielsen ratings, even the network news departments continuously struggle against corporate pressures to water down their product and make it more entertaining. If audience tastes were truly omnipotent, the network newscasts would have adopted the "happy talk" format and soft news orientation of so many local stations.

Serious journalists are probably even more resistant to market research as a factor in news decisions than they are to abstract theorizing about the nature of the news. That leaves them to depend on their instincts about what the news is on any given day.

But instinct is largely a catch-all term for the internalized values of the news organization and the common culture of the news-room. This point has been noted often by outside observers. For example, social scientist Leon Sigal argues that news decisions are partly the product of the journalists' creed, which includes a "set of conventions for choosing which information to include in the news and which to ignore . . . however, conventions are rarely subject to conscious scrutiny by newsmen; they are just the way things are done around the newsroom."[32]

Analysts like Sigal and Edward J. Epstein have stressed the external dictates of the journalists' creed, especially those of the news organization.[33] But students of bureaucratic politics have mostly ignored the internal factors that impinge on journalists' news decisions. It is considerably easier to chart processes of decision-making in the newsroom than in the anteroom of the journalist's consciousness. That is the contribution we hope to make, by exploring some uncharted recesses of the media mind. A journalist's instincts are not only internalized imperatives of an organization. They are also the external manifestations of his or her own inner world.

From this perspective, journalists may not focus on competition and conflict between powerful people solely because they are taught to do so, or because that is what their audience wants to learn about, though both factors definitely play a role. Journalists may also be drawn to such themes because their own inner needs are gratified by the sense of involvement with powerful forces and the contest for high status. By describing the struggle for power from close quarters, they partake of it. They gain a surrogate feeling of self-importance by virtue of sheer proximity. Simultaneously, politicians and other would-be newsmakers become dependent on the journalist to get their message out. This provides the latter with a more direct sense of personal influence.

In this way, partly unconscious conceptions of the news may gratify journalists' needs for power and narcissistic gratification, even as they are rationalized as part of the unquestioned set of conventions. The point is not that underlying motivations produce the outward consensus over news decisions. Rather the internal (psychological) and external (organizational) factors may interact, and sometimes reinforce each other, to bring about certain attitudes and behavior. The news can serve an expressive function for journalists, even as it is shaped by organizational requirements. **The Adversary Appeal.** The potential match between journalists' power motives and their professional emphasis on power and competition shows how the news product can express the needs of those who produce it. This is a rather simple and direct example of the psychic baggage journalists may carry with them. Yet the expression of a particular motive is only the tip of the iceberg. More interesting is the way underlying motives interact or conflict with each other to produce unexpected outcomes of behavior. For example, we found not only relatively high power needs among the media elite, compared to the business elite, but a relative ambivalence toward power as well. This combination may suggest the presence of conflicts over acquiring and exercising power. People with this motivational pattern both want power and are afraid of it. One way of dealing with these contradictory feelings is to attack others who are perceived as powerful. Such attacks may be rationalized as serving some good cause or public duty. Some rationalization in terms of the public good is crucial to ward off feelings of guilt. It allows one to experience power while denying (to oneself most of all) the personal satisfaction of aggressive activity.

This process is familiar to those who study personality from a psychodynamic perspective. Consider how well it might explain some aspects of the journalists' relationship to the political world. In fact our data bear a remarkable similarity to the speculative psychological portrait of Washington reporters sketched in Leo Rosten's classic study half a century ago:

> The energies which lead men into newspapers are . . . the desire to startle and expose; the opportunity to project personal hostilities and feelings of injustice on public persons under the aegis of "journalistic duty"; inner drives for "action" plus inner anxieties about accepting the consequence of action. The last is particularly important. There is a sense of invulnerability at-

tached to newspaper work. . . . The Washington correspondent outstays presidents and cabinets. He is, as it were, self-sufficient in the small world of his newspaper organization. His first vested interest is his status as a privileged observer. He can attack senators at their most vulnerable point—the reading public. Not even the president can claim immunity from him.[34]

While Rosten wrote in the print era, contemporary complaints about adversarial journalism tend to focus on television correspondents who skewer politicians and other luminaries nightly. But we find no significant differences in the TAT scores of print and broadcast journalists. This suggests that, as a group, they may share the same urge to confront the powerful, to stand up to those in authority. As Dan Rather puts it, "When I am gone, the best someone could say about me to my children would be: 'He did not buckle. Not before President Johnson, not before President Nixon. He stood his ground.' "[35]

Disdain for politicians as unprincipled power-seekers permeates the national media. Columnist Richard Reeves expresses his distaste this way: "Politicians are different from you and me. The business of reaching for power does something to a man—it closes him off from other men until, day by day, he reaches the point where he instinctively calculates each new situation and each other man with the simplest question: What can this do for me?"[36] And *New York Times* reporter James Naughton offers the succinct dictum, "You should never place your trust in a politician."[37]

This opinion is so widespread that professional advancement is enhanced by a macho approach to reportage—doing the "toughest" interview or story. The *Atlantic* correspondent James Fallows writes, "The true lesson of Watergate is the value of hard digging, not only with scandal but everywhere else. The *perceived* lesson of Watergate in the White House pressroom is . . . that a surly attitude can take the place of facts or intelligent analysis . . . one sees reporters proving their tough-mindedness by asking insulting questions."[38] This passage reflects the indignation of a one-time presidential speechwriter. But the phenomenon is recognized widely within the profession. During the 1984 presidential campaign, *Washington Post* columnist Tom Shales criticized the "aggressive" and "contentious" style of interviewing candidates. He asked ABC's Sam Donaldson whether reporters "try to out-macho one another, to be tougher than their competition." Donaldson agreed that, "some reporters, being human, have that attitude."[39]

Being human implies that anyone might have this sort of motive. But some people are more macho than others. The real question is, are journalists more susceptible to such tendencies than people in other professions? If so, it would help explain the disparity between many journalists' self-image as champions of the people and the public's tendency to see journalists as rude, callous and disrespectful. The journalistic justification of public service may be crucial to the inner dynamic we have hypothesized. Journalists are in a continual struggle for control over the news product. In effect, they are engaged in a power struggle with politicians, interest groups, flacks, and others to set the public agenda by controlling the flow of information. Every day, for example, the White House has an idea of what central message and pictures it wants television to convey to the public. Producers and correspondents are well aware of this, and they strive mightily to communicate their own version of what the "real" story is.

Television journalists have various options in fighting back. They may seek to undercut a politician's game plan by focusing on only a small bit of his or her speech, thereby stressing a point the speaker was trying to downplay. They may suggest to the audience that a politician is either abusing the medium by substituting slick images for substance (a persistent criticism of Ronald Reagan) or is inept in using the medium, hence a poor communicator (the rap against Walter Mondale). The treatment of Reagan's and Mondale's communication skills during the 1984 campaign illustrates how both good and bad television performances can expose a politician to media criticism.

Another technique is the instant rebuttal, in which a filmed report is negated by the correspondent's closer. For example, on the first anniversary of the U.S. invasion of Grenada, CBS covered an emotional speech in which Ronald Reagan paid tribute to a soldier who was killed in the battle. In closing, the correspondent noted that Reagan did not tell his audience that the young man was killed by "friendly fire." That is, he was mistakenly shot by American forces. The effect was a jarring denial of the emotion produced by the preceding film clip.

This brings to mind Michael Robinson's thesis, discussed in Chapter Five, that journalists attack incumbents and leaders in election campaigns. He notes that, "Reporters simply feel that they have a special mission to warn Americans about the advantages any incumbent has." Reagan's 1984 election coverage was especially negative because, "When the press knows that this is the last shot voters will have—against a front-runner, no less—getting out the bad press becomes a near messianic mission."[40]

Yet the voters were hardly crying out for the press to rip off the president's alleged Teflon coating. But it was also the media's last shot at a Reagan campaign. Is it not possible that their sense of "mission" derives from a desire to unmask the one contemporary politician who seems impervious to attacks from the fourth estate? This would certainly accord with Robinson's own view of media campaign criticism as "a last minute effort to get the bad news out before it was too late, with Reagan likely to go scot free. . . ."[41]

Private Needs and Public Interests. Many observers may see this behavior as a power struggle between two elites (media and politicians) for control of the news. But many journalists do not see it that way at all. Instead they regard their concerns as expressions of the public interest. As *New York Times* correspondent Steven Wiseman puts it, "the press is not simply a purveyor of news, but a kind of surrogate for the public, questioning Presidential performance and, to some degree, holding the President accountable for his statements and actions."[42] The problem with this self-definition is that many in the public do not accept the press as their surrogate. Thus journalists were caught by surprise when the public did not share their overwhelming outrage at being excluded from covering the Grenada invasion. Wiseman reports with chagrin, "The Administration's negative view of the press seems to be shared by much of the public. . . . Many Americans apparently view the problem of withholding access as a defeat for the press, with little concern for the loss of information to the public."[43]

The journalist's response to such setbacks is usually similar to that of a defeated politician: we must not have explained our case to the public well enough. The notion that the public might understand and still reject this patronage rarely is considered. One reason for this is that the journalists' self-image as public tribunes serves important psychological functions. It permits them to engage in power strivings without having to acknowledge the nature of the striving. It allows them to behave in ways that might otherwise give them pause (asking rude questions, intruding on private emotion at times of sorrow or tragedy, sometimes hiding their true identities, etc.), under the aegis of performing a public duty.

Here again, such feelings may have long been commonplace among journalists. Rosten writes that "one of the most seductive phases of the reporter's life is the sanction which his calling receives from society. He is above the law in a sense. . . ." Rosten tells of a reporter who signed another man's name to a telegram to get an exclusive story. The reporter wrote later that, "my conscience was untroubled. . . . I was living up to the standards of my fellows. . . . I was exultant, not ashamed." Rosten notes, "It was not merely the exultance of having scored a journalistic triumph, it also contained the pleasure of breaking a taboo serene in the knowledge that society forgives much 'in the line of their duty.' The reporter's business is often to get secrets and tell them. Any vestigial guilt about this practice is defended by the statement 'that's the job of a newspaperman.' "[44]

Much has been written of some journalists' tendency to become "First Amendment ideologues," i.e., to justify any journalistic practice as an expression of First Amendment freedoms. In former CBS News president Fred Friendly's words, "If you say [to reporters] . . . 'you didn't report that story . . . very well,' they're offended. Suddenly you're fighting the First Amendment."[45] The journalistic justification of public service is even more significant psychologically because it protects its upholders from within rather than from without. If a questionable news practice is legal, it is only permissible. But if it is a public duty, it is a badge of honor. This is not to say that journalists are hypocrites who create such justifications for public consumption. The fact that ideas serve one's interests makes them easier to believe. Nor is this merely a mask for private interest. The journalist's sense of public patronage has a truth-value that transcends the motivations behind it. It must be evaluated on its own terms.

Here, however, we are seeking to understand the functional significance of a sense of mission. This notion may also play a role in maintaining the delicate internal balance required by an ambivalence toward power. The self-image of journalist as public tribune alleviates psychic tension. It permits one to strive after and enjoy the experience of power while denying that this experience colors one's behavior. Again, the public justification is not merely a cloak for personal aggrandizement. The two go hand in hand, just as all behavior expresses a welter of competing internal and external drives and constraints. For example, media consultant Tony Schwartz cites CBS correspondent Bill Moyers' self-image as a teacher or entrepreneur of ideas. But he adds,

> At the same time, television provides Mr. Moyers an arena in which to serve more personal needs. "I own and operate a ferocious ego," he acknowledges, and through television he has gained not only a national forum but a considerable measure of celebrity. By approaching his work as a form of public service, he can enjoy both—the wide exposure and the applause—in good conscience. He is quick to enumerate the people in high places and the everyday viewers who have written in praise of his "Journal"—but always in the context of being "useful," of "having an impact."[46]

Schwartz is mainly sympathetic to Moyers. Indeed it is no criticism of a journalist's abilities to say that he has a "ferocious ego." This passage simply illustrates the way, in political scientist Harold Lasswell's phrase, private motives can be displaced onto public objects.[47] If journalists engage in this displacement more than other people, it is because their work carries them regularly into the public arena.

Should journalists' claims to serve the public interest be treated with more reverence than similar claims voiced by representatives of business, labor, or self-described public interest groups? All claim to serve the public as a whole, while treating the claims of their competitors as partial at best. The public has learned to accept most of these claims with skepticism, just because competing conceptions of the public interest tend to favor private or professional interests as well. Therefore, journalists should perhaps be less surprised by public reluctance to accept their claims at face value. After all, the head of General Motors was long ago laughed off the public stage for voicing essentially the same claim for his company. Why, then, should people automatically agree that what's good for the media is good for America?

Thin-Skinned Critics. The reluctance of many journalists to accept this verdict may provide a clue to a related psychological dynamic. We have argued that inner ambivalence toward power may be displaced outward as antagonism toward the seekers and holders of power. By opposing those in power, the journalist protects against an inner striving for power, which can produce decidedly mixed feelings. This inner struggle against aggressive desires is displaced onto the external world, and negative feelings toward oneself are projected onto politicians and the high and mighty in general. The notion of the press as public tribune protects journalists against the guilt that would otherwise result from making personal attacks in the line of duty.

Narcissistic mechanisms may produce an analogous dynamic that protects one's self-image and fends off criticism from within and without. In their TAT stories, journalists differentially display a self-centered orientation and tend to attribute negative traits to other people. According to psychoanalytic theory, such efforts to inflate one's self-importance and devalue others are probably born of insecurity. They represent efforts to shore up a shaky foundation of self-esteem. Such people will be resistant to criticism, even to the point of self-righteousness. This is not because they have a good opinion of themselves; quite the reverse. The internal criticism is so searing that it is turned outward onto others. Thus, external criticism must be rejected because it threatens to open a Pandora's box of self-doubt or worse.

Such an account, if applicable, could help explain the siege mentality journalists often display in response to outside critics. Some journalists readily admit to this tendency in their profession. One is former *Fortune* editor Louis Banks. He writes, "most of my friends who write, edit, publish or broadcast the news work behind . . . a shield of righteousness, defensiveness, and self-protection which blocks other elements of our world."[48] Another who chided his colleagues for not countenancing critics was Edward R. Murrow, perhaps the most widely respected of all television journalists. In a recent interview, former CBS News president Fred Friendly recalled, "Ed Murow used to say that newspeople don't have thin skins—they have no skins. They believe that people are ganging up on them."[49]

Since media criticism has become a growth industry in recent years, journalists have had ever more opportunities to circle the wagons. Indeed the upsurge of negative feedback has engendered great resentment in many newsrooms. When the Janet Cooke scandal broke, and the *Washington Post* reporter was stripped of her Pulitzer Prize for fabricating a story, famed investigative reporter Seymour Hersh complained that the ensuing criticism was "wildly out of focus. The White House can put out an absolutely fallacious statement and everybody says that's the way the world works, but we hold ourselves to incredible standards."[50]

The strongest backlash, however, is reserved for critics on the political right. Some eminent journalists argue that a conservative conspiracy is at the root of public disaffection with their profession. Haynes Johnson of the *Washington Post* writes, "there has been a deliberate attempt to portray the press as the agent of America's problems, the enemy within . . . the political zealots, the hard-eyed haters and the lunatic conspiracy theorists have combined with public figures to poison the well about the press."[51]

Longtime Washington correspondent James Deakin goes even farther. He concludes his recent memoir, *Straight Stuff,* with a warning: "There are people in the United States who very much want the public to believe the worst about the nation's journalists." These people are the "far right," and they are trying to create "the gravest possible distrust of the news media." Why? Because "the extreme right hopes to take the American nation as deeply as it can into authoritarian regions and absolutist doctrines *. . . But the news media are standing in its way*" (author's emphasis). He concludes, "The ancient spirits can be summoned from the vast deep, *and they will come.* Nixon summoned the old ignorances, suspicions, and dreads. And they came. *And they have stayed . . . .* 'The dead,' wrote Aeschylus, 'are coming to slay the living.' If we let them."[52]

Despite this rhetorical flourish, it seems unlikely that right-wing opposition is responsible for a decline in popular support for the press. After all, polls show that public confidence in journalism was higher fifteen years ago, in the days when Spiro Agnew and other Nixon associates were marshalling the political clout of the White House against the media.

It is understandable that journalists might overlook a less palatable explanation. As ordinary people come to perceive them as wealthy and influential in their own right, populist reactions against the major media have begun to match similar sentiments against big labor, big business, and big government. It is a sign of the times that David Halberstam's popular work on national media organizations is titled *The Powers That Be.*

Resentment is the Janus face of envy. The same public that grants celebrity status to what used to be called the "working press" also relishes the chance to take this new elite down a notch. *Time's* 1984 cover story on the press notes that, "The failings of journalists have been compounded in the public's mind by the perception that as their power has increased, so has their presumption of self-importance." Among the complaints listed: "They are arrogant and self-righteous, brushing aside most criticism as the uninformed carpings of cranks and ideologues."[53]

It is ironic that such criticism mirrors the response that many journalists themselves have toward the powers that be in other sectors of society. One can well understand their failure to appreciate this irony, if our inferences from the TAT findings are correct. The same narcissistic mechanisms that may lead journalists to relish a prosecutorial role would also make them vigorously resist the role of defendant.

Narcissism and Negativism. Some journalists have come to similar conclusions about their profession. Economic columnist Robert Samuelson recently published a kind of mea culpa New Year's resolution that includes the following observations: "The press's most offensive characteristic is its obsessive self-righteousness, which can border on nastiness . . . Instinctively, I fixate on what I think are others' mistakes. . . ."[54]

The late Joseph Kraft went even further, complaining of a "new narcissism" in his profession: "those of us in the media have enjoyed an enormous surge in status and power in recent years . . . But while we have acquired confidence and self-assertiveness, there is no security. We are driven to keep moving forward, and in an adversary way. We are thus prone to the disease of the times —narcissism. The narcissism of the journalist, of course, is not mere conceit. It consists in the belief that because we describe events, we make them happen."[55]

The end of this passage refers to a traditional narcissistic gratification of this profession—the journalist's association with movers and shakers. To be with those who make history is to feel important. One absorbs a sense of self-esteem by sheer proximity to the powerful. Former *New York Times* editor Clifton Daniel illustrates this feeling in his recent memoir:

> There have been 40 presidents of the United States since our Constitution was adopted in 1789, and, although I am barely in my dotage, I have known one-quarter of them. That doesn't necessarily mean that they knew me. However, five of them called me by my first name, and one of them, through absolutely no fault of his own, became my father-in-law.[56]

Few journalists will ever marry a president's daughter (in this case Margaret Truman), but many are on a first-name basis with would-be "great men." And they would hardly be unique in feeling nearly great for being near the great.

Journalists not only go where the action is, they get there

before the rest of us. Another ego salve is the feeling of being there first, knowing the inside story, living the privileged life of the inside dopester. Timothy Crouse rhapsodizes over "the methedrine buzz that comes from knowing stories that the public could not know for hours and secrets the public will never know."[57]

Yet these traditional ego-feeders pale in comparison to the narcissistic feasts of recent years. Members of the national media need no longer depend on associating with the powerful. Suddenly, many have become wealthy and influential public figures themselves. In the words of Joseph Kraft, "We have advanced almost overnight from the bottom to the top; from the scum of the earth . . . to the seats of the high and mighty. We have become a kind of lumpen aristocracy in American society, affiliated, as priests at least, with the celebrity culture. . . . [Thirty years ago] being a newsman had a certain raffish quality. But nobody could have been attracted by the thought of becoming rich, or important, or powerful. Fame was not the spur. It is now."[58]

As Kraft's earlier comment indicates, though, the media elite's new status has hardly eliminated narcissistic needs. They have simply found a different outlet. Thus Sander Vanocur, a longtime network correspondent, criticizes his colleagues for accepting "the idea that the interviewer is at least as important as the person being interviewed."[59] This notion can lead to reporting that calls attention to the reporter rather than the newsmaker. Former NBC News president Reuven Frank cites instances like Roger Mudd's request for a Teddy Kennedy imitation from presidential candidate Gary Hart. Frank comments, "These interviews are pointless. Nobody ever remembers the answers. All anybody ever remembers are the questions."[60]

Calling attention to oneself is only one side of the narcissistic coin. The flip side is knocking other people down, which brings to mind the phenomenon of media negativism, the tendency for negative stories to drive out the positive ones. In its own assessment of the media, *Time* comments on "the suspicious attitude among reporters [that] leads to a negativism in news coverage. . . . One key cause of this kind of error: a tendency among younger reporters to believe the worst, to see a potential Watergate, hence their fame and fortune, in almost every story." *Time* quotes one editor who complains, "Every kid I get out of journalism school wants to have some major exposé under his byline. Sometimes they cannot accept the fact that something is not crooked."[61]

Negativism is not only expressed in suspicions and accusations. It can also be a matter of adopting a constantly critical tone that finds ineptitude everywhere. An example is one *Washington Post* columnist's nonpartisan assessment of the 1984 election aftermath:

> While the Democrats go off to the U.S. Virgin Islands to ponder their future, without, of course, any sign of agreement either on the problem they face (if in fact they even recognize that they have a problem) or its solution, the Republicans demonstrate that they are the party of ideas—crazy though some of them may sound.[62]

A colleague provides a pithier example, in summing up the second Reagan-Mondale debate: "It was even in negative terms. Both candidates seemed equally lacking in stature."[63] Or consider a few front-page headlines culled randomly from the *Post*: "Senate Fritters Day Away Over Rights Impasse"; "Congress Lifts Debt Limit, Flees Town"; "Making of a Diplomatic Debacle."[64] In cases like these, it is not simply a matter of conveying bad news faithfully, but of choosing verbiage that almost gleefully puts the worst face on things.

More systematic evidence is available on this point. In their study of 1980 presidential campaign coverage, Robinson and Sheehan find that television news gave every candidate more negative than positive coverage. Overall "the ratio of bad press to good press for principal candidates was two-and-a-half to one . . . "[65] They argue that television's critical tone is borrowed largely from the prestige press, such as the *New York Times* and the *Washington Post*. Finally, they link negativistic campaign coverage to increasing public dissatisfaction with political institutions:

> Probably the one "political" dimension in which [the] networks have sought to achieve a purpose has been the area of public

cynicism. Network reporters do seem to want to make the public more aware of the frailties and inadequacies of their elective leadership. The networks have succeeded. If there is one clearcut example of media power in the age of television news it must be the networks' contribution to our increasing political malaise.[66]

Whether or not one accepts this as a consequence of media negativism, the phenomenon itself has been noted widely. What Robinson and Sheehan call reporters' "fear of flacking" is a logical outgrowth of their ambivalent, sometimes adversarial relationship to politicians and others who wield power. In the last analysis, they would rather be mistaken for prosecutors than press agents. As Richard Reeves puts it, "If there's anything good about the guy, f—— it, the press officer will get it out."[67]

The Dogs That Didn't Bark. We have concentrated on journalists' narcissism and power concerns because the TAT results highlight these needs. But what about the personality traits that are less salient to them? Like the newsworthy item that is not reported, the motives that are missing may be more telling than those that are heightened. For example, a somewhat diminished capacity for personal intimacy may be highly functional in a profession that must treat tragedy and human suffering as opportunities for stories rather than occasions for empathy—hence the often heard complaint about reporters' intrusiveness at moments of personal grief or tragedy. The necessity to observe and report rather than intervene or assist is a hard lesson, one that to be fully learned may require a certain predisposition.

Occasionally, this professional norm is pushed to the limit, as in the aftermath of a 1983 terrorist attack on U.S. Marines in Lebanon that killed 239 soldiers. CBS News filmed and broadcast the moment when one victim's family was notified of their son's death, while NBC decided not to show a similar scene. In another widely criticized incident, a crew from a local television station filmed an attempted suicide by self-immolation. They let the cameras roll to record the event before stepping in to put out the flames. The hard-boiled or cynical persona adopted by many journalists may be seen as making a virtue of necessity. You're not likely to score a beat by stressing the virtues of courtesy and restraint. Nor are concerns for harmony or humanitarianism the most useful tools of a highly competitive trade.

Even more intriguing and potentially far-reaching is the lack of achievement motivation we measured among journalists. This does not mean that they lack the desire to do good work or attain professional prominence. The issue is not whether one wants success but why. What are the rewards that propel journalists forward? The TAT results suggest that efficient performance is not its own reward for the media elite. Measuring up to an internal standard of excellence may help corporate executives to meet quotas, but it is not where journalists get their satisfaction. These are not people who value the chilly virtues of efficiency and delayed gratification. Instead, they seek out the stimulation of new sensations, the excitation of experience. As Stephen Hess writes of Washington correspondents, reporters live "at the cutting edge of the moment . . . in a business of instant gratification, variety, excitement."[68] Each day brings new stories, new dramas in which journalists participate vicariously. Theirs is a life centering around activity and immediacy. Its appeal lies at least partly in what Rosten calls "the remorseless vitality of the moment . . . the exhilarating chase after the Now."[69]

A half century ago a *Baltimore Sun* correspondent offered a paean to this world of heightened experience. "These are men predestined from their mother's womb to regard this world as a garish, outlandish and somewhat bawdy, but infinitely amusing and thrilling show. . . . They yell more, sweat more, hiss more, start more tears and goose flesh in the course of their lives than a dozen ordinary men. They have a helluva good time."[70]

Timothy Crouse described the same stimulation in his account of life on the press plane during the 1980 presidential campaign. His stories of illicit drugs, alcohol, sex, and various hijinks aboard what he calls the "zoo plane" seem calculated to produce apoplexy among the straitlaced.[71] To illustrate this point in a less contentious fashion, consider his description of a typical campaign stop, beginning with the plane's arrival at the airport:

> There were greetings, new stories, fresh rumors, a curious delight at seeing these familiar faces in a new city. . . . Everyone would dash for the buses, which were waiting in a row. Then the motorcade would start off, with motorcycles roaring and police sirens screaming, and the buses would slice through the traffic of some great city; nobody would admit it, but it was more fun than riding a fire engine. There was all the noise, pomp, and license that only a presidential candidate could generate, and it was these things that gave the press the energy to survive the eighteen hour days.[72]

From Moment to Moment. Granting that journalism lures its practitioners more with the prospect of stimulating experiences than with notions of efficient performance for its own sake, how might this motivation shape the news? Perhaps by encouraging the very type of reportage that journalists profess to abhor. If there is one criticism that journalists will allow, one complaint that is heard throughout the profession, it is the constant condemnation of shallow, superficial reportage. Reporters bemoan the lack of willingness to really dig, to follow through, to get beneath the surface. In part, this is a limitation of the genre. Daily deadlines rarely encourage depth of intellectual analysis. It would be difficult to improve on Rosten's description of life on a deadline:

> The Washington correspondent lives in a twenty-four hour cycle of time. He must make "snap decisions." This tyranny of the immediate makes it difficult to achieve perspective, or apply . . . "the long view." Each day the newspaperman is faced with new challenges and fresh sensations. Each day presents a deadline which must be met. This telescoping of crises into a daily cycle stamps tension and obsession into the behavior of the journalist.[73]

It's enough to push you into a more leisurely job, as a few journalists-turned-professors would no doubt attest. But there are also those who thrive on the superheated atmosphere, the constant confrontation with "the iron moment of the deadline" that "involves the crisis of an internalized drama."[74] There must be some mesh between the thirst for immediacy and a willingness to accept its constraints. In short, the very traits that attract many reporters to journalism—the need for excitement, variety, constant stimulation—also militate against the reflective temperament required to gain distance and perspective on the day's events. There will always be the exceptions, of course—the Walter Lippmanns, the I.F. Stones. But they may always be just that—exceptions in a profession that welcomes and shapes a quite different personality type.

New York Times columnist Tom Wicker recently argued that more thorough and insightful reporting can only come about through the cumulative efforts of individual journalists to "do better." He calls for "more and more people in the press [to] sincerely try to do a better job."[75] But this hope ignores the reality that good reporters might make bad archaeologists. A disposition oriented toward speed, action, and variety may be badly suited to endless digging, no matter how priceless the artifact buried far below. No less a pillar of the profession than Dan Rather speaks for many of his peers: "When it gets down to the choice of action or reflection, I'll probably take the action. I am from a school, professionally, that says, 'Damn it, grab a pencil and get out of the office' . . . journalism is not a haven for philosophers, intellectuals, academics."[76] So one should not be too surprised at Hess' assessment of the motivations that impel the Washington press corps: "One might expect that those covering the national government would have a deep interest in political ideas. Instead . . . the attraction perhaps is to excitement and powerful personalities."[77]

Conclusion: The Media Mentality

For most observers, the journalistic mentality starts and stops with the belief systems and the norms and restrictions journalists' organizations impose upon them. This chapter has tried to probe deeper into some underlying and perhaps unrecognized motivations of the media elite. It has tried to show how their shared personality traits might subtly shape the process and the product of their unending search for news.

Compared to successful businessmen, leading journalists are at once relatively power-oriented and ambivalent toward power. They are relatively narcissistic, needing to build themselves up at the expense of others. In the same comparison, the journalists score differentially lower in achievement motivation, and (to a slight extent) the capacity for intimacy. This collective personality profile can shed light on the allure of their profession and the ways they practice it. The media elite move in a world of excitement, variety, stimulation, and quick gratification. They enjoy proximity to famous and powerful people and are privy to inside information. Recently they have even gained the opportunity to become wealthy and influential in their own right.

Many people attracted to this milieu are fascinated by machinations for power, by struggles among those who seek and hold it. Indeed, the spotlight they place on the race and the prize may dim their awareness of events and processes that take place outside its glare. News of the battle drowns out consideration of its causes and effects, partly because journalists are so fascinated by the thrill of battle itself.

At the same time, the media are increasingly willing to enter the fray themselves, eager to unmask the hypocrisy and puffery of the combatants. This more aggressive style of reporting provides several internal rewards. By deflating the claim of all sides that their own selfish interests represent the public interest, journalists can demystify politics, laying bare the struggle for power and preventing politicians from using them as unwilling flacks to delude the public. They can also reclaim control over the news product, telling the truths that newsmakers try to hide. Finally, they can establish themselves as the final repository of the public interest, the only actor without an axe to grind. All this can produce a gratifying self-image as guardian of the little guy against the establishment, the truth against flackery, the common good against partial interests.

Thus political journalism, at its pinnacle, can offer the opportunity to play at politics while looking down on politicians, to become the public's tribune while patronizing the "boobseoisie," and to engage in aggressive behavior with confidence that the ends are worthy. Ideally, the media elite can live the insider's life while holding onto the outsider's self-image. Indeed, it can be argued that good, tough, unyielding journalism is fostered by just the mentality we have described. An orientation that makes one both outwardly critical and sensitive toward incoming criticism may be just the driving force needed to pry stories loose from recalcitrant sources, while offering protection from dangerous self-doubt. Similarly, an ambivalence toward power may help to sustain a productive adversarial relationship with entrenched interests who have something to hide.

In this scenario, good reporters don't give anyone the benefit of the doubt. Nice guys get scooped. Former *New York Times* investigative reporter Sidney Zion argues, "The press understands that the government must by definition be the adversary. . . . The press is most effective when its reporters write about someone they don't like—Nixon, say, or Begin—and can play the adversary role to the hilt."[78]

Yet this temperament can also have its costs, in the quality of the news that it generates. When journalists consider themselves to be the public's proxy, they may brush off criticisms of reportage as threats to the public interest. Meanwhile, a sometimes inflated sense of self-importance may express itself in self-referential reporting that shifts the focus from the news to the reporter as celebrity or crusader. This self-importance may also contribute to an approach that treats the news gatherer as the newsmaker's competition in a struggle for the public's attention and affection.

All this suggests that the media's collective mentality may have both positive and negative effects on the news product. Indeed, some effects may be viewed as either positive or negative, depending on one's perspective. The larger point is that personality can influence a journalist's work, in both direct and indirect ways, no less than ideology or social structure. The news is a genre whose changing character reflects the requisites of large organizations, the conventions of a profession, and, not least, the drives and desires of honorable and fallible human beings.

131

THE RASHOMON PRINCIPLE

"Our business is truth as much as news."
—Bill Moyers, CBS

THE RELATIVITY of all reportage was beautifully expressed by the Japanese film *Rashomon,* which presents a single event as observed by several different characters. The story changes as the viewpoint shifts, leaving the audience to decide what really happened, or to ponder over our inability to ever be sure. An equally important question raised by the film is why each witness portrays a different picture. It is not a defect of the eye but of the ego. Each tells the tale in a way that reflects best on himself. Even a dead man, who tells his story through a medium, has his reputation and memory to protect.

It is time to turn our gaze from the teller to the tale itself. The media elite are a group apart—urban and cosmopolitan in background, liberal and skeptical in outlook, self-involved and aggressive in personal style. But does it all make any difference in the end, in the final product that rolls off the presses or appears over the airwaves?

We began by describing the media elite—their upbringings, their beliefs, their wants and needs. The "Rashomon principle" operated in their choice of sources, their summaries of news stories, the stories they created from TAT pictures. This helped explain who journalists are, what they think, what they want, who they trust. What does it really tell us about the news they produce?

So far, we have explored only speculative similarities between leading journalists' personalities and their propensity for certain themes such as horse race stories and negative news. In the remainder of this book, we will pull apart the news and sort out its components, to try to discover the ways it may bear the marks of its creators. But first we must explain just what we intend to do and why it is necessary.

In this chapter, therefore, we will first discuss the problematic relationship of news to reality, using examples drawn from national media outlets. Then we will describe a scientific method of examining the news and the role it will play in our study of the media elite. Finally, in Chapters Six through Eight, we put this method to the test.

What's the Story?

News from Nowhere? If the news were either the bare facts or the whole truth, there would be no need to study the people who report it. So it is not surprising that journalists sometimes find it convenient to treat the product of their labor as reality unadorned by man-made garb. In the words of former CBS president, Frank Stanton, "What the media do is to hold a mirror up to society and try to report it as faithfully as possible."[1] Similarly, a *New York Times* piece defended media coverage of racial riots against congressional critics with the argument, "Congress, one would hope, would not conduct an examination of a mirror because of the disquieting images it beholds."[2] CBS correspondent Morley Safer even suggests that news judgment consists of reality revealing itself to the reporter: "Journalism is erratic. It's often irrational. It's the way certain facts fall into place. There *is* no process."[3]

According to these practitioners, the news has little to do with journalists. Aside from this perhaps reflexive defense against criticism, however, journalists usually recognize that the news is neither the truth pure and simple, nor a perfect reflection of reality. News is like a prism that breaks a single object into multiple images. The image we perceive depends equally on the object, the eye of the beholder, and—not least—the prism itself.

This is most easily demonstrated by comparing cases where images diverge. Consider America's two leading general-interest dailies, the *New York Times* and the *Washington Post.* Take a straightforward event covered by both papers, the release of a scientific report on the theory of a "nuclear winter." The *Times* headlined its story, " 'Nuclear Winter' Is Seen as Possible." The lead sentence reads, "A panel of scientists told the federal government today that despite great uncertainties there was a 'clear possibility' that a major nuclear war would generate enough smoke and dust to blot out the sun in the Northern Hemisphere, causing severe drops in temperature." The story goes on to stress the "enormous uncertainties" involved, and later quotes the panel's chairman as saying, "There's great uncertainty . . . but it's not impossible."[4]

Now turn to the *Washington Post*'s treatment of the same event on the same day. The *Post*'s headline reads, "National Academy of Sciences Backs Nuclear Winter Theory." The lead sentence begins, "The National Academy of Sciences, the nation's most prestigious body, gave its seal of approval today to the controversial theory that a nuclear war could drastically alter the earth's climate. . . ." The term "uncertainty" does not appear until the twenty-second paragraph of the story, and then only to be rebutted: "Although the panel stressed that there were many uncertainties in its calculations, Paul Ehrlich, the Stanford University ecologist, said that this was almost irrelevant in terms of nuclear winter's effect on life."[5] The article notes that Ehrlich was not a member of the committee but had "written extensively" on the issue. Finally, the story features a bold-faced insert of a statement by the theory's main proponents, claiming vindication.

What does this comparison tell us? Both news organizations had access to the same report, the same press release, and the same sources. But *Times* readers learned that a controversial theory was "not impossible," though the jury was still out. On the other hand, *Post* readers learned that the verdict was in—the scientific community had endorsed the theory. And readers of both papers were left to puzzle over why the news this day resembled a funhouse mirror casting such inconsistent reflections.

Consider another example, even briefer and more straightforward. What could be more factual than a simple listing of cases on the Supreme Court docket for the coming term? In the *Times* we read,

> The Court is to decide the constitutionality of a Tennessee law, similar to laws in 23 other states, that authorizes the police to use deadly force to stop a fleeing suspect. In Tennessee vs. Garner, a Federal appeals court ruled that the law violated the Fourth Amendment by not requiring the police to have grounds for believing that the suspect was armed and dangerous.[6]

Compare this straightforward, rather terse account with the *Post*'s rendering of the same case:

> In Tennessee vs. Garner, the justices are to consider the constitutionality of a Tennessee "fleeing felon" law. The law was used to justify the police shooting of an unarmed 15-year-old as he attempted to flee an unoccupied house from which he had stolen two $5 bills and a small ring. The case has drawn the attention of the NAACP, which claims that black suspects are disproportionately victimized by police shootings allowed under such laws.[7]

In the nuclear winter story, it seemed that at least one of the accounts must be wrong, or at least misleading. Here both accounts may be equally true, but the stories are very different. This illustrates the impact of "framing" a set of facts with additional information. The *Times* story tells us the constitutional issue but not the specific facts of the case. The *Post* presents the facts in a way that engages the reader's emotions against the law. Instead of a "fleeing suspect," it presents a very sympathetic figure. We read of a young boy who posed no threat to the public (unarmed, he fled an unoccupied house). Moreover, his punishment far outweighed the crime (petty theft). Finally, there is the suggestion of racism in the NAACP's claim. The implication is that the law is unjust, or at least had unjust consequences in this case.

Which item is closer to the truth? The *Times* is more factual, less interpretive. The *Post* adds an interpretation and point of view, which may either illuminate or obscure the legal and social issues before the court. The two images intersect and diverge. The reader learns something different from each, without either necessarily being wrong.

Our final pairing is drawn from the increasingly popular realm of the background story. It is considered news and not editorial content. Yet it is intended to be more interpretative than the typical account of the day's events, to go beyond the "who, what, when, and where" to explain the "hows and whys" that underlie those events.

This example concerns a letter on the U.S. economy that the Roman Catholic bishops released just after the 1984 elections. The letter criticized many Reagan administration policies and endorsed economic practices associated with New Deal liberalism. Both the *Times* and the *Post* ran an interpretive piece marked "news analysis" alongside their more straightforward recounting of the bishops' proposals. But the analyses themselves differed dramatically.

The *Post*'s story is aptly summed up by its headline, "Bishops Review Proposals Abandoned as Unworkable, Too Costly." The thesis, elaborated at considerable length, is that the bishops' recommendations "have been tried and abandoned as unworkable or too costly even by many liberal economists and politicians." The point-by-point refutation that follows consists mainly of variations on a stock criticism: "virtually no economist, liberal or conservative thinks . . . all but ignoring the virtual consensus in the economics profession . . . approaches [advised by the bishops] have been tried extensively during the past two decades with minimal results . . ."[8]

Now consider the *Times* counterpart, headlined, "A Call for Economic Change Based on Moral View." The writer calls the report "eloquent" and asserts, "Though the Federal budget seems overstrained, it appears there would be room for a greater effort on social programs if the nation willed it." After dismissing the report's critics, he concludes that, "Many economists [will agree] the bishops have brought together competent economic analysis and a clear-eyed view of actual conditions in the United States and other countries. They will applaud the bishops for hitting so hard and challenging the nation to rethink its policies in the name of the well-being of its people."[9] Whether most economists would agree or disagree, it is clear where this reporter's sympathies lie. It seems equally clear that this "news analysis" must be partly the product of his own beliefs about economics and social policy, no less than for his *Post* counterpart who voices the opposite conclusion.

The point of these comparisons is not to ridicule two major newspapers simply because they sometimes differ in their versions of events and their significance. If anything, one might argue that they differ too little. If uniformity were the only goal, the vehicle would be a single national newspaper, using the vast resources of the government to ensure the most authoritative version of each day's events—a "solution" that already exists in many countries. It is no coincidence that the Soviet Union's official news organization is named *Pravda,* the Russian word for truth. The American approach is quite the opposite, presuming that the truth is more likely to emerge from the welter of many independent voices competing for attention. But this takes for granted that each voice is necessarily partial. The most informed consumer of the news product is the reader or viewer who partakes of many different news sources while understanding the partiality of each.

As much as most journalists subscribe to this approach in theory, they are understandably less enthusiastic about exploring the partiality of their own work. Hence the occasional defensive identification of their product with reality, as well as confusing the goal of impartiality with its attainment. By comparing the above stories from the *Post* and the *Times,* we simply show how two news outlets, equally committed to impartial reportage, can portray the same event in a quite different light. The fact that they differ shows how each can tell part of the truth while differing in their news agenda, use of sources, and interpretation.

These pairings also illustrate several unavoidable choices for journalists, which push their stories in one direction or another, always moving closer to one part of the truth at the cost of pushing another part aside. By understanding some of the problems facing journalists, readers can better evaluate the ways the news both expands and limits their own information about the world around them.

Observers and Participants. Our starting point is the ineradicable tension between the journalist's role as impartial observer, on one hand, and social critic or reformer, on the other. American journalists have perched on the horns of this dilemma for roughly a century, since the ideal of news as impartial information began to replace the earlier tradition of a proudly partisan press.[10] By the early twentieth century, the profession's new standard-bearers were the wire services and the *New York Times*, with their new model of relatively neutral reportage. Yet there was never a danger of the newspaper becoming a daily dictionary of events. As George Herbert Mead observed, "the reporter is generally sent out to get a story, not the facts." Reporters remained story-tellers who were expected to entertain as well as inform audiences. The difference was that tall tales, or highly partisan accounts, were no longer permitted.

Then as now, however, the facts had to be framed within a story. The story imputes significance to the facts with the aid of such conventions as the lead and closer, the inverted pyramid, the news peg and the angle. As Lewis Lapham writes, "stories move from truths to facts, not the other way around, and the tellers of tales endeavor to convey the essence of a thing. . . . Journalists have less in common with diplomats and soothsayers than they do with vagabond poets."[11]

In the process of getting a story, even the most meticulously objective reporter makes subjective choices, from the moment he contacts a source (and fails to contact another) to the time he turns in copy that includes some facts and neglects to mention others of arguably equal relevance. In fact, a subjective element precedes his work, since certain values and choices figure into an editor's story selection and assignment. And subjective choices will certainly guide the editors who revise and place (or kill) the story after it leaves the reporter's hand. In television, the process is somewhat different, but subjective decisions are just as critical from story assignment to airtime.

The matter of source selection, an integral part of the reporter's daily routine, should be considered. We saw in Chapter Three how the media elite systematically favor some types of sources over others, in ways that seem related to their own social values. The stories we cited on the bishops' letter show how sources can be invoked to bolster the authority of a reporter's conclusion. The *Post* reporter cites the "virtual consensus in the economics profession" that the bishops' proposals are unrealistic. The *Times* reporter assures us that "many economists" will applaud the same proposals. Both are undoubtedly drawing on their own discussions over the years with economists whose analyses they have come to trust. Both undoubtedly could have quoted prominent economists in support of their conclusion, had they chosen to do so. But it is equally clear that their contrary conclusions reflect their own judgments and values, which were not wholly formed in the few hours each had to research and write the story. It is only the conventions of objective journalism that demand that they place their conclusions in the mouths of those with expert standing on the topic.

The professional norm holds that the reporter is transmitting his knowledge of other people's opinions, rather than his own. The resulting convention is the quashing of first person singular in news copy. Despite the inroads of the new (personal) journalism, the rule still holds at the major media outlets where we interviewed. It is the same rule that guided CBS radio commentator H.V. Kaltenborn, when he drafted his analysis of a 1940 campaign speech. He wrote, "I listened to Wendell Willkie's speech last night. It was wholly admirable." By airtime, however, his listeners heard a slightly altered version: "Millions of Americans of both parties listened to Wendell Willkie's speech last night. Most of them agreed it was wholly admirable."[12]

There is an ongoing dialogue between reporters and sources, through which reporters simultaneously acquire information and learn where to go for a good quotation. Even if they trust their own instincts and knowledge, though, they still must respect the conventions. In the pithy phrase of one observer, "Somewhere a city editor is always saying, 'You can't write that unless you quote somebody.' "[13]

The choice of sources illustrates the many unavoidable decisions that determine the flavor and "spin" of any news story. Just as important as what goes in the story, though, is what gets left out. Often this is an unconscious decision. The reporter can't include what he doesn't know about, and he may not think to include something he would consider irrelevant. Other times reporters may be forced to exclude material they believe is relevant, but which cannot be verified to an editor's satisfaction. In the early 1950s, many reporters transmitted Senator Joseph McCarthy's charges of communists in the government, despite their personal reaction of disbelief. Even though they felt they were being used, the conventions of objective journalism did not allow them to rebut McCarthy's assertions in their stories.

In recent years these conventions have eased sufficiently for reporters to rebut public officials by reminding readers of things they did *not* say. Take the following *Washington Post* account of a 1983 press briefing: "White House spokesman Larry Speakes . . . [read] a long list of federal food programs and the increased levels of funding from 1980 to 1983. Speakes didn't mention, however, that Reagan had tried to cut spending for many of the federal food programs."[14] Similarly, a *New York Times* account of a presidential speech focused on an omission: "In saying he had reversed 'America's retreat' in foreign policy, the President referred to some of his favorite 1980 themes, the Soviet invasion of Afghanistan and the seizing in Iran of American hostages. He did not refer to . . . the death of 241 American servicemen last October in Lebanon in a terrorist bombing."[15] Finally a *Times* piece on a miners' strike in Britain began, "The Labor Party's annual conference today [accused] the police of perpetrating violent acts against striking miners. It made no mention of violence on picket lines."[16]

In all three instances, journalists could well argue that the public was better informed for learning about facts that the speaker failed to mention. The point is that the reporter's choice to include such information is obviously intended to change the reader's impression of the event reported, to keep the speaker from getting away with omitting material the reporter considers relevant. Equally important, the previous generation of reporters was less likely to have the option of including this sort of material. They had to find a third party to make the point. For example, a Democratic spokesman might have been quoted on the Reagan administration's attempts to cut the federal food program or on its handling of the situation in Lebanon. Of course, that would have meant contrasting two partisan positions, instead of presenting the refutation as a simple matter of fact. The latter approach obviously carries greater rhetorical weight. It also subtly reminds readers that the press is their objective protector against the partisan leanings of politicians.

Indeed, the reminder is not always subtle. In the following item, the process of filling in what the speaker left out turns into a full-scale refutation. This *Washington Post* report concerns Alabama Senator Denton's proposal to make English this country's official language. In straightforward fashion, the report cites Denton's concerns over illiteracy and especially bilingual education. It cites his belief that the latter "alienates immigrants from the mainstream of American society." However, this information is framed by commentary that is anything but straightforward. The article's lead reads, "It seems that there often is some kind of 'foreign' threat out there for Senator Jeremiah Denton. This time the foreign threat is truly foreign. It's foreign language." This sarcastic opening is matched by the "missing" information the reporter supplies after presenting Denton's argument that bilingual education hampers immigrants' assimilation and advancement. "Denton didn't mention the millions of immigrants who came to America, spoke their native languages at home and yet learned English and became an integral part of their new country without English being constitutionally mandated."[17]

Here the inclusion of what "wasn't mentioned" goes beyond factual material and places a politician's assertion in a new light. It drives home the point that Denton's proposal is the frivolous product of a nativist cast of mind. Yet there exists a serious and widespread debate among scholars and educators over the virtues and vices of bilingual education. By dismissing Denton's argument without reference to this debate, the story actually imposes an interpretation under the guise of supplying new information. Even as it claims to alert readers to political posturing, it averts their attention from a serious issue.

If news always falls somewhere in between fact and fiction, or objectivity and subjectivity, this last story clearly moves toward the subjective end. So far we have reflected on the subjectivity that suffuses even the most objective journalism. But throughout this work we have alluded repeatedly to trends that are giving leading journalists greater interpretive latitude. They range from the decline of the press lords and the professionalization of the journalist's role, to the impact of the 1960s *Zeitgeist,* the new journalism, and even television. The upshot is a widening of the sphere of news judgment and an increased opportunity for top journalists to function as social critics, crusaders for justice, or patrons of the disadvantaged. But the increasingly interpretive and combative approach of the national media also increases the subjective elements in the news.

One such element is a more provocative, even pugnacious style. Consider these lead sentences from two *Washington Post* stories:

> Like a child trying not to eat the vegetables, Congress is likely to push Central American issues to the side of its plate next week, hoping they will get cold and go away.[18]

> Crying spies, data leakage and one-way benefits for the Soviets, the administration wants to withdraw the United States from a unique, 10 year-old detente-era institute here where 100 scientists from East and West co-operate to seek solutions to problems that plague mankind.[19]

These items share a tone that might once have been relegated to the editorial pages. They seek not to inform but to persuade, not to describe but to criticize. They forgo a balanced account in favor of confronting miscreants. In short, they cast off the conventions of objective journalism to take up the muckraker's cry of *j'accuse.*

The question here is not whether this is good or bad journalism. Rather it is a different order of journalism from the dry, factual wire-service style that purports to provide a mirror of reality. As such, it invites analysis of the journalist's own attitudes, since it makes no apologies for presenting the news with a distinctive point of view.

Moreover, a reporter need not insert his or her own perspective quite so directly. It may appear in passing, by a choice of descriptors. Consider a reference to "Phyllis Schlafly, the noisy leader of the successful scuttling of the Equal Rights Amendment . . ."[20]

In the same vein, though at the other end of the political spectrum, is a description of Eleanor Smeal, president of the National Organization of Women: "Smeal . . . is a charismatic ideologue whom her backers consider a visionary."[21] Here a negative description (ideologue) appears as fact, while a positive trait (visionary) is presented as an opinion held by supporters. It would be easy to present the same information with a very different implication: "Smeal is a visionary whose detractors consider her a charismatic ideologue."

It is not just flamboyant language or a punchy style that makes for more interpretive or reformist journalism. What is often referred to as the "staid" *New York Times* sometimes combines a quiet tone with an equally strong dose of criticism. For example, we find in the midst of a story on defense spending, "Administration officials are effusive in the arming of the forces and in applauding the quality of people in them. But they glide over the shortcomings in readiness and staying power. Part of this is partisan politics."[22] This item uses the motif of adding what wasn't said ("they glide over") and even provides an explanation for the officials' shortcomings—partisan politics.

Occasionally, this tendency blossoms into a full-blown story whose sole news value lies in its rhetorical value as a rebuttal. For example, in 1984 a dispute arose over the extent of hunger in America. A government-sponsored study suggested that hunger was quite uncommon. Liberal critics replied angrily that they were personally familiar with many cases of hungry people. Presidential counselor Edwin Meese rejected such criticism as "anecdotal," hence an inadequate response to the study's overall statistical findings. The controversy generated an opportunity for the *Times* to run the following story:

> Sometimes a current political issue is crystallized for observant Washingtonians by a glimpse or two of ordinary people, rather than a spate of Congressional oratory or a prearranged White House "photo opportunity."
>
> Early on a cold Sunday evening, for example, a car from the Maryland suburbs carrying a couple and a small child pulled up to the curb on 17th Street near the Ellipse, beside a sidewalk grating. The passengers called to four homeless people who were huddled over a heat source, gave each of them a covered plateful of food and drove away. A passerby found some irony in the fact that the episode took place within clear sight of the White House, where evidence of hunger has been called "anecdotal."
>
> A day or two later, in a somewhat lighter vein, a bedraggled man stood at the corner of 17th Street and Pennsylvania Avenue, two blocks from the first scene. He held a sign that read: "I'm hungry enough to eat a stuffed Meese."[23]

To rebut an argument that evidence is merely anecdotal, the reporter responds with another anecdote, which he considers particularly devastating. (An alternative approach would have been to cite an opposing study, which in fact soon surfaced.) Also notable here is the technique of pseudo-attribution. A "passerby" finds the episode ironic, and it will be meaningful to "observant Washingtonians," presumably those who share the reporter's viewpoint and the "passerby's" sense of irony.

Humor, irony, and pointed ancedotes can enliven the news. But this style of reportage is a long way from the Joe Friday "just-the-facts-ma'am" approach. It is a more personalized form of journalism that allows reporters to put their own thoughts and feelings more overtly into their work. The *Times* style is perhaps more subtle than that favored by the *Washington Post* articles cited above, but the interpretive quality is easily as great.

Poetic License. In recent years some reporters have taken a more controversial step along the road toward subjective news by taking artistic rather than literal truth as their standard. The new journalism of the 1960s popularized such techniques as reconstructed dialogue (direct quotations verified only from second- or third-hand sources) and composites (combining characteristics of several different events or people into a single "representative" scene or individual).

The use of composites burst into public view with the 1981 Janet Cooke scandal. Cooke, a *Washington Post* reporter, was stripped of a Pulitzer Prize when it was revealed that "Jimmy," the twelve-year-old heroin addict featured in her winning series of articles, did not exist. He was a composite, a creation intended to represent several youthful drug addicts she had met. Cooke had earlier denied charges that her subject was fictional, and her editors accepted her word. She had also lied about her educational credentials in her job application. When the truth came out, she was fired.

The Cooke case stands at the fringes of our line of inquiry. The issue seems far from the realm of legitimate interpretive journalism. A reporter played fast and loose with the facts and lost her job because of it. Yet later events suggest that the issue is less cut and dried, and certainly less unique, than it first appeared. In 1984 a longtime *New Yorker* writer revealed that, in the words of a news report, he had "spent his career creating composite tales and scenes, fabricating personae, rearranging events and creating conversations in a plethora of pieces presented as nonfiction."[24]

Two factors made this case very different from the Janet Cooke affair. First, the reporter, Alastair Reid, defended his style as accurate in spirit, indeed more accurate than a purely factual approach. He told an interviewer, "Facts are only a part of reality. . . . You have to get over this hump that it's fact or else. There is a truth that is harder to get at and harder to get down towards than the truth yielded by fact."[25] Second, some prominent journalists came to Reid's defense. The *New Yorker* is famed for its meticulous, almost religious observance of factual accuracy. Yet its editor, William Shawn, at first defended Reid's approach. Although he later condemned the use of composites, he took no disciplinary action against Reid.[26] Several *New Yorker* colleagues also came to Reid's defense. A former *Atlantic Monthly* editor, Robert Manning, also called this approach "legitimate," while cautioning that "it's quite easy to level with the reader."[27]

Perhaps most telling was the response of *Washington Post* columnist Jonathan Yardley. He argued that the practice was not only justifiable but commonplace:

> Only the most doggedly literal-minded would deny him or any other writer the freedom to compress material or to speak in an assumed voice; it happens all the time, journalism being as inexact a craft as any other that relies on the human eye and ear, and there seems little reason to believe that Reid's uses and/or abuses of journalistic license have been significantly more griev-ous than anyone else's.[28]

At the same time, many "mainstream" journalists rejected Reid's methods. For example, the *New York Times* editorialized that "fictional facts are forever counterfeit."[29] Even if the critics outnumbered the defenders, though, both sides had their say in print. The crucial point is that Reid's methods were seen as con-troversial rather than indefensible.

The contrast with the Cooke affair is instructive. Reid volun-teered information that Cooke tried to conceal; he professed jour-nalistic methods that Cooke admitted to under intense pressure. Reid was and is a respected member of his profession. Cooke was a novice whose word became suspect after background checks revealed that she had lied to the *Post* about her educational cre-dentials. The Cooke case was thus seen as a matter of right and wrong; in Reid's case, two legitimate *modi operandi* were counter-posed. No one defended Cooke's deceptions, while a prominent *Washington Post* columnist justified Reid's methods as a matter of widespread and necessary practices coming out of the closet.

Reid himself claimed to be surprised by the controversy. In his view, "there is a more serious measure of accuracy than merely the factual one—accurately reflecting moods and opinions. . . . The real moral question comes over whether there is any intention to deceive and falsify. And the intention is rather to clarify than to deceive and falsify."[30]

With this approach we reach the far end of the subjectivity spectrum. The most objective journalist, as we saw, must pick and choose in moving from reality to news. Advocates of subjective journalism claim the right to rearrange reality to conform to their own inner vision of the truth. In either case, journalists' predispositions may influence their product. Objective journalists cannot escape this possibility; their subjective colleagues embrace it.

The subjective school, while probably a minority position, is no longer unthinkable in the world of daily journalism. In fact, it may be the wave of the future. *Harper's* editor Lewis Lapham believes the new pressures in this direction stem from the rising status of journalists, which we outlined in Chapter Two. He writes of the bright, self-assured new breed who began filtering into the profession in the early 1960s,

> Having enjoyed the privileges of both affluence and education, the new generation of journalists felt inhibited by the older conventions. They thought of themselves as "creators," as the possessors of "the truth" brought down from [Harvard] in bound volumes, as novelists manqués, as the social equals of the politicians or popular celebrities about whom they are obliged to make romances. . . . [They thought] the devices of literary fiction could be applied to the data base of the news.[31]

Enter Television

The Video Version. At precisely this historical moment, the new breed also discovered a new journalistic medium that could more readily meet their needs for self-expression and creative reporting. Television news began as little more than a talking wire service, occasionally enlivened by newsreel footage. During the 1960s, however, the medium was rapidly transformed by technological advances, increased resources, and a turbulent decade that seemed made for television coverage. Newspapers could not compete with the immediacy and vividness television coverage gave to assassinations, race riots, space exploration, combat abroad, and antiwar demonstrations at home. As the nation's eyes turned from the printed page to the television screen, broadcast journalism evolved into a distinctive and highly interpretive genre.

The public generally gives television news its highest marks for fairness, accuracy, and even thoroughness.[32] Numerous scholars have argued that this has more to do with the power of visual images than any true superiority.[33] The cracker-barrel sages who once intoned that seeing is believing now propound a high-tech version: "The camera never lies." This adage is fallacious in either form. The network news story the viewer sees in the evening is as painstakingly constructed as the one he reads in his morning newspaper. It employs the same techniques of selection and editing, with the additional set of news judgments that determine the proper mix of sight and sound. A three-minute film report represents the careful distillation of an hour or more of film footage, created under the editorial guidance of a field producer who operates under instructions from an executive producer.[34] If the seams don't show, chalk it up to the expertise of the tailors.

If anything, television's rejection of traditional wire service conventions makes it substantially more subjective than the daily paper. As media analyst Paul Weaver has noted, television news adopts the more personal voice of the omniscient reporter-narrator; it imposes a more unified interpretation on the day's events; and it is attracted to the drama and spectacle that produce good film. As a result: "Whereas newspapers focus on a diverse mass of specific events, television depicts something more directly thematic and melodramatic—the spectacle adorning the national dramas of the whole and the parts, of conflict and consensus, war and peace, danger and mastery, triumph and defeat, and so on."[35]

Robinson and Sheehan's systematic comparison of CBS and UPI campaign coverage confirms television's intrinsic interpretive cast. These researchers found that the network tended to mediate or interpret the facts rather than just report them. CBS was also more analytical, providing explanations rather than descriptions. And it was more thematic, feeding separate news items into cohesive story lines. Robinson and Sheehan conclude, "while the wires still provide information (who, what, where, when), the networks increasingly offer instruction (why and how). . . . In the last analysis we have two different genres of political reporting, old and new, traditional and contemporary. . . . Traditional print [the wire services) continually spits out fact-laden news. Much more often network journalism presents a short story, complete with moral. Print works to be informative, while network news shades markedly toward the didactic."[36]

Leaving aside the elements of narration, visuals, and storytelling, the camera itself can lie by selectively presenting visual information. An extreme close-up can exaggerate the tension in a speaker's face, showing glistening perspiration and unflattering shadows, suggesting an untrustworthy demeanor. By contrast, a camera aimed slightly upward at a speaker from middle distance can produce a more authoritative and forceful impression. The camera can grant respect or take it away.

A remarkable West German study put some of these intuitive principles to the test. The researchers first surveyed network news staffs to determine their political preferences. Then they asked cameramen how they would go about making subjects look good or bad, if they so chose. The prevailing response was that shots sharply angled from above or below produced the most unflattering images. The researchers then coded the camera angles used to photograph major party candidates for chancellor in a national election. They found that the Social Democratic candidate was more favorably photographed than his Christian Democratic opponent. What party did most television journalists favor? The Social Democrats, by a margin of 70 to 20 percent.[37]

The New Ombudsmen. The nightly newscast is television's least subjective journalistic format. Documentaries and so-called newsmagazine shows like "60 Minutes" and "20/20" allow far more leeway in presenting stories with a point of view. "60 Minutes" pioneered the concept of using news as entertainment. Much of its appeal lies in its ability to merge the muckraking aspects of print journalism with the personal and thematic imprint of television news.

Executive producer Don Hewitt is well aware of this achievement. His credo is clear and simple: "Our purpose is to make information more palatable and to make reality competitive with make-believe. There are shows on TV about doctors, cowboys, cops. This is a show about four journalists. But instead of four actors playing these four guys, they are themselves."[38] Yet Hewitt gives the tradition of Edward R. Murrow equal time with that of Fred Silverman. "You know what we are?" he proclaims. "We have become America's ombudsman!"[39]

Being America's ombudsman requires considerable editorial discretion. For a "60 Minutes" segment fifty times as much film may be shot as is finally used—about double the ratio for an evening news story. Similarly, far more time and resources can be devoted to a story, allowing much greater development of a story line. No wonder Mike Wallace says flatly, "You have the power to convey any picture you want." In fact, he goes on, "we once thought about doing a 'Rashomon'—getting a piece of material and editing it several different ways—to demonstrate that fact."[40]

Audiences have yet to see such a multiperspective approach. Moreover, Wallace's proposed story would not really fit the bill, since the "60 Minutes" staff would be in charge of presenting all the viewpoints. A true *Rashomon* effect would emerge only if "60 Minutes" subjects produced their own competing reports. This actually occurred in 1979, after the show aired a segment criticizing the Illinois Power Company for cost overruns on a nuclear reactor they were building. Unlike the typical subject of a "60 Minutes" exposé, Illinois Power fought fire with fire. They had videotaped all the interviews themselves. So they produced their own filmed report, showing the footage CBS left out and adding information the program omitted.

Among other things, the original broadcast contained some factual errors that put the company in a bad light, which CBS later retracted; it misinterpreted a scheduling chart to Illinois Power's detriment, ignoring a company representative's explanation of how to read the chart (as Illinois Power's film showed); and it relied heavily on the testimony of a former employee, without informing viewers that, as CBS knew, he had falsified his educational credentials. As Paul Good later reported in *Panorama,* "in virtually every case, the Illinois Power film shows "60 Minutes" omitting portions of interviews that offer evidence challenging its contentions against the power company. Certainly, Illinois Power tries to put its best face on things. But "60 Minutes" follows a pattern of believing the worst and artfully neutralizing elements that might disturb that pattern."[41]

The point is not that "60 Minutes" produced a sloppy or unfair story. Rather, the story looks very different when told from the other side, the side the viewer ordinarily never sees. When confronted with this unexpected opportunity to participate in an actual *Rashomon*-type story, CBS proved reluctant. In a written reply to Illinois Power, a network vice-president warned that "your own use and distribution of the ["60 Minutes"] material constitute in themselves an infringement on our copyright."[42]

In fact such usage is protected under the "fair use" doctrine, and CBS never followed up on its implied threat of legal action. CBS did, however, sue to stop Vanderbilt University from taping news broadcasts for scholarly use. CBS contended this archive of TV newscasts, which enabled historians, political scientists, and other media analysts to review network broadcasts, was in violation of their copyright.[43] News executives are just as susceptible as the rest of us when faced with the temptation of presenting their own version of events as the authorized version. There is a natural tension between their usual staunch espousal of First Amendment principles and their reluctance to lose control over the information they produce. The danger is that this tension may undermine their position as unwavering advocates of the public's right to know. It helps explain the disturbing conclusion of one survey of public attitudes toward the media: "For many Americans, it is the media who may be the enemy of freedom of expression, since the media have the power to select and limit the information available to the public."[44]

Talking Back to the Tube. Following the example of the "60 Minutes" Illinois Power episode, the public recently received another unusual look behind the scenes of a now-famous 1982 CBS News documentary, "The Uncounted Enemy." The broadcast charged that General William Westmoreland conspired to deceive the president and the American public about enemy troop strength during the Vietnam War. Four months later, two investigative journalists, writing in *TV Guide,* called the broadcast a "smear" that was "misshapen by personal bias and poor supervision."[45] They charged that the program's executive producer, George Crile, set out to prove a conspiracy and ignored or omitted evidence to the contrary.

In response, CBS carried out an internal investigation headed by senior producer Burton Benjamin. His report unexpectedly became public as a result of a libel action subsequently brought by General Westmoreland. The Benjamin report substantiates many of the *TV Guide* charges. It cites eleven "principal flaws," including "an imbalance in presenting the two sides of the issue"; failure to prove a conspiracy; failure to identify a key accuser as "a *paid* consultant"; allowing another accuser to be interviewed twice and to see screenings of other interviews; and other "coddling of sympathetic witnesses."[46]

These criticisms concern both the process and the product, and they show how the two are interwoven. The producers' contention of a conspiracy led them to favor some witnesses and exclude others, and to use some interview footage and leave others on the cutting room floor. The effect of this unbalanced approach on the actual broadcast was measured in various ways. For example, the report compared the number of Westmoreland's accusers and defenders shown on the program. Nine different accusers were shown, compared to one defender, aside from Westmoreland himself. Alternatively, it measured the amount of air time allotted to each side. Westmoreland and his supporter spoke for just under 6 minutes; his accusers spoke for over 19 minutes.

Thus, the Benjamin report not only confirms the charge that the production process was one-sided, it shows systematically how this resulted in an unbalanced presentation. This is a critical point, and we shall return to it momentarily. The main service the Benjamin report renders, though, is to give us an inside look at a network documentary. It shows how a single viewpoint, that of the executive producer, can shape the facts to conform to his own vision of the truth.

Later, millions of viewers would get a taste of the report's findings, as network news programs showed outtakes from the documentary to illustrate points at issue in the Westmoreland libel suit. General Westmoreland dropped his case, perhaps seeing the futility of trying to prove CBS' "reckless disregard for the truth," a rigorous legal standard. But a generation of television viewers for the first time glimpsed the difference between the smooth product they take for granted and the difficult process of creating it.

"The Uncounted Enemy," like the "60 Minutes" Illinois Power story, illustrates the problems that may give rise to an unbalanced broadcast. Unfortunately, we are most likely to obtain a look behind the scenes when the angry subject of an exposé fights back. When the story is less pointed, journalists find no reason to expose their techniques to public view. Indeed they sometimes go to jail on principle, to protect their notes or recollections against judicial intrusion. But this protectiveness in "hard cases" often leaves scholars in the position of the psychiatrist who tries to generalize about human nature on the basis of the neurotic patients he sees in his practice. The best analysts realize that neuroses provide insights into irrational processes common to us all, without reducing all human behavior to mere neurosis. Just so, we must recognize that the controversial story helps us see behind the scenes without implying that the exercise of news judgment automatically produces unfair outcomes.

Our effort is aimed at eliminating the false dichotomy between a "true" and a "biased" story. News judgment necessarily reflects partial perspectives, which are filtered through the conventions of the journalistic profession. The news will always represent the interaction of individual perspectives and group conventions. But neither term in the equation is static. Both vary with changes in the profession's personnel and norms. We have tried to show how the rise of a new generation of more cosmopolitan journalists has worked to introduce more overtly subjective elements in the norms and conventions of their work. Now we must determine how these elements operate, day in and day out, to produce patterns and perspectives in news coverage over the long run.

In "The Uncounted Enemy," whatever the producers' intentions or methods, the final measure of their work lies in the broadcast itself. In commissioning the Benjamin report, CBS News was concerned to see whether its employees followed company standards designed to ensure fairness. For example, reinterviewing a friendly witness and allowing him first to see other filmed interviews violated those standards. Our concern is with the end result. Which viewpoints are expressed and which are omitted, regardless of the procedures and decisions that shaped the piece? If certain viewpoints are favored over others in a story, and if the favored viewpoints are those held by the reporter, that would be *prima facie* evidence of a journalist's attitudes influencing his work. From the audience's perspective, it doesn't matter whether the influence is conscious or unconscious, intentional or unwitting, a violation of standards or their fulfillment. What matters is what the audience sees, and what it never gets the chance to see.

It is not enough, however, to assert that the news favors one view over another. This must be demonstrated in ways that transcend the critic's own subjective outlook. The Benjamin report provides an example of this, by measuring the amount of time given to Westmoreland's attackers and defenders. This is a reliable and quantitative way of asking whether a story meets the standard of balance. An equivalent approach to a newspaper story would be to compare column inches of space allotted to sources on different sides of an issue. The great advantage of this quantitative approach is that various critics with different perspectives can agree on the result. They might differ in interpreting the result. For example, one might argue that the weight of the evidence was on the side of Westmoreland's critics; therefore, they deserved more air time. One network wag, buffeted by demands for "balanced" stories, once suggested doing a balanced documentary entitled, "Hitler: Pro and Con."

Journalists must not only decide how to balance two competing views, they must decide when there are two (or more) legitimate sides to an issue. So one might quibble over the standard of fairness being applied. Nonetheless, the quantitative approach provides a core of less subjective information, a datum that provides a common ground for interpretation. Without that starting point, we are lost in the wilderness of subjective criticism stemming from our own self-interest and self-delusions. Business and labor, Democrats and Republicans, conservative and liberal groups all complain that the news is biased against them and in favor of their opponents. Journalists sometimes feel that the best measure of accuracy is having an equal amount of flak descend from both sides. In fact, however, one side (or both) may be wrong. The journalist's problem may lie either in choosing between them or in finding an appropriate middle ground. It is rarely a simple choice.

The Role of Content Analysis

To sort out competing claims, it is necessary to depend on reliable and accurate measures of the news. The tool that social scientists apply to this task is called content analysis. This term refers to a set of techniques that allows us to classify information in an objective and systematic way.[47] It involves proceeding by explicit rules and judging by clear criteria that minimize our own subjective predispositions. The goal is to produce valid measures of news content. The hallmark of success lies in reliability. Other investigators who apply the same procedures to the same material should obtain the same results. Again, they may differ in interpreting those results. For example, General Westmoreland and CBS producer George Crile differ on the fairness with which "The Uncounted Enemy" treated its subject. But both would have to agree that Westmoreland's defenders received less airtime than his critics, however differently they might interpret that fact.

Analyzing Campaign Coverage. How can content analysis help to resolve disputes about media coverage? Consider the quadrennial complaints of presidential candidates that the media are biased against them. Accusations of media hostility are a regular feature of contemporary political campaigns, transcending the boundaries of party and ideology. In 1984, supporters of Jesse Jackson and Ronald Reagan were probably equally certain that the media held a grudge against their respective candidates, while backers of Gary Hart and Geraldine Ferraro complained bitterly about the fickle media turning against those candidates. Each group could cite numerous unnecessarily critical stories, along with puff pieces that allegedly assisted a rival. Journalists tend to discount such complaints as predictable partisan carping. But even paranoids may have enemies, and even partisans may have a valid case. The problem is how to assess their claims in a nonpartisan fashion.

How do you assess a highly subjective matter like media fairness in a manner that is itself fair? In principle, the answer is simple—by establishing objective criteria of fairness and applying them systematically to media coverage of all candidates. For example, one standard of fairness is equal access. A straightforward (if laborious) way of comparing candidates' extent of coverage is by measuring the time each receives on television and radio and the space allotted to each in newspapers and magazines. Here the measuring instruments are objective and precise—a stopwatch and a ruler.

Yet, candidates are concerned not only with the amount of coverage they receive but also with its tone. Only the darkest of dark horses would dare accept the adage that what the press says doesn't matter so long as they spell your name right. When a candidate's press revolves around whether his name is spelled "Hart" or "Hartpence," he begins to worry that bad press is worse than no press at all.

Good and bad press are harder to measure objectively than the mere fact of coverage, but the task is by no means impossible. First you decide which topics are relevant, e.g., discussions of the candidate's competence, integrity, consistency, et cetera. Then you determine the tone of each statement dealing with one of these topics. The result may be coded as positive ("Reagan is a great communicator"), negative ("Reagan often gets his facts wrong"), balanced ("Reagan is a master at using anecdotes, but he often gets his facts wrong"), or neutral ("Reagan's use of anecdotes has stirred debate").

Some judgments are more difficult than these, and coders must be guided by clear rules. In making each decision, coders should be applying rules, not expressing their own opinions. If the rules are sufficiently clear, two coders working independently should come to the same conclusions, regardless of their own opinions about the subject matter (this is called "inter-coder reliability").

These procedures are easier to describe than to attain. For example, the analysis must be exhaustive. Edith Efron's study of the 1968 presidential election concluded that Humphrey received much more favorable television news treatment than Nixon.[48] However, most coverage was neutral or ambiguous. The difference between the two candidates' coverage is small relative to the entire body of campaign news.[49] On the other hand, Richard Hofstetter's careful study of the 1972 election may include too much material in its definition of good and bad press. One of his criteria for positive or negative news was the success of the campaign. Thus, reports about Nixon's big lead in that landslide year may have inflated his positive totals, with the converse holding true for McGovern. Hofstetter found that each candidate received a roughly equal amount of good and bad press. Yet Nixon's positive horse race coverage may have obscured more negative portrayals of his character and policies.[50]

Such examples show that content analysis is not a panacea. Any method can be applied in various ways, for better or worse. The great virtue of this method is that it reduces, to some degree, questions of opinion to questions of fact. We may disagree over how well Hofstetter measured the fairness of 1972 campaign coverage. But his findings provide a point of departure for debate. If we accept his definition of the issue and his interpretation of the findings, we are led to the same conclusion that he reached. We are arguing about the significance of facts rather than the facts themselves. And this is a great leap forward from the realm of purely subjective opinion.

Moreover, by studying controversial topics systematically with a scientific method, we replace endless partisan wrangling with the search for generally acceptable answers. The failings of one study become the problems that the next study seeks to solve.

Thus, Robinson and Sheehan, learning from Hofstetter, were careful to distinguish between the horse race and substantive issues coverage when they assessed the fairness of 1980 campaign coverage.

We do not posit a positivistic utopia in which all controversy eventually gives way to timeless principles of numerical evaluation. History is too sly to be reduced to physics, and events always seem a step ahead of interpretations. For example, Robinson and Sheehan found in 1980 that television news was about equally hard on Democrats and Republicans, liberals and conservatives—it had a bad word for everyone. So they argued that the real problem with television journalism was not partisanship but negativism. In 1984, however, Robinson and his colleagues found that the Mondale campaign received favorable television coverage, while Reagan and Bush were treated much more harshly, some nine times as negatively as their Democratic opponents. Was this a new wave of partisan bias by the liberal media? Not so, argued Robinson. It was bias against the front-runner, another trend he had spotted in 1980.[51]

Edith Efron would no doubt disagree with this interpretation. She might claim vindication for her disputed 1968 findings, arguing that 1980 was an aberration that reflected the media's dislike for Jimmy Carter. So are we back in the realm of partisan wrangling, having gained nothing from twelve years of scholarship? Not quite. We have a much clearer picture of what campaign media coverage is like than we used to, even if we are not yet sure of why it is that way.[52] The very fact that the coverage can vary so much from one election to the next militates against simple conspiracy theories.

Further, some alternative hypotheses can be eliminated in light of evidence that has accumulated since 1980. Pro-Mondale coverage in 1984 shows that the networks are not always evenhanded in the general election; nor are they necessarily negative toward all candidates. That leaves the anti-front-runner hypothesis standing. Television journalists may see themselves not as liberal crusaders but as giant killers whose job is not to follow the leader but to fell him.

In principle, we should be able to submit the competing "liberal bias" and "anti-front-runner" hypotheses to the test—especially if we analyze television coverage of the 1964 campaign, the last landslide victory of a liberal Democrat over a conservative Republican. Unfortunately, there are no thorough and accessible records of that coverage, since it predates the 1968 creation of Vanderbilt University's Television News Archive. While we're waiting for the next Democratic landslide, some enterprising scholar might examine coverage of highly partisan statewide races that attracted national television attention, such as Jim Hunt vs. Jesse Helms in North Carolina, or Lew Lehrman vs. Mario Cuomo in New York.

Granted, we still lack definitive answers on television's partisanship in political campaigns. But content analysis has given us some preliminary and partial answers, has helped us to better formulate the questions, and directs our strategies for getting better answers in the future. It has also increased our understanding of campaign journalism enormously over the past fifteen years. Content analysis has replaced the assertions of columnists and speechwriters with a growing body of knowledge. If all the answers are not yet in view, at least the questions can be posed in a more sophisticated and fruitful fashion.[53]

Beyond Elections. Campaign journalism, however, offers a poor test of how journalists' outlooks and sensibilities color their portrayals of social conditions. Political campaigns are far from typical arenas for social change. The hothouse atmosphere and high drama they generate, their often abstract rules and fixed schedules, and their clear-cut denouements are more reminiscent of the sports section than the front page. Election coverage is too idiosyncratic to permit generalizations about how reporters are guided to some topics but not others, some sources but not others, some conclusions about how society works but not others.

In addition, campaigns offer a uniquely personalized setting for social conflict, and journalists must respond simultaneously to individuals and the issues they raise. All issues are shaped and carried partly by the personalities of their adherents, but in political campaigns they are carried too far to be disentangled. John

Kennedy's good press may have been less attributable to his liberalism than to his persona. Sophisticated, urbane, self-confident, witty, and ironic, he represented a kind of ego ideal for reporters who were charmed even if they differed over specific issue positions. No such residue of good will aided his liberal successor, Lyndon Johnson, whose own insecurity and resentment toward the "eastern establishment" only fanned the flames of press suspicion toward his backwoodsy manner. Nor did Jimmy Carter's piety fare well with the more freewheeling Washington press corps.

To minimize the effects of such ephemeral or extraneous factors, we decided to examine how the media covered controversial social issues over long periods of time. We looked for issues that not only engendered ongoing controversy, but also generated questions whose answers required some expertise. The strategy was to follow major media coverage of several complicated issues for several years, permitting comparisons among media outlets across diverse topics.

Chapters Six through Eight focus on three long-term social and political controversies: the safety of nuclear power, the use of busing for racial integration of public schools, and the role of the oil industry during and after the energy crises of the 1970s. The results of our studies are presented in these three chapters. However, first we should explain why we chose these particular topics, and what we hoped to learn about the media by examining them. These issues are diverse, encompassing aspects of science and technology, the sociology of race relations, and business and economic policy. They also generated ongoing, and occasionally massive, coverage over long periods of time, providing material for the comparisons we wanted to make. Finally, all three produced disputes among both the general public and the intelligentsia.

Nuclear safety, busing, and the economics of petroleum are all issues that are at once highly technical and profoundly political. They evoke passionate responses from the man in the street even as academic experts debate their meaning in scholarly journals. This presents both an opportunity and a problem for journalists. These are "hot" issues that people want to know about, and they bring forth partisan claims and counter-claims. At the same time, scholars have been spewing forth a great deal of information on these very topics, but much of their work is arcane, couched in scientific terminology, and resistant to quick conclusions that make for clear and concise reporting. Thus, such topics offer an opportunity to see how reporters attempt to transmit information on matters that they rarely have time to explore fully. This allows us to ask what kinds of sources they seek out, how broadly and deeply they penetrate into uncharted terrain, and how they attempt to simplify complex arguments without oversimplifying them.

The Search for Standards. There was an even more important reason why we chose such difficult and complicated issues. A crucial problem for content analysis is the standard by which the content is judged. In the case of campaigns, analysts usually assume that political candidates representing the two major political parties should receive roughly equal treatment. This is an arbitrary standard, as evidenced by the complaints of third-party candidates, but it probably reflects a consensus of both scholars and the general public. Even in this case, though, problems arise. What if the candidates behave differently, or one performs better than the other? Shouldn't that difference in reality be reflected in the coverage? If an incumbent president runs a "rose garden" campaign that generates less news than his opponent does, should his coverage be inflated to produce parity? If one candidate's campaign runs smoothly and elicits enthusiasm, while the other falters and fails to move the public, shouldn't the news reflect the difference? Such considerations bring us back to the question of whether variations in media coverage are simply reflections of reality. This problem is compounded when studying issues, since there may be many "candidates," all claiming to represent the solution to a problem, some inevitably worthier than others.

Scholars have wrestled with this "reality" problem for decades. In a seminal study conducted over thirty years ago, sociologists Kurt and Gladys Lang neatly solved the problem by comparing television coverage of an event to the notes of on-the-spot observers they had stationed there in advance.[54] They concluded that the television news broadcast distorted the reality of the event, a parade in honor of General Douglas MacArthur. More recently, political scientist David Altheide has shown how on-spot observation in the television studio can contribute to our understanding of distortions in a newscast.[55] Unhappily, such methods work better for judging coverage of events (especially those that can be anticipated) than long-term coverage of issues. Even if we had stationed observers at Three Mile Island, or in South Boston during court-ordered busing, such eyewitness accounts could tell us little about such abstract issues as reactor safety or "white flight."

Therefore, we adopted a quite different strategy. Coders were directed by scholars who, by virtue of advanced training in relevant fields and extensive study before the content analysis began, were experts on each topic. Each of these project directors began by studying the academic literature and following the debates among specialists, noting the scholarly consensus where it existed and the particular points of contention where it did not. Once this was done, we worked with each project director to develop a content analysis system that examined coverage of the most important issues they had identified. Then each project director trained a team of coders, first giving them a substantive background in the topic and then teaching them the coding system.

This procedure was laborious and time-consuming, but it permitted much more thorough analyses than commonly are obtained. For example, these studies go beyond whether a story is positive or negative to explore the themes it elaborates, the sources it quotes, the way issues are phrased, and whether a topic is treated as controversial or consensual.

Finally, we compared media treatment of each topic to state-of-the-art knowledge among scholars. This is not to say that the scholars always had the final answers. Indeed, one recurring question is whether journalists accurately transmitted their uncertainties where they existed. The assumption is that media coverage should reflect the best knowledge available on a topic, even if that means reporting a lack of knowledge. For example, one would expect an article on extraterrestrial life to cite many different views, reflecting the lack of either certain knowledge or scientific consensus on this issue. Yet, one would not expect to see equal time given to those who reject the theory of evolution, because scientists overwhelmingly endorse it. Claims to the contrary should be treated as distinctly minority views, if journalists accurately reflect the intellectual consensus. As these examples suggest, our standard for judging the news is not truth but the accurate transmission of available information. One may never be sure what the truth is, but good reporting tells us what is agreed on, what is disputed, and what is unknown, so we can judge for ourselves.

Analyzing Issue Coverage. In each of the following chapters, we lay out a major social issue with its attendant controversies, then show how national media outlets presented the issue. We ask first what the experts thought, then what the media told us, and finally, whether there was a discrepancy between the two. If the media portrait diverged from the best available knowledge, in the direction of journalists' own attitudes, that would be *prima facie* evidence that their attitudes, however unconsciously, influenced their coverage.

The case of nuclear energy was our most extensive area of inquiry. The first task was to gain an overview of expert opinion on the controversies that rage about the safety of this technology. To find out what the experts think, we not only surveyed the literature but the experts themselves. This involved sending lengthy questionnaires to large samples of leading scientists and engineers, as well as key decision-makers in industry, government, and academia. Their responses provide a portrait of that community's views on controversial issues, ranging from the effects of low-level radiation to the probability of nuclear accidents. Simultaneously, the same questions were asked of America's most influential science writers. Finally, to complete the comparison, the media elite were asked a few questions about their attitudes toward nuclear power.

After the surveys were completed, we worked with a scholar specializing in energy policy to prepare an overview of the scholarly literature on the points of debate. Dr. Robert Rycroft,

Associate Director of the Graduate Program in Science, Technology, and Public Policy at George Washington University, identified the major points of contention and the various perspectives in the scientific literature. This document was the basis for a content analysis system to measure how well media coverage captured the key elements of this debate. Then a team of coders was assembled that included individuals with diverse viewpoints on nuclear energy. The coders were trained until they agreed at least 80 percent of the time on how information should be classified for all categories in the content analysis. Levels of agreement were usually much higher than the 80 percent minimum, which is relatively standard in this field.

One point is essential to understand this process: coders were not asked to make subjective judgments based on their own feelings about nuclear energy. Instead, they were taught to follow a system of highly specific rules designed to minimize the effect of personal feelings on coding decisions. The success of these rules is measured by the high levels of agreement among the coders.

The research team then embarked on the arduous task of coding fourteen years of newspaper, magazine, and television coverage. When they were finished, the data were computerized and the results analyzed. Finally, we compared this information about media coverage with the attitudes measured in the surveys.

The results of the nuclear power content analysis are detailed in the next chapter, followed by similar accounts of busing and oil industry coverage, excluding the surveys of experts. This overview of the research strategy is intended to convey the scope and method of this undertaking.

We also chose at the outset not to try to match the attitudes of particular reporters with the stories that they covered. Everyone we surveyed was promised complete anonymity, and all records matching names with survey responses were destroyed. Ethical concerns aside, we were far from certain that this approach would be fruitful. For one thing, it overlooks the crucial editorial component of mainstream journalism. Editors may not receive bylines, and television producers may never appear onscreen, but their role can neither be ignored nor precisely measured.

The Rashomon Principle

On a more theoretical level, we are less concerned with the attitudes of particular individuals than with the intellectual milieu to which their ideas contribute. One of the most important characteristics of the media elite is its social and intellectual homogeneity. Such homogeneity both informs and limits conceptions of the news. Organization theorists have pointed out how reporters absorb the culture of the newsroom. But they also help create that culture, by contributing to perspectives that become so widely shared that they are taken for granted.

This chapter has shown how such perspectives might influence the news product. The most straightforward news report is the outcome of unavoidable choices that reflect the journalist's sensibilities in weaving together fact and interpretation. We have illustrated the ways stories can vary according to choices of emphasis, source selection, descriptive vs. insinuational language, and even poetic license that reshapes the facts to fit the truth. These choices are not constants but variables. They vary from one individual to another, and one era to another. The choices made by mainstream journalists shifted toward a more self-consciously objective approach with the rise of the wire services a century ago. Today, under the influence of television, they seem to be incorporating more subjective elements.

The techniques of content analysis can show whether and how these elements shape the contours of media coverage. Thus, the analyses presented in the next three chapters attempt to determine whether the intellectual climate within which leading journalists operate influences their coverage of specific social controversies over the long run. Ben Bagdikian has written, "The central function of journalism is to permit a more valid view of 'reality.' "[56] To assess the "reality" that journalism presents, requires a scientifically valid view of the news.

MEDIA MELTDOWN

"Even while the awesome force of the atom spreads, we still do not fully comprehend its dangers—except that it poses the possibility of our extinction and the death of the earth."
—"The Fire Unleashed," ABC documentary

ONE SPRING night in 1985, ABC did something highly unusual. The network preempted its entire prime-time schedule in order to confront what host Peter Jennings called "the most crucial issue ever to confront the human species—the degree to which the atom has come to dominate this planet." Thus began "The Fire Unleashed," a three-hour documentary on the dangers of nuclear weapons and nuclear energy, which the program treated as malevolent Siamese twins.

Narrators spelled out the "deepening dangers and uncertainties" of "the atom's fearful power":

> Nuclear power . . . in the U.S., the industry is staggering with economic and safety problems. The worst nuclear plant accident in history. Radioactive nuclear waste, with elements that will remain a threat to life for hundreds of generations to come. Nuclear proliferation . . . the nuclear arms race. . . . These issues of the nuclear age raise the largest question of all—whether it's

possible we've brought forth a power beyond our power to control. A power posing for the first time the possibility of our actual termination. The termination of our whole past and place. The earth. Our home.[1]

This is strong stuff. It continued for three hours, accompanied by a panopoly of visual effects and sophisticated computer graphics. It was the state of the art taking on the fate of the earth. And it was powerful. One study of a randomly selected group of viewers found that the show produced a 36 percent increase in those opposed to the use of nuclear energy to provide electricity. This impact was still evident when they were resurveyed five months later.[2]

Opinion shifts such as these tend to be short-lived unless reinforced by other sources. But it certainly shows that the media can affect public attitudes toward nuclear power. And it raises broader questions about the role media coverage has played in the dramatic decline in public support for nuclear energy.

Public attitudes toward nuclear power have completely turned around since the early 1970s.[3] In 1971, the proportion of Americans willing to have nuclear plants in their own communities was double the proportion opposed (57 to 28 percent). By 1978, a year before the Three Mile Island (TMI) accident, opponents already outnumbered supporters. In 1980, a year after TMI, the number of opponents was more than double that of supporters (63 to 28 percent). Moreover, polls show that nuclear power has become the least popular energy alternative in recent years, mainly because of fears about safety.[4]

The media undoubtedly have played some role in this process, simply by transmitting information to millions of people who lack the time, inclination, or expertise to read the technical literature on nuclear energy. Several studies by the Battelle Institute in Seattle, Washington, concluded that major media coverage has been predominantly negative toward nuclear power.[5] And a study by the Media Institute in Washington, D.C., found that, on television newscasts, critics get about twice as much airtime as supporters to make their case.[6] Yet, if nuclear power is as dangerous, and its critics so numerous, as "The Fire Unleashed" suggests, such coverage may be entirely appropriate.

Thus, we return to the conundrum raised in Chapter Five. How do you evaluate the coverage independent of the event being covered? How does media criticism rise above blaming the messenger? What is an appropriate standard for judging media coverage of nuclear safety? To evaluate the coverage, it is necessary to understand something about the topic. To do this, we will turn to both the people who spend their professional lives dealing with these often arcane issues and, more broadly, those whose advanced scientific or technical training instills the ability to comprehend such issues. That means, first, reviewing the technical literature to determine the terms of the debate over nuclear safety, problems, and issues. It also means polling the scientific and engineering communities to gain an overview of their views on these matters.

A Framework for Analysis

Nuclear energy is by far the most sophisticated high technology energy alternative. The fuel cycle through which uranium is transformed into usable electricity involves many stages: mining, milling, conversion, enrichment, fuel fabrication, reactor operation, reprocessing, waste management, and transportation. Each of these steps involves a host of intricate technological activities, and at every stage of the process certain questions remain to be answered. We will first outline the types of questions that have been raised and the types of answers that have been proposed. Then we will apply these concepts to the specific topics in the nuclear debate.

QUESTIONS: What gaps in our current knowledge must be filled if nuclear power is to overcome the substantial hurdles in its path? Three areas of uncertainty can be identified: design, impact, and management.

Design questions have to do with performance. They concern the scientific and engineering requisites that create technologies and develop them to the point of commercial use. The key performance question is: How will the technology execute the functions for which it is designed? Behind this lurks a second question: According to what criteria?

Impact questions concern the distribution of economic benefits and the costs and risks to health and environment that result from placing a technology in a particular location. Here the key question is: Who wins and who loses? The state of the art in this area is less well developed than in that of design uncertainty.

Management questions involve who participates in making decisions at each stage of the technological process. This is the murkiest area of policy uncertainty, because it deals with social and behavioral science questions. The task is to develop institutions that can control the impact of modern technology while still assuring adequate performance. This is the arena where trade-offs between efficiency and equity must be resolved.

ANSWERS: We turn now to the process by which significant design, impact, and management uncertainties are addressed. This is not simply a matter of finding the right answers but of deciding what kind of answers to seek. Do definitive solutions exist, even in principle, or are the "answers" limited to deciding how best to live with enduring uncertainties? In the terms employed below, are we confronted with problems to be solved or issues that can at best be resolved?

Problems are the domain of the expert, where the solution involves "the application of knowledge and choice in a definitive way.[7] Technological problems are most amenable to rational decision-making when there is relatively detailed understanding of the system involved and only small changes are required to develop a solution. Problem-solving involves the reduction of risk—the use of expertise to decrease the likelihood or the magnitude of a potential hazard.

Issues, on the other hand, are the domain of the politician. They involve fundamental enduring conflicts among objectives and those who pursue them. Problems can be solved, issues cannot. Issues can, however, be resolved. Their resolution requires the adaptiveness to compensate for incomplete understanding, and the flexibility to reach a balance between competing interests. Unlike problems, issues deal with situations where risks cannot be reduced. These matters are "trans-scientific," because they are not resolvable by science—they transcend science.[8]

The distinction between problems and issues has been critical for nuclear power. To a great extent, the debate between nuclear advocates and opponents has been structured according to whether a complex design, impact, or management question fell into the problem or issue category.

Applying the Framework

How do these categories apply to the major questions about nuclear safety? Dr. Rycroft's survey of the scientific and social scientific literature identified ten major topics in the nuclear debate: the nuclear fuel cycle, reactor safety during and after accidents, safeguards against the loss or destruction of radioactive materials, proliferation, health and safety risks of normal reactor operation, environmental hazards, radioactive waste disposal, siting and licensing of nuclear technologies, risk assessment, and citizen involvement in decision-making. We will briefly describe major areas of concern about each, on the basis of the current debate. Each topic will be framed according to the main type of questions that are asked and the solutions that are offered. Opposing positions will be presented regardless of the support each commands. Thus, this section will set forth the terms of the debate. In the following section, we will ask which opinions predominate among energy specialists.

Design Problems. Performance questions to which current scientific and technological expertise can be applied include: the adequacy of the nuclear fuel cycle, reactor safety, and safeguards.

Nuclear fuel cycle adequacy refers to questions about the process undergone by materials used as fuel in nuclear power production. Uranium extraction technologies are similar to the strip- and underground-mining techniques used in the coal industry. Milling activities involve the processing of ore to create material that is enriched to produce fuel for the nuclear reactor. Before this material can be used, however, fuel rods must be manufactured and assembled. These initial stages in the process are together termed the "front end" of the fuel cycle. After the reactor has used the fuel, the "back end" activities come into play. They include storing the spent fuel, reprocessing fuel to recover plutonium and residual uranium, and waste disposal.[9]

At least three of these steps have been a source of concern: estimates of uranium resources, insufficient enrichment capacity, and the lack of fuel reprocessing. (Waste disposal is such a major public concern that it receives separate treatment below.) Since the nuclear industry has gone into decline, these design problems have been assigned a much lower priority on the policy agenda. Nonetheless, some critics regard the current lack of reprocessing facilities as a major obstacle to successful waste disposal. Storage capacity at reactor sites for spent fuel has been limited in anticipation of the development of a reprocessing stage. The lack of reprocessing also increases pressures for more uranium and enrichment. Other analysts, however, have argued that any advantages of reprocessing are outweighed by the increased danger of nuclear proliferation.[10]

Reactor safety, along with waste disposal, has been one of the two most controversial nuclear power concerns. The most important debate concerns the reactor's vulnerability to core meltdowns. Despite the fact that American reactors have operated for a quarter century with one of the energy system's most impressive safety records, there is continued concern about their safety performance.

The controversy over core meltdown problems (given a certain emotional edge when described as the "China Syndrome") centers on the probabilities and magnitude of a sequence of uncertain events. First, reactor fuel could be melted by the failure of the cooling systems and release of radioactivity beyond the capabilities of the control rods. Second, if the core did melt, the containment vessel could fail from too much pressure or heat. Most experts believe this is a very unlikely but very dangerous combination of circumstances.

A number of highly publicized Atomic Energy Commission (AEC) and Nuclear Regulatory Commission (NRC) studies have emphasized the extremely low probability and magnitude of effects associated with a core meltdown. The most controversial of these was the "Rasmussen report," which found the likelihood of being killed by a nuclear reactor mishap comparable to that of being struck by a meteor. Even among supporters, this analysis was cause for concern—not for characterizing nuclear plants as safe, but for the degree of certainty that was attached to this finding.[11] On the opposition side, such blanket endorsements have been used as ammunition for an attack on the credibility of all official risk studies.

Ironically, the controversy surrounding the potential for catastrophic accidents in nuclear reactors may have obscured a number of less dramatic safety problems. In the wake of TMI and other nuclear reactor malfunctions, the nuclear community has begun to take a closer look at several problems that traditionally have been given low priority. These include concerns about reactor vessel cracking,[12] human reliability failures, the physical chemistry of fission product behavior in accidents,[13] and the problems of degraded reactor cores.[14] Thus, the reactor safety problem may be undergoing a subtle change toward incorporating a number of more likely but less dangerous risks, instead of focusing entirely on catastrophic events.[15]

Safeguards are required throughout the fuel cycle to reduce the risks of theft, terrorism, or other losses of radioactive materials. Debate in this category centers on two factors. First, are existing measures adequate to manage and control these materials, especially uranium and plutonium? Second, is it possible to design and implement a sufficiently stringent system of accountability and security?

Many opponents of nuclear power have argued that total accountability is either impossible to achieve or can be attained only through significant loss of civil liberties. Fears of a "plutonium police force" or other Draconian measures often are cited by groups concerned about the possible trade-off between safeguards and personal freedoms.[16]

In response to these questions on the safeguards problem, proponents point to various technological solutions. In addition to more sophisticated monitoring and security techniques, these include the use of innovative siting approaches, such as clustering nuclear facilities in fewer locations. This would minimize vulnerable transportation and communications linkages, simplify control over fissionable materials, reduce access to the most hazardous products, and permit scientific and engineering expertise to be easily mobilized in the event of a threat to the system.[17]

Design Issue. *Proliferation* is the only major performance question whose complexities appear to transcend the rational application of scientific and technological expertise. In this context, proliferation concerns the spread of nuclear weapons, which may occur through the spread of nuclear power. Because weapons-grade materials are potential outputs at almost every stage of the fuel cycle, the global political community for years has attempted to constrain the military potential of nuclear energy.[18]

United States policy for some time has emphasized an attempt to limit the spread of scientific and technical expertise and institutional capability in nuclear weapons. Underpinning this approach is the central issue in the proliferation debate: What difference does it make for world proliferation whether the U.S. has breeder reactors or any other component of the plutonium economy?

It is this conflict between a desire to limit the spread of nuclear weapons and a recognition that American policies cannot, "with a wave of the hand," prevent other governments from becoming nuclear, that leads some energy analysts to call proliferation the "irreducible risk" of nuclear energy.[19]

Impact Problems. When one moves from questions about technical performance to the consequences of placing a technology in a particular location, the uncertainties become greater and the problems more difficult to solve. In part, this has to do with the limited level of development of impact assessment. It is also a function of the highly complex nature of the costs, risks, and benefits of sophisticated technological systems.[20] There appear to be two important impact problems in the nuclear power arena: health and safety risks and environmental hazards.

Health and safety risks include the exposure of both nuclear workers and the general public to low-level radioactivity. Both workers and the public routinely come into contact with small quantities of radioactivity that are either impossible or

173

uneconomical to segregate from the environment. The dispute concerns the consequences of these releases and contacts.[21]

Opponents of nuclear energy argue that exposure to radioactivity in the mining and milling of uranium products has led to an epidemic of lung cancer in the work force.[22] Industry supporters deny this and point out the much more hazardous threats to health and safety posed by a number of non-nuclear sources of radiation.[23]

In essence, this debate has become enmeshed in a conflict over very different perceptions of the appropriate framework for evaluating health and safety consequences. Critics of nuclear power tend to adopt a "no-risk" framework, arguing that the public and nuclear energy work force should be exposed to no additional or unnecessary risks. By contrast, nuclear advocates argue for either a "risk-risk" consideration, which balances the beneficial and adverse health effects of energy technologies against one another, or a "risk-benefit" orientation, in which the hazards and rewards of nuclear power would be compared systematically.

Environmental hazards of nuclear energy are subject to many of the same uncertainties and controversies as health and safety problems. Three areas of concern dominate this category: air pollution, water pollution, and land use. Nuclear facilities have ecological consequences in each of these areas.

Air quality can be affected by routine releases of radioactive gases from reactors and reprocessing facilities. But these emissions are maintained at very low levels—lower than the background radiation from naturally occurring radioactive minerals or gases, for example.[24]

Thermal pollution is a well-known consequence of reactors that circulate water from a river or lake and then return it. However, there is a relatively straightforward technological fix for this problem—closed-cycle cooling systems, which reduce the heat.

The most significant land-use impacts are those associated with the mining and milling of uranium. Trace amounts of radioactivity are left behind at each step of extracting and processing uranium ore. Significant amounts of land are also required to construct and operate or clean the facilities.

Impact Issue. *Radioactive wastes* are generated at every stage of the fuel cycle, in both high-level and low-level form. The latter includes contaminated materials such as clothing. By far the greater concern is with the disposal of high-level radioactive spent fuel from reactors. Discharged nuclear fuel has been accumulating in interim cooling pools at the various power plants. The questions surrounding waste disposal raise the issue of whether any generation has the right to leave such a potentially hazardous legacy to its descendants.

Waste disposal always has been seen as perhaps the most technologically demanding stage of the fuel cycle. But until recently, radioactive waste management policy appeared to stagnate. Critics demanded that nuclear industry expansion should be limited until an adequate disposal method is found and demonstrated. Of course, this places the government and industry in the position of demonstrating something that, by definition, would take hundreds of years.

Nuclear proponents, on the other hand, argued that technologically feasible disposal methods were available, constrained only by politics. Fortunately, this stalemate may be ending. There is now substantial optimism within the energy community about our ability to dispose of nuclear wastes with current technology. However, there are still questions about the impact of such a program.[25]

The choices facing the technical community have to do with the type of disposal, the barriers that separate radioactive materials from the environment, and the geological structure within which the wastes will be deposited.[26] For the first time in the American nuclear experience, however, the design and construction of waste disposal facilities seems feasible. The 1982 Nuclear Waste Policy Act established schedules and procedures for locating and constructing a permanent nuclear waste repository by 1998.[27]

Management Problems. As with the transition from design to impact problems, the move from impact to management concerns brings into play an additional layer of uncertainty and a new group of experts—the social and behavioral scientists. Moreover, management problems and issues involve the general public in the nuclear energy debate to a much greater extent. Two management problems have been critical to the evolution of American nuclear power: licensing and facility siting and risk assessment.

Licensing and facility siting obstacles are a complex combination of procedural requirements, governmental jurisdictional conflicts, and public resistance to the location of nuclear technologies. The length of time it takes to bring a nuclear power plant from the planning stage to operation is a sign of the poor state of the industry's health. Fragmented rules at all levels of government have been a major factor in this problem. Unanticipated regulatory changes are cited by industry officials as a key economic uncertainty facing the electric utilities.[28]

Risk assessment is at the very root of the debate over design, impact, and management concerns. Risk is an empirical measure of the probability and severity of the adverse effects of nuclear power. Safety, or the degree to which risks are acceptable, must be a judgmental and, therefore, political standard. It is easy to note that risk is not purely a technical problem, not something that can be left to the nuclear energy community in isolation. But building such an appreciation into the policy process is not easy.[29]

We must distinguish between two concepts of risk: first, as a problem arising from insufficient technical evidence (in which case the response is to ascertain scientific truth); and second, as a consequence of a lack of public acceptance (to which a number of responses, including public education or public participation, might be reasonable). Most nuclear energy problems and issues appear to fall into this second category of risk. A host of institutional and management factors must be addressed, to bring about their resolution.[30]

Management Issue. *Citizen involvement* in scientific and technological decision-making generally takes four forms: exchange of information, administrative interaction, the making of actual decisions, and support for participation.[31] Mechanisms for exchanging information, such as hearings, are by far the most common methods of gaining citizen input. Administrative interaction refers to ways in which the public and representatives of technical agencies are brought into contact, such as through the use of task forces

and advisory committees. Actual citizen decision-making authority is vested in such mechanisms as the citizen review board or
referendum. Finally, support for participation involves supplying
interest groups with technical or legal expertise, or funding.

The evaluation of these mechanisms, however, has been mixed.
Most are highly inefficient. The trade-off required by citizen involvement is the very difficult choice between expensive and time-
consuming participatory structures and the constant pressures for
greater efficiency. Almost as troublesome, existing research raises
warning flags regarding the ability of public involvement to resolve conflicts in nuclear energy decisions. For example, European
experiments in citizen participation found that increased involvement merely reinforced existing views of the nuclear controversy.[32] Nevertheless, the success of nuclear policies ultimately
depends upon public acceptance. Who should control? This is still
the main unanswered question.

Polling the Energy Community

We have outlined both sides of each disputed question to convey
the dimensions of this debate. But this does not imply a balance
of opinion on any question. To provide a standard for judging
media coverage, we need to know not only what the questions are,
but where the energy community stands.

Nuclear energy is often cited as the classic example of a scientific and technical controversy in which conflict is heightened by
divisions among experts.[33] In 1975, for example, Ralph Nader
secured the support of five Nobel laureates for a public statement
opposing further development of nuclear energy. In response,
Hans Bethe and eleven other Nobel winners signed a petition
favoring nuclear development. Prominent scientific critics of nuclear energy, such as Barry Commoner and Amory Lovins, are
known to millions, as are fervent supporters like Edward Teller.
So it is hardly surprising that the public has come to expect
disputes between experts in the nuclear policy arena.

Yet what does the public really know about the views of the
energy community, aside from a few highly publicized activists?
The best way for us to find the answer to this question was to ask

them directly. In 1980, we sent a detailed questionnaire on nuclear energy to leading American energy scientists and engineers.[34]

Initially, energy scientists were selected randomly from listings in *American Men and Women of Science* of prominent scientists trained in seventy-one energy-related fields. Their areas of training represent such diverse specialties as conservation, environmental health, radiation ecology, reactor physics, and solar energy. Then, engineers were selected randomly from fourteen energy-related fields listed in *Who's Who in Engineering*. Examples of these disciplines are energy engineering, nuclear engineering, and environmental engineering.

Our next step was to select nuclear specialists from a larger study of nuclear decision-makers surveyed by Dr. Robert Cohen of the survey research firm Yankelovich, Skelley and White.[35] This group represents a reputational sample of influential researchers in the nuclear field, such as senior scientists at national laboratories and social scientists who have directed large-scale foundation-funded studies of energy policy.

High response rates in all three surveys were obtained, ranging from 71 percent of the nuclear specialists to 82 percent of the engineers. This provided samples of 358 energy scientists, 279 engineers, and 42 nuclear specialists. Most of them are based at universities. Thus, 57 percent of the scientists sampled are academics, 20 percent work for a government organization, and 23 percent are employed by industry.

Finally, in order to evaluate media coverage, we wished to compare scientific and engineering opinion to that of leading journalists. To accomplish this, we sent the same survey to leading science journalists at major media outlets. This group included veterans of the science beat at the national media network (as defined in Chapter Two), as well as other influential science journalists identified in a previous study.[36] Forty-three responses were received, a rate of 60 percent. In addition, a short follow-up survey was mailed to all journalists included in the media elite sample, in order to assess the opinion milieu of the national media. They were asked their opinions on nuclear development, reactor safety, and willingness to live near a nuclear plant. The return rate among this group was 65 percent.

Table 7 shows that the three groups of energy specialists were consistently supportive of nuclear energy and sanguine about dealing with its uncertainties. It also reveals a gulf between these groups and the journalists, who were more pessimistic about

Table 7—Attitudes of Scientists, Engineers, and Journalists
Toward Nuclear Energy

	Energy Scientists	Engineers	Nuclear Specialists	Science Journalists
Favor rapid nuclear development	70%	82%	69%	24%
Favor nuclear moratorium	5	3	5	24
Present risks not acceptable	20	11	12	40
Very confident of problem-solving knowledge	65	68	74	18
Reactors are very unsafe	3	4	5	16
Would live near a reactor	71	83	88	47
Rate as "very serious" problems:				
Training personnel	47	51	32	61
High-level waste disposal	46	40	23	65
Proliferation	31	30	50	54
Consequences of accidents	26	18	25	48
Plant construction	24	23	8	35
Transporting waste	16	19	5	42
Plant design	21	22	5	35
Low-level waste disposal	18	23	5	37

Table 7 *(Continued)*

	Energy Scientists	Engineers	Nuclear Specialists	Science Journalists
Likelihood of				
accidents	17%	18%	13%	40%
Sabotage	19	20	18	19
Release of				
radioactivity	10	9	2	23
Decommissioning				
plants	12	11	2	33
Risks to workers	4	6	0	24
Rate as "very important" factors:				
Engineering/				
technical	85	86	74	81
Scientific/theoretical	45	48	31	41
Environmental	46	38	41	65
Economic	54	55	79	61
Moral	20	20	10	28
Political	29	34	46	37
Rate performance as "good" or "excellent":				
Industry experts	76	79	86	40
Academic experts	71	65	57	49
Government experts	58	51	67	37
Reactor technicians	48	65	67	33
Reactor owners and				
licensees	43	59	52	9
U.S. government				
regulators	26	30	31	14
State and local				
authorities	14	12	7	9
The public	12	11	14	24
Congressional				
committees	10	10	14	12
Number of Cases	358	279	42	43

virtually every aspect of this subject. Perhaps the most significant implication is the substantial optimism among the energy community about the problems and prospects of nuclear power. Across the entire range of potential problems confronting the nuclear energy alternative, these scientists and engineers generally exhibited confidence in the technology and in their understanding of the key performance, impact, and control dimensions of the nuclear controversy.

Large majorities favored rapid nuclear development, and no more than 5 percent of any group supported a moratorium on plant construction. Moreover, they did not regard most of the problems and issues discussed above as serious impediments. Of thirteen problem areas listed, only the training of reactor personnel was rated as very serious by a majority of any group. Fewer than one in four applied this level of concern to any of such hotly debated topics as the design and construction of reactors, risks to plant workers, the likelihood of accidents, transporting nuclear waste, or the dangers of sabotage.

In general, their ratings accord with our review of the technical literature. They suggest that the major issues (in our narrow sense of the term) confronting nuclear power within the energy community are radioactive waste disposal, reactor maintenance, and proliferation. All this is consistent with much of the public debate. But care must be taken in interpreting these findings.

First, recognizing a problem does not necessarily imply an inability to reduce risks, even when the problem is viewed as very serious. Thus, most energy specialists were very confident that they already possessed the knowledge to solve scientific and technical problems posed by nuclear power.

Second, as one defines expertise more narrowly, the pattern of overall support for nuclear energy increases. For example, by limiting the analysis to those scientists who have actually written articles on a particular subject, much more positive reactions were obtained. For example, only 33 percent of those who have written on waste disposal regarded it as a very serious problem. The same general pattern held for the other problems.

In addition, the identification of even serious problems didn't seem to dampen confidence in the current safety of nuclear reactors. Despite their expressed concern over reactor personnel, majorities of all groups rated nuclear plants as very safe, and no more than 5 percent of any group rated them very unsafe.

We asked not only what energy specialists thought about nuclear energy but also how they thought about it. Their views were guided primarily by technical and engineering considerations, and secondly by scientific, economic, and environmental concerns. They gave short shrift to either political or moral aspects of this issue. Since they regard the current state of the art as safe and relatively well understood, and future development as worth the risk, it makes sense that they would have the politicians and moralists give way to the technicians and economists.

This may also help to explain their focus on technical design problems (safety, etc.) as the perceived key to resolving the nuclear stalemate. Almost as striking, however, was the importance they attached to environmental considerations. In fact, impact problems narrowly surpassed even scientific/theoretical factors. Such a perspective might underlie the emphasis on waste disposal noted above.

The perceived irrelevance of political factors also holds implications for their assessments of management issues. An indication of their tendency to downplay such concerns lies in how they rated the performance of various groups in dealing with nuclear problems. They gave high marks to the scientific and engineering professions, while reserving failing grades for government regulators, Congressional committees, and the general public.

One last sign of their confidence in nuclear development was the relatively high ratings these groups gave the nuclear industry. They rated the performance of both reactor owners and technicians higher than that of either regulatory or Congressional oversight groups. And these scientists and engineers, most of whom are academics, reserved their most positive evaluations for industry experts, ranking them ahead of their peers in both government and universities.

Finally, it is unlikely that these views have changed markedly since this 1980 study. In 1985, we sent a short follow-up survey to the scientists, again asking about reactor safety, willingness to live near nuclear plants, and knowledge about nuclear problems. On all three questions, the results were almost identical to those of the earlier survey. So scientists' confidence in nuclear power proved not only strong but stable.

In sum, energy scientists and engineers were quite optimistic about the current safety and future potential of nuclear power. They did show concern about particular design and impact problems and issues; however, they perceived even serious problems as amenable to technical solutions. The scientists and engineers were very conscious of the importance of environmental and economic considerations, but did not view broader political or moral issues as significant to the nuclear debate.

The agreement among energy specialists highlights the divergence of media attitudes. On virtually every question the journalists were more skeptical about nuclear safety, often by wide margins. Leading science journalists were as likely to favor a nuclear moratorium as they were to support rapid development, and only a minority would live near a reactor themselves. They were from two to five times more likely than the other groups to rate current reactors very unsafe, reject the risks involved, and express doubt about current knowledge of nuclear problems.

On the few questions they were asked, the media elite responded in similar fashion. They were slightly more likely than science journalists to support rapid nuclear development (by 31 to 24 percent) and less likely to favor a moratorium (16 vs. 24 percent). But they were slightly less willing to live near a nuclear reactor (40 vs. 47 percent), and about the same percentage rated reactors very unsafe (17 vs. 16 percent).

Thus, the two media groups were as united in their skepticism toward nuclear power as the three energy specialist groups were in their support of it. This gulf is illustrated most succinctly by their respective reactor safety ratings. Within each media group, the percentage rating current reactors very safe equalled the percentage rating them very unsafe. By contrast, the other groups were up to almost twenty times more likely to pick the very safe category (e.g., by 58 to 3 percent among energy scientists).

It is important to realize that science journalists did not frame the safety issue very differently from scientists and engineers. They, too, gave their highest priority to problems of training reactor personnel, waste disposal, and proliferation. They, too, rated engineering factors as the most important. They were simply more critical than energy specialists toward the technology and its oversight.

Thus, journalists rated virtually every problem as more serious and the performance of most groups as poorer. They gave their most serious rating to problems of avoiding reactor accidents, transporting wastes, risks to plant workers, and the release of radioactivity over twice as often as the expert groups. In assessing performance, they were especially critical of industry representatives. They were about half as likely as the energy specialists to rate industry scientists and engineers as good or excellent, and about one-fifth as likely to give high marks to reactor owners and licensees.

Overall, these surveys reveal an energy community that mainly supports nuclear safety and a journalistic community that is equally as critical. The views of scientists and engineers are not presented here as a norm from which journalistic opinion should not deviate. There is no single "legitimate" perspective on the nuclear debate. But the sharply different outlooks of these groups provides an opportunity to consider the role that values may play in news coverage. In Michael Robinson's terms, how "mediating" are the media on this topic—do they mainly transmit the perspective of the energy specialists, or do they translate the issue into a framework that reflects their own concerns? In short, does the news about nuclear safety more closely resemble the perspectives of the energy community or those of the journalistic community?

Media Coverage of Nuclear Energy

The Nuclear News Agenda. We analyzed nuclear energy coverage from 1970 through 1983 at seven national media outlets—the *New York Times;* the three major newsmagazines, *Time, Newsweek,* and *U.S. News and World Report;* and the evening newscasts of ABC, CBS, and NBC. During these fourteen years, nuclear power received extensive national media coverage—nearly 6,000 stories in the *Times* alone, well over 1,000 stories on the network news, and over 250 stories, many running several pages, in the major newsmagazines. This means that the news audience was confronted by an average of over one story per day (nearly ten a week) in the *Times,* one newsmagazine story every two to three weeks, and almost two evening news broadcasts a week devoted to this topic.

For this study, coders examined all the magazine articles, half the television broadcasts, and a randomly selected 10 percent of the *Times'* coverage of this subject.[37] On all categories discussed below, agreement between coders exceeded 80 percent.[38]

All three media formats produced increased coverage over the years, even aside from the deluge of stories unleashed by Three Mile Island. For example, in the early 1970s, the *New York Times* ran only about one nuclear energy story every other day. By the middle of the decade, the flow had doubled to roughly one a day. Then in 1979, TMI opened the floodgates, and the paper published almost a thousand stories, virtually three a day. In the 1980s, the news flow abated somewhat, but still remained above pre-TMI levels.

Most of these stories did not address nuclear energy as a whole, but rather one of the narrower problem areas identified in the framework for analysis. These include the nuclear fuel cycle, reactor safety, safeguards against the loss of radioactive material (including terrorist threats), proliferation, health and safety risks of normal reactor operations, environmental hazards, radioactive waste disposal, sighting and licensing of nuclear technologies, risk assessment, and citizen involvement in decision-making.

With regard to these topics, the media's nuclear agenda was everywhere virtually identical. By far the most coverage went to reactor safety. It was followed by a second tier of topics that garnered moderate attention, including licensing and siting, proliferation, waste disposal, health and environmental hazards, safeguards, and citizen participation. Finally, risk assessment and the nuclear fuel cycle got short shrift at most outlets, accounting for only a few stories throughout the entire sample period.

Not only the amount but the focus of nuclear coverage has changed markedly over the years. For example, the predominance of reactor safety stories is confined to the post-TMI era. Almost 75 percent of the reactor safety magazine articles and 88 percent of the television stories on this topic appeared since 1979. The shift in news priorities following TMI carried some other topics into the public eye. Health and safety hazards were accorded new prominence in the print media, as articles on the risks associated with even routine releases of radioactivity from reactors increasingly appeared. New attention also was given to the role of the public. The print media began running many more stories on citizen involvement in decision-making, while television gave its first sustained coverage to licensing and siting disputes, picking up where the *Times* left off.

QUESTIONS: We turn now from the relatively simple questions of what, when, where, and how much, to the more substantive issues of how nuclear coverage is structured. First, how are the questions framed? Does the news focus mainly on questions of design, impact, or management? And do journalists' news judgments agree with the experts' assessments about which topics fall into each category?

In addition to the questions that arise, there are those answered along the way. So we also coded all stories dealing with uncertainties that were overcome. Such stories were few and far between in all outlets, ranging from only one in twenty newsweekly stories to one in seven television newscasts and just over one in six newspaper articles.

Typical of such stories was a CBS report on alleged health hazards to nuclear plant workers: "A ten-year study of radiation effects . . . rejects charges that radiation levels at certain nuclear power plants are dangerously high. The report . . . contends that current government standards provide generally adequate protection for workers exposed to radiation.[39] This category also included stories about the disposition of licensing disputes and the outcome of anti-nuclear protests.

For the questions that remain, our review of the technical

literature placed several major topics into each category of uncertainty. The major uncertainties concerning the fuel cycle, reactor safety, safeguarding radioactive material, and proliferation are widely regarded as design questions. How do you make the technology perform properly, and how should you assess its performance? These design questions underlie a range of topics, from the need for secure uranium enrichment and reprocessing facilities to the performance of emergency core cooling systems.

For example, an early *Time* article dealt with design questions about reactor fuel rods: "There is also disturbing evidence that the nuclear fuel rods in one kind of atomic plant have bent, crushed or cracked during normal operation . . . the rods, designed for and proved in a previous generation of smaller reactors, may simply not stand the higher pressures and temperatures of today's big reactors."[40]

By contrast, such topics as everyday health and safety concerns, environmental hazards, and waste disposal are treated primarily in terms of their impact on the human and natural environment. What health risks does low-level radioactivity pose for reactor workers? What ecological impact do nuclear facilities have on the surrounding land, water, and air? What are the long-term consequences of creating highly toxic waste products? These questions transcend the proper performance of technologies. They call for an understanding of the continuous interplay between technology and the environment.

Thus, a *Newsweek* piece highlighted uncertainties over the impact of low-level radiation: "Too much radiation can cause cancer. But how much, and at what levels? So when low-level radiation leaked from a nuclear power plant last week, some experts called for an immediate evacuation of the area, while others said the leak was less dangerous than a chest X-ray."[41]

Finally, even greater uncertainty attends the topics that are mainly matters of management. How should government decide where and when to build and license nuclear plants? What kinds of involvement by concerned citizens are necessary and appropriate? How do we decide whether the inherent risks of nuclear power are acceptable? These questions include design and impact concerns but are more fundamentally dependent on institutional and management factors.

For instance, a *Newsweek* article dealt with the management of nuclear development: "Until now, nuclear regulation was solely the province of technical experts in Washington—first at the Atomic Energy Commission and later at its successor agency, the Nuclear Regulatory Commission. But now that nuclear worries are coalescing into a popular crusade in several states, Washington's regulatory monopoly is ending."[42]

Since major areas of uncertainty fall into all three categories, one might expect to see considerable news coverage devoted to each. Instead most coverage focused on management uncertainties (see Table 8). This was so only partly because the media were highly attentive to questions most experts regard as management matters, such as licensing procedures and citizen participation. In addition, they concentrated on the management aspects of other topics that scientists and engineers tend to address in terms of design and impact uncertainties. The result was to magnify the uncertainties attached to nuclear power, by presenting these topics to the public in a fashion that highlighted the most difficult questions and downplayed the more tractable.

All seven media outlets placed more emphasis on management questions than on any other category. In fact, everywhere but at the *New York Times,* management uncertainties received several times as much coverage as any other type of question. On televi-

Table 8—Types of Question Posed on Nuclear Safety			
	New York Times	Magazines	Television
Solution	22	5	14
Design	23	4	9
Impact	11	9	14
Management	44	82	63
	100%	100%	100%
Number of Cases	486	213	582

sion, nearly two out of every three broadcasts were confined to management questions. And at the newsweeklies, over four out of every five stories focused on management concerns. There was only token variation from one outlet to the next within a given news format.

Just as significant is the divergence between scientists' and journalists' treatments of particular topics. The technical literature tends to treat questions related to the fuel cycle, reactor safety, proliferation, and safeguarding fissionable material in design terms. Yet none of the seven national media outlets portrayed any of these topics primarily in terms of design. Only the *New York Times* addressed more than a small minority of its coverage to the performance of technologies associated with any of the four topics. Thirty-eight percent of *Times* stories dealing with reactor safety, and 33 percent concerned with the fuel cycle, dealt with design uncertainties.

To be fair, this probably understates the paper's congruence with the technical literature on these topics. The *Times* was more likely than the other outlets to report on the resolution of technical uncertainties, and many such stories were concentrated on these two topics. So it is likely that a majority of *Times* articles on the nuclear fuel cycle did address design questions.

The pattern was very different, though, when the *Times* came to covering efforts to prevent the diversion of uranium for nuclear weapons. Only 8 percent of its proliferation stories, and not a single article on safeguards, dealt with design questions.

If these results distanced the *Times* from the experts, they put the paper squarely in the media mainstream. The networks covered design questions in about one broadcast out of five on reactor safety, in a single fuel cycle story, and in none of the stories on proliferation or safeguards. The newsweeklies dealt with design questions in only 6 percent of their reactor safety stories and in none of the pieces concerning safeguards, proliferation, or the fuel cycle.

Thus, on three of the four topics the experts associate with design questions, the networks and the newsweeklies together produced a total of two design-oriented stories during the fourteen-year period. Not a single story on the design questions involved in nuclear safeguards ever appeared in the seven media outlets coded. (Because we coded only samples of the *Times* and network coverage, such stories may have appeared occasionally. But the number of them would almost certainly have been very small.)

What happened to the stories that did run on design topics? In most cases they were framed as management questions. For example, this was true of every article on safeguards in the weeklies, over 90 percent of the television broadcasts, and over 80 percent of the *Times* articles. Thus, NBC aired a proliferation story following the 1981 Israeli air strike against an Iraqi nuclear installation. The correspondent said, in part, "Physicist [Theodore] Taylor thinks nuclear power and nuclear weapons are so closely linked, controlling one requires giving up the other."[43]

The trends were similar, although not so dramatic, on fuel cycle and reactor safety stories. As a result, many of the nuclear design questions that scientists and engineers debated were rarely or never aired in the major media. Instead readers and viewers persistently were confronted with management questions, which became the entire story by default.

The correspondence was somewhat greater on two topics whose uncertainties scientists see mostly as matters of impact—health and safety risks and environmental hazards. On waste disposal questions, though, the media stressed the management questions involved. News judgments best mirrored expert judgments on topics the latter deemed to be management questions. Since the media treated virtually all topics as management questions, it is not surprising that they agreed with the scientists on topics like sighting and licensing plants, citizen participation, and risk assessment. In fact, of the ten topics considered, television and the major newsweeklies treated nine primarily as management questions.

Thus, the pattern is consistent—management stories drive out stories about the performance of nuclear technologies and their impact on people and the environment. Since management questions are inherently less amenable to resolution than design and impact questions, the uncertainty surrounding nuclear energy is heightened by the news process.

This one-sided view is not a fact of nature. The coverage does not have to be this way. Indeed it has not always been this way, at least not to the degree that it has recently. In the early 1970s, when nuclear power was less of a story, it was also a somewhat different story.

From 1970 to 1972, 30 percent of *New York Times* stories, 27 percent of television broadcasts, and even 12 percent of the highly management-oriented newsweekly articles reported on difficulties of nuclear energy that were resolved or uncertainties that were overcome. Soon thereafter, though, this kind of coverage virtually disappeared. For the rest of the decade only 4 percent of network newscasts and 2 percent of magazine articles reported on newly found answers to nuclear questions. In the newsmagazines, only two such stories appeared from 1973 through 1975, one story from 1976 through 1978, and no stories at all during the saturation coverage of 1979. The drop-off at the *New York Times* was more gradual, but no less inexorable—from 30 percent to 25 percent during 1973 through 1975, to 15 percent thereafter, half the original figure (but still more than the newsmagazines ever carried).

As the coverage of problems being solved dwindled, the attention given to management questions accelerated. The key period again was 1973 to 1975. During those years the proportion of management stories jumped from 58 to 78 percent at the networks, from 71 to 86 percent at the magazines, and from 15 to 34 percent at the *Times*. The *Times'* coverage of management questions continued to rise slowly until they finally comprised a majority of all stories after 1980.

These figures indicate that the media's struggle over how to frame nuclear power questions effectively was over by 1973. The outcome emphasized the questions least likely to be resolved. In the early 1970s, nuclear coverage featured a mixture of questions about the performance of this technology, its costs and benefits, and the difficulties of managing it, with a liberal sprinkling of reports on questions that were being answered. Thereafter the inherently open-ended management questions began to drown out all others. While Three Mile Island raised new questions about nuclear power in the public mind, the form new questions would take was determined much earlier. And the form of the questions goes a long way toward determining the shape of the answers.

ANSWERS: There are always more questions than answers in news on technological controversies. When an answer is discovered, or a problem solved, it may momentarily make news. But once that moment has passed, it is replaced by new controversies that crowd their way into the news. In analyzing coverage, then, the main consideration is not necessarily whether answers get reported, but the kinds of answers that are sought in ongoing controversies.

The way we assess a new technology may depend greatly on whether we can reasonably expect technological "fixes" to help solve current problems, or whether we must live indefinitely with uncertainties and conflicts. In short, what kinds of outcomes can be expected? Will the technology eventually do our bidding, or must we adapt ourselves to its inherent uncertainties? In the terms used here, are the questions confronting nuclear energy *problems* that require technical solution? Or are they trans-scientific *issues* that, at best, may submit to social or political resolution?

A technology as complex and as controversial as nuclear power must involve both problems and issues, both technical and political elements. But the particular mix of these elements, and their distribution across the various topics in the nuclear debate, are anything but preordained. Moreover, the distinction between these two types of answers is often critical for assessing nuclear power.

Our surveys of the technical literature and the scientific and engineering communities suggest that three major topics are regarded primarily as political issues transcending scientific approaches: proliferation, waste disposal, and citizen participation. The experts regard proliferation as a political issue not only because of its international character, but also because the creation of weapons-grade materials is an unavoidable by-product of nuclear technology. As one *Time* article put it, "But can anything really be done to stop nuclear proliferation? . . . Strategic and political concerns work mightily against shutting down the 'plutonium economy.' But it can still be checked. One approach might be to give international controls more power."[44]

Waste disposal is far more amenable to technical problem-solving, and many technological questions have been raised and resolved. Yet the Faustian bargain that demands many generations of vigilance seems unavoidable. Moreover, the burden must fall mainly on a few localities, so that the entire nation may benefit. Issues such as these are quintessentially political, as a *Time* article illustrates: "The thorniness of the disposal problem was aptly summed up by one Senate Committee aide: 'We don't need to do it in my backyard,' he said. 'But we need to do it.' "[45]

Finally, citizen involvement in decision-making is the *sine qua non* of political issues. There are costs as well as benefits to citizen participation, but any cost-benefit calculus must itself reflect social values and conflicts of interest that cannot be reduced to the purely technical realm. Perhaps the most political of all questions is, who should control? An NBC story on one dispute didn't mince words in presenting this perspective: "For the people of New Mexico this question: How much control do they have over the project? How can they know which is the right decision? It's a problem for the people of New Mexico and for their political leaders."[46]

By contrast, the remaining seven topics have major components that can be addressed in technical terms. Scientists and engineers can at least strive for technological solutions to problems such as fuel enrichment, fuel reprocessing, pollution, the release of radioactivity during normal reactor operations and in accidents, choosing plant sites, and protecting these sites against thieves and terrorists.

Since the media concentrate on topics like reactor safety, which the experts regard more as a problem area, one might expect the coverage to focus on efforts to find solutions to such technological problems. Yet just the opposite occurred. In all seven media outlets, the potential answers to nuclear questions were framed as social and political issues that can at best be resolved.[47]

All seven outlets portrayed the answers to nuclear questions more as social or political issues than as technical problems (see Table 9). At the newsweeklies, the margin exceeded five to one. All media outlets agreed with the experts in treating most stories on proliferation and citizen participation primarily as political matters. The *Times* and the newsweeklies also portrayed waste disposal predominantly in a political context, while the networks gave a slight edge to the technical side of this topic (although most broadcasts combined both elements).

The media's deviations from the specialist community occurred mostly on those topics in which the specialists look to the technical realm for answers. At the *Times,* fuel cycle adequacy was the only topic whose answers mainly were sought in the technical realm. Reactor safety turned into a virtual dead heat, with issues edging out problems by 51 to 49 percent. Every other topic consistently spilled over into the political arena. The story was much the same at *Time, Newsweek,* and *U.S. News.* On only two topics did problems edge out issues—risk assessment, on which only four articles were published, and waste disposal, which the technical literature ironically treats more as a social or political issue.

The often maligned television networks came much closer to the energy specialists than did any of the print outlets. They mirrored the technical literature in looking mainly for technical

Table 9—Types of Answers Presented on Nuclear Safety

	New York Times	Magazines	Television
Problem	42	9	34
Issue	58	48	42
Combination	—	42	24
	100%	*99%	100%
Number of Cases	486	213	582

*Total reflects rounding error

solutions to problems dealing with reactor safety and safeguards, health and environmental hazards, and risk assessment, while presenting political resolutions for problems of proliferation, citizen involvement, and waste disposal. The only major differences cropped up on broadcasts dealing with the fuel cycle and plant siting and licensing. The specialists regard these mainly as technical problems, while television presented them mostly as political issues.

Despite the relatively good correspondence between television and the experts on several topics, the overall pattern contains more differences than similarities. When the specialists seek answers to the questions raised by nuclear power, they primarily look to the technical realm. The media, by contrast, tended to present the greater uncertainties of political resolution as the best we can hope for. This was particularly true in the print media, and above all, at the newsweeklies. Thus, magazine journalism continued to frame nuclear energy topics in ways almost diametrically opposed to the specialists' approach.

Like the questions, the character of the answers in media coverage changed over time. Moreover, the nature of the change was quite similar, with the approach that most emphasized uncertainty gradually gaining ascendancy. But whereas management questions came to the fore in all media outlets at about the same time, the timing for the changeover in answers varied widely.

In the newsweeklies, the political realm dominated the technical throughout the entire period under study. The only change over time concerned the extent of its dominion. During the first half of the 1970s, 30 percent of the magazine articles posed potential answers in political terms, compared to 10 percent that relegated them to the technical realm. The majority of stories at that time (60 percent) combined the two elements. From 1976 to 1978, the proportion of "pure" political solutions doubled, to 60 percent, while the technical side dropped to only 4 percent. Since then, the magazines have remained the realm of political issues *par excellence*.

The mid-1970s were also a watershed for *New York Times* coverage of nuclear uncertainties. From 1970 to 1975, a majority of *Times* stories looked for solutions in technical terms. Since then the *Times* has presented political resolutions a majority of the time. During the first six years of the study, problems outnumbered issues by 55 to 41 percent in the pages of the *Times*. Thereafter issues outnumbered problems by 61 to 35 percent.

An even more dramatic shift took place on the airwaves, though it came a bit earlier. From 1970 to 1972, television presented virtually no nuclear topics in terms of pure political issues. Technical problems outnumbered issues by 42 to 4 percent. The next three years witnessed a major reversal. Two out of three broadcasts looked to political solutions, while the stories stressing technical answers were almost halved, dropping to 22 percent. From 1976 through 1983, issues easily outnumbered problems every year but one. The exception was 1979, when TMI brought a host of (mostly brief) stories about design problems. That year stories posing technical solutions outnumbered those posing political resolutions by 37 to 35 percent.

In sum, all media outlets shifted early on toward a more political orientation. But the starting point, the timing, and the extent of the change varied from one format to the next. We have followed these shifts in some detail because they provide some important evidence about nuclear coverage. First, they reinforce the point that the coverage was not set in stone. Changes did occur over time, and they again emphasized aspects that were less amenable to definitive solutions—in this case the political realm. Once again the inherently uncertain human element increasingly took precedence, with the political displacing the technical dimension.

Equally important, though, was the varying pattern of changes over time. The character of the news is not only communicated through the events reported, but is colored by the journalists' characterization of those events. It might be argued, for instance, that the coverage became more political because the subject became more political. (A note of caution may be needed here, if this proposition seems self-evident. A political conflict between environmental groups and industry over the safety of a reactor would be coded as capable of technical solution, if the opponents objected to alleged design inadequacies of some component. The process of conflict might be political while the solution remains in the technical realm. We coded the way answers were framed, not simply the presence or absence of a dispute.)

How do we know that changes in the nuclear story over time reflected changes in journalists' perceptions above and beyond any changes in the events they were reporting? The answer is that, at a given time, different media outlets were reporting the same story very differently. From 1970 through 1972, the *New York Times* and the television news departments emphasized technical solutions, while the newsmagazines favored political resolutions to the questions they raised. From 1973 through 1975, television discovered the political dimension, while the *Times* stuck to its technical stance. In 1979, all the print outlets emphasized the political elements of TMI and other nuclear stories, while television again stepped up its coverage of the technical realm.

These variations represent the outcome of choices about how to cover a changing story, and reasonable people may differ in making such choices, even among a community of skilled professionals. The fact that different news organizations made different choices at different times suggests that the story did not simply impose itself on the media. It was mediated by the news judgments of practicing journalists.

Story Slant. This is the aspect many people regard as the bottom line of content analysis. In which direction does the coverage tilt? Is it mostly pro-nuclear, anti-nuclear, or evenly balanced? After all is said and done, doesn't it all come down to this value judgment?

We think not. People ask too much of such shorthand assessments of news stories, expecting them to convey the entire flavor of the news in a single global judgment. A story's slant may be less important than the questions it asks, how it frames potential answers, which sources it cites (and omits), and how it brings expertise to bear on the subject matter. All these things may subtly influence how the audience comes to view an issue, even if it rejects a journalist's conclusions. Readers may keep the road map even as they bypass the destination. That is why our analysis tries to traverse the entire route, rather than leapfrogging right to the end.

Though its importance can be overstated, the tilt or slant of a story is a significant element of the news. But deciding where it lies can be deceptively difficult. Other studies have classified stories as pro- or anti-nuclear, positive or negative, tending to favor or oppose nuclear energy, and so forth. The problem with such classifications, as journalists are quick to point out, is that they depend heavily on the events reported. When something goes wrong at a nuclear reactor, such as a radiation leak, a report on the problem will be bad news (hence anti-nuclear) almost by definition. Whether only the bad news is reported and the good news ignored (the reactors that don't have problems, the successful stoppage of the leak) is another question fraught with its own difficulties.

Consider a *New York Times* report that began, "More than 2,600 gallons of low-level radioactive water spilled onto the floor of a building at the Public Service Electric and Gas Company's nuclear power plant in Salem County."[48] That might be considered negative or bad news, or perhaps news that leads a reader to become more critical of nuclear energy. Industry advocates might argue that such an occurrence should not be considered news at all. Whatever else it may be, though, it is a strictly factual accounting without overt interpretation or judgment.

At issue here is how to differentiate the slant from the facts. When people think of slanted or one-sided coverage, they usually have in mind the "spin" the reporter adds to a story, not the tenor of the facts reported. To minimize this problem, we gave particular attention to areas where journalists have the most discretion in shaping their stories. These include the lead that draws attention to the story while stating its major theme, the closer that summarizes a piece and draws conclusions about it, the use of emotional or insinuational language, and the choice of sources cited. The same event might easily produce a neutral or slanted story, depending on how reporters and their editors or producers choose to frame it with a lead and closer, whether their language provides a neutral or emotional tone, and whether sources on both sides of a controversy are represented.

Stories were coded as pro-nuclear, anti-nuclear, balanced

(both sides about equally represented), or neutral (no tilt in either direction). A good example of a pro-nuclear article, by these criteria, appeared in *Time* during 1978. Opposing views were presented, only to be rejected: "Irrational opposition to nuclear power can only delay a solution to America's energy problems." After noting the controversy over waste disposal, the weight of expertise was invoked: "the overwhelming majority [of scientists] believe the waste disposal problem can be satisfactorily resolved." The article concluded "the time to start building [nuclear] plants is now. Otherwise, they will not be ready when the nation really needs them."[49]

The lead paragraph from a 1973 *Newsweek* article was equally direct in expressing a preference for nuclear development: "But the nation's $3 billion nuclear energy program is almost certainly the most viable long-term answer to the [energy crisis]—the key question is how fast it can be speeded up."[50]

Introductions and conclusions such as these obviously go beyond reporting facts to suggest appropriate conclusions, and even policy judgments, to be drawn from the facts. But the same techniques can just as easily be used to paint a very different portrait of nuclear power. A CBS report on a controversial nuclear plant began with an alliterative anchor calling the project, "overdue, over budget, and overloaded with other problems." This was followed by a field reporter's well-cadenced lead sentence: "Seven years behind schedule, a billion dollars over budget, and riddled with reports of construction mistakes, cover-ups, employee fraud and crime, [this reactor] is called by Congressional experts the best example of how not to build a nuclear power plant."[51] Similarly, emotional language was used to great effect in a *Newsweek* piece on TMI titled, "In the Shadow of the Towers":

> With the crippled reactor still belching gusts of radiation, hardly a soul except the Showalters was left on their abandoned suburban block . . . When the bad dreams came true last week, the people in the shadow responded with a mix of resignation and alarm that somehow stopped short of panic, even as the scarifying sights and sounds of crisis unfolded around them. A

contagion of fear and anger spread through the countryside
. . . fear of an invisible plague . . ..[52]

It is also easy to bolster one side of an argument through the selective use of quotations or references to authoritative sources. For example, a *Newsweek* article on the failure of a California initiative to ban nuclear plants began with a quotation from no less a scientific icon than Albert Einstein: "To the village square, we must carry the facts of atomic energy. From there must come America's voice."[53] This quote was followed by a remark from a nuclear power lobbyist proclaiming victory over a distinctly un-American sounding group of anti-nuke types: "We have broken the back of the opponents—that vast collection of food faddists, perennial bitchers, deep-breathers, nature lovers and anti-Establishment counter-culturists who came together in California." Three years later, however, the same magazine ran a piece on an anti-nuclear march on Washington that provided a forum for the protesters.[54] Those quoted included Richard Pollock of Critical Mass ("this will be the major social movement of the 1980's"), activist minister William Sloane Coffin ("You can't trust the utilities . . . and you can't trust the regulatory agency . . . ."), Daniel Ellsberg, Dave McReynolds of the War Resisters League, and others, with only one mild dissent from a Carter administration aide.

As this pairing of articles shows, tilt cannot be adequately assessed on the basis of a single article or an unsystematic recollection of apparently partisan examples. It must be based on an exhaustive or representative reading of the materials, to determine how much spin exists and whether pieces slanted in either direction cancel each other out.

Our systematic survey of the major media yielded results that were consistently negative toward nuclear power. At six out of seven media outlets, anti-nuclear stories outnumbered pro-nuclear pieces, often by a wide margin. The closer one looks at the coverage, though, the more diversity one finds (see Table 10). There was considerable variation in the amount of spin, the extent of its one-sidedness, and the timing of its appearance.

Table 10—Story Slant

	New York Times	Magazines	Television
Pro-Nuclear	7	25	17
Anti-Nuclear	10	46	42
Neutral/Balanced	83	29	41
	100%	100%	100%
Number of Cases	486	213	582

The *New York Times* featured the most even distribution of one-sided stories, as well as the lowest proportion of stories tilted in either direction. Only one *Times* story in six was tilted for or against nuclear power. The majority of these were slanted in a negative direction, although the difference was slight—10 percent were anti-nuclear and seven percent pro-nuclear.

By contrast, a substantial majority of television stories displayed spin, and the anti-nuclear side predominated by a margin greater than two to one. The individual networks ranged from a two to one negative margin at CBS (40 to 19 percent) to three to one at NBC (47 to 15 percent).

The newsmagazines produced the most spin of any news format. Seventy-one percent of all magazine stories tilted in one direction or the other. The direction of the tilt was strongly negative, by 46 to 25 percent. Unlike television, though, one outlet differed sharply from the others. *U.S. News and World Report* produced a plurality of pro-nuclear stories, by 40 to 33 percent. This is hardly a massive pro-nuclear tilt, but it certainly set *U.S. News* apart from its larger competitors.

A typically upbeat 1974 article began, "While nuclear power plants are a hotly debated issue in the U.S., for much of the rest of the world there is just one question: How fast can new plants be built and rushed into use?"[55] The piece described nuclear power as a "kind of salvation" from soaring oil prices and quoted a "top expert" who said, "Nuclear power is available and it's getting cheaper in relation to other energy sources." Additional comments were solicited from an Atomic Industrial Forum official and the president of Westinghouse Power Systems Company, the world's largest manufacturer of nuclear plants. Another pro-nuclear lead read, "Unless present facilities for processing uranium are greatly expanded, there will not be enough atomic fuel to run the nuclear power plants counted on to supply a growing share of U.S. needs for electricity."[56]

In *Time* and *Newsweek*, by contrast, a majority of all stories were tilted against nuclear power. The margin was greatest at *Newsweek*, 51 to 17 percent, with *Time* close behind at 51 to 23 percent. That means the two largest newsmagazines were even more anti-nuclear than the television networks.

To create an overall spin index, we subtracted the percentage of negative from positive stories. By this measure, the major media were arrayed as follows: *U.S. News*, +7; *New York Times*, −3; television networks, −25; *Time* and *Newsweek*, −31. The varying extent of slanted coverage probably reflects the different traditions of the three news formats. The *New York Times* has long been America's exemplar of self-consciously objective journalism. It eschews emotion-laden or highly interpretive coverage in favor of a low-key style and balanced presentation. The approach of the newsweeklies is far different. Interpretive coverage has been their hallmark since the format was created by Henry Luce, who treated *Time* largely as an extension of his personal viewpoint. Even with the passing of such media barons from the scene, the weeklies retain a more subjective flavor than one normally encounters in the most respected daily newspapers.

This difference in tone can be illustrated by comparing two leads from roughly contemporary stories on proliferation that appeared in the *New York Times* and *Newsweek*, respectively. The newspaper story, a lengthy front-page think piece, began, "The construction of nuclear reactors around the world for the production of electricity and the resulting spread of material that could be used for making atomic bombs are putting increasing pressure on the United States to devise new policies on nuclear energy and international control."[57] The magazine led with a verse from a Tom Lehrer song: "The Lord's our shepherd, says the psalm, / But just in case we'd better get the bomb. / Who's next?"[58]

Television news stands somewhere in between, though certainly closer to the style of magazine journalism. In the 1950s, network newscasts were little more than wire service reports with pictures. Since the sixties, television journalism has been evolving toward its own genre of dramatic, personalized, subjective news. So it is not surprising that television's spin factor should be hot on the heels of the magazines. A CBS story on missing uranium began portentously, "Modern life is rich in fuel to feed paranoid fantasies. The theft of radioactive uranium has been the starting point for countless books and movies and nightmares and this week . . . life caught up with art."[59]

Even more variable than the amount of spin was its focus. Although the three news formats all offered more negative than positive spin, they distributed their one-sided coverage among quite different topics. At the *Times,* the fuel cycle was the only topic treated in a largely positive light. Proliferation, waste disposal, risk assessment, and reactor safety all elicited relatively negative coverage. The magazines placed the problems of environmental hazards in a mainly positive light, while reserving negative coverage for health risks, reactor safety, safeguards, and citizen participation. Television set the standard for consistently accentuating the negative. Not a single topic came across positively over the airwaves. There was rough parity among topics, with most treated in an equally negative light.

Two features stand out from this potpourri of topical variations. First, anti-nuclear spin was not restricted to particular concerns shared by all the major media. Rather, a more generalized tendency toward anti-nuclear coverage seemed to attach itself to different topics at different media outlets. Second, the critical question of reactor safety generated a consistently negative tilt. It was never the focus of the most severely anti-nuclear sentiments, but it always attracted heavily negative coverage. In all three news formats, the anti-nuclear stories on reactor safety outweighed the pro-nuclear by margins of at least two to one.

The consistently negative coverage of reactor safety raises a more general question of timing. To what extent did the media's negative view of nuclear energy stem from the accident at Three

Mile Island? The answer reveals the first major clear-cut division between print and broadcast media. In the *Times* and the magazines, anti-nuclear spin can indeed be traced to TMI. On television, however, TMI fit into a well-established pattern of anti-nuclear coverage. At the *Times* its effect was transient; at the networks it was negligible.

The briefest blip occurred in the otherwise balanced pages of the *Times*. Aside from 1979, coverage there was evenhanded throughout the period studied. In that exceptional year, anti-nuclear pieces captured 15 percent of the *Times'* coverage, compared to only 6 percent that were pro-nuclear. So the *Times'* anti-nuclear tilt was attributable almost entirely to TMI.

A more striking and lasting change occurred at the newsmagazines. Before TMI, the magazines were as evenhanded as the *Times*. Afterward they were overwhelmingly anti-nuclear, outstripping even television's tilt. From 1970 through 1978, anti-nuclear stories at the magazines outnumbered their pro-nuclear counterparts by a single percentage point (35 to 34 percent). Then, in 1979, an anti-nuclear slant colored 56 percent of all articles, compared to only 15 percent in the other direction. From 1980 through 1983, the anti-nuclear portion held steady at 56 percent, while the pro-nuclear rose to only 20 percent. Thus, the magazines shifted from a decade of balanced coverage of nuclear energy to a three to one negative tilt in the post-TMI era.

No such shift was needed to bring the networks into the anti-nuclear camp. As far back as the early 1970s, network news spin was running eight to five against nuclear power (39 to 25 percent through 1975). In the latter seventies, the anti-nuclear margin increased to three to one, or 36 to 12 percent. The year of TMI, it increased only slightly to 47 vs. 17 percent, and has changed little since then.

To summarize, major media coverage of nuclear energy had a markedly critical flavor. This anti-nuclear tone survived efforts to separate the spin from the story. It emerged from the language used, the sources cited, and the tone of the leads and closers chosen. Of the seven outlets, only *U.S. News and World Report* displayed a slightly pro-nuclear tilt. The *New York Times* had the most evenly balanced coverage, with a slight nod toward the negative. The other major newsmagazines and all three television networks held a strongly anti-nuclear stance. For the print media, this was a recent phenomenon, which apparently stemmed from Three Mile Island. Television presented a predominantly anti-nuclear tilt from the start.

Judging the Issues. Global judgments of a story's overall slant are common in content analysis. They are easy to make, if sometimes harder to defend, and they catch the eye. Yet the highly specific judgments within the story may be more significant in understanding nuclear coverage.

How did the media assess the breeder reactor, the risks of catastrophic accidents, the choice of waste disposal technologies, and the many other hotly debated topics that, in the aggregate, make up the nuclear debate? To find out, we analyzed every major controversy on nuclear safety, coding every rationale for judging each controversy, as well as the pro- or anti-nuclear tenor of each judgment published or aired. For example, we identified four major competing judgments about current reactor safety regulations: current regulations are sufficient to ensure safety; the regulations are appropriate, but better enforcement is needed; the regulations themselves need strengthening; or the regulations are already overly burdensome. Each position has its advocates, and each found expression in the stories analyzed.

Overall, we identified 151 areas of controversy. They ranged from six separate disputes about nuclear safeguards (e.g., how adequate is current safeguarding of nuclear materials in transit?) to twenty-three areas of debate over reactor safety (e.g., how significant are the safety risks of routine radioactive emissions from nuclear facilities?). These controversies in turn gave rise to 1,425 judgments, almost ten per topic.

The most notable finding was the divergence between expert assessments and the judgments rendered in the media. The media judgments tended to be much more critical. Overall, 60 percent of all judgments coded were negative, and 40 percent were positive (see Table II). For example, the technical literature treats water pollution from reactors as a minor problem amenable to technical

Table II—Media Judgments of Nuclear Safety Issues

	New York Times	Magazines	Television
Positive	45	45	34
Negative	55	55	66
	100%	100%	100%
Number of Cases	449	387	588

solutions. Yet the media judged this as being a major problem fifteen times and as a minor problem only nine times. One *Time* article concluded:

> Along with radiation, critics of the reactor program are alarmed about the effects of thermal pollution on marine life. The problem is that nuclear plants use cool water from rivers and bays, and then return it hot. . . . [Heat] makes existing pollutants more toxic, disturbs the reproduction cycle of fish and spurs the growth of noxious blue-green algae. . . . All this suggests that knowledgeable critics have a point in urging a reassessment of the present nuclear program.[60]

This critical tone prevailed in nine out of the ten issue areas. Only on questions of fuel cycle adequacy did positive assessments outnumber negative ones. By contrast, negative judgments appeared over 60 percent of the time on waste disposal, reached 70 percent on proliferation, and topped 80 percent on safeguards.

In the highly contested area of plant siting and licensing, one key source of positive stories was public acceptance of existing facilities. A *U.S. News* story on the Hanford Energy Center in Washington state typified 17 positive pieces: "The welcome mat is out in a Northwestern community for nuclear business others don't want. Result is a continuing boom—and strong local pride."[61] The story quotes one resident: "I worry more about traffic when riding my bicycle to work than I do about radiation." Such paeans to the peaceful atom were outweighed, however, by mainly negative evaluations of other issues. Thus, media judgments rejected, by a 24 to 13 margin, the industry's charge that current siting requirements are unduly cumbersome. One *Newsweek* piece quoted Senator Edward Kennedy's attack on a regulatory speed-up: "It's more important to build these plants safely than to build them quickly."[62]

Judgments in the media also favored, by a 17 to 7 margin, the need to solve remaining safety problems prior to any industry expansion, even if that requires a licensing moratorium. For example, CBS News reported that, "The Center for Science in the Public Interest said [today] there are too many unanswered questions about safety, and it said a moratorium would allow time to resolve the questions in a manner that is more in accord with our moral responsibilities."[63] Table 8 showed that 95 percent of America's energy scientists reject such a moratorium. That is not to say that this particular item was not newsworthy. But by presenting such judgments over twice as often as the contrary position, the media gave credence to a view with very little support in the scientific community.

Nearly 10 percent of all pro-nuclear assessments concerned the lack of alternatives to nuclear power. By the overwhelming margin of 53 to 3, judgments on the adequacy of alternative energy sources came down on the side of continued nuclear development. Typical of these was a *New York Times* story that quoted a group of pro-nuclear scientists: "There is no reasonable alternative to increased reliance on nuclear power to solve our energy needs . . . nuclear power offers a temporary easing of this worldwide need for energy and time to seek more effective and permanent solutions through other sources."[64] And a *Time* essay posed the question, "Where will the country get the energy to satisfy the need [for electricity]?" After systematically rejecting the options of coal, oil, natural gas, and solar energy, the essay concludes, "In short, after weighing the alternatives, nuclear power is necessary."[65]

Yet this single pro-nuclear category could not balance out the many other topics on which the judgments went the other way. Some of these judgments seemed in line with the scientific community's views. For example, nearly half the energy scientists surveyed termed human reliability problems very serious. Eighty percent of the media judgments stressed the significance of this problem. In other areas, though, the coverage seemed to diverge from the scientific consensus. For example, only one in four energy scientists portrayed the performance of emergency systems in reactor accidents as a very serious problem. (The scientists were polled a year *after* the Three Mile Island accident.) Yet nearly two-thirds of the media judgments came to the opposite conclusion. After TMI, for example, *Time* and *Newsweek* ran pieces comparing the accident to the anti-nuclear movie, *The China Syndrome*. Both magazines concluded that the real-life accident was far more serious than the fictional version. *Newsweek* commented:

> Now the nation knows all too well about the China Syndrome, reactor meltdowns, and life's chilling ability to imitate art even in the nuclear age. . . . Where life and art part company, the real events proved more frightening."[66]

One of the clearest differences between the experts and the media appeared in overall assessments of reactor safety. In our surveys, 58 percent of energy scientists categorized nuclear plants as currently very safe, compared to only 3 percent who thought them very unsafe, a margin of almost 20 to one. By contrast, over 63 percent of the media-based judgments presented safety risks as unacceptable.

We were especially interested in how these judgments varied across media outlets and over time. In both cases the results echo the findings on story slant. Thus the *New York Times,* which accounted for nearly one-third of all media judgments, presented slightly more negative than positive assessments, by 55 to 45 percent. *Time* and *Newsweek* were close to the overall media average of 60 percent negative to 40 percent positive. The most negative judgments were presented on television, where the ratio reached two to one. And the only outlet to present more positive than negative judgments was *U.S. News,* by a margin of 57 to 43 percent. So the judgments presented in various media outlets stack up to one another just like the overall spin: *U.S. News* is slightly positive, the *Times* slightly negative, the other newsmagazines decidedly so, and television news the most negative of all.

The same similarities appear in the changes from year to year. During the first half of the 1970s, positive and negative judgments were almost perfectly balanced. The years immediately prior to TMI witnessed a slight shift toward more negative judgments, by 55 to 45 percent. In 1979, the anti-nuclear judgments outweighed the pro-nuclear by a margin greater than two to one. Since then the pendulum shifted back somewhat, to a margin of 42 percent positive and 58 percent negative. Nuclear assessments were never predominantly positive, and they have remained negative, in varying degrees, ever since 1976.

Why is it so significant that the judgments passed on nuclear energy move in tandem with the overall spin imparted to news stories? Because it suggests that these judgments are related to the general orientation of the media rather than the opinions of energy specialists. Story slant was coded on the basis of discretionary elements such as language, sources, and leads, which give a story its overall tone or flavor. The judgments, by contrast, are highly specific assessments of topics that often permit direct comparison with expert opinion. Yet the judgments presented in the media were a poor match for the actual judgments of the scientific and engineering communities. They provided a much better match with the story elements that expressed the tone the journalist wished to convey.

Sources and Experts. So far, the results of the content analysis form a fairly consistent pattern. Scientists and engineers see nuclear energy primarily in terms of design and impact questions; the media ask mainly management questions. The energy community is most concerned with problems that call for technical solutions; the media emphasize the political answers. Most energy specialists regard nuclear power in a positive light; the media present it with a negative spin, backed up by unfavorable judgments on specific issues.

These findings raise some important questions about the media's transmission of expert opinion. If the energy community and the media are so far apart, how did the latter portray the views of the former? To gain a sense of how independent scientists and engineers fit into the overall pool of source material, academic scientists and engineers (along with scientific bodies like the National Academy of Sciences) were separated out from the welter of government, industry, and interest group sources that were cited in news stories.[67]

How often did the media present "expert" testimony? Over 5,000 citations were coded from all sources. Of these, academic scientists and engineers accounted for only 2 percent of those cited on television and in the *New York Times,* and 5 percent of those mentioned by the newsmagazines. That works out to about one per year at each of the television networks.[68]

Moreover, the use of academic scientists and engineers declined over time. In the early 1970s, they accounted for over óne source in ten cited by the networks and the newsmagazines. After 1976, they declined to less than half that number at the weeklies and to only 1 percent at the networks. A similar decline took place at the *New York Times,* from 4 percent of all sources in the early 1970s to only 1 percent a decade later.

Journalists might argue that their job is not to explain nuclear energy but to report the news about it. And news is more likely to revolve around government, industry, and interest groups than college campuses. This argument contains some truth, although it can easily become circular. It is journalists' news judgmer.ts that ultimately usher one source into a story and close the gate on another. But the consensual definition of news does focus attention on events in the political and economic spheres, until some noteworthy problem or breakthrough brings the experts' esoteric world into contact with that of the ordinary citizen. Whether this should be so is itself a difficult value judgment. Indeed, the recent increase in science reporting, as evidenced by a regular weekly section in the *New York Times,* shows how such judgments can change.

One need not judge the news decisions of journalists, however, to ask a simple question of fact. Did the expert testimony presented in the media agree with the actual views of the energy community? For the most part it did not. Instead, it reflected the overall tenor of media coverage. Even the variations among views cited or quoted in different media outlets reflected the variations in coverage already observed among those outlets.

Thus, the academic experts cited by the networks and the newsmagazines dealt primarily with management questions, while those appearing in the *New York Times* were far more likely to consider design and impact uncertainties, as well as questions that have been resolved. When it came to framing answers, energy scholars cited in the *Times* and the networks split their discussions between the technical and political realms, while those appearing in the newsmagazines strongly emphasized the latter dimension.

In addition, most university-based scientists and engineers who were cited treated nuclear power primarily in a negative light, although the ratios were far greater at the networks and *Time* and *Newsweek* than at *U.S. News* and the *New York Times.* The *Times* ran a story citing physicist Hans Bethe's statement that it is "eight times safer living next to a nuclear plant than in a brick house," because bricks give off eight times as much radiation as a nuclear reactor.[69] The story noted that Bethe was a Nobel laureate. By contrast, a UCLA geologist appearing on NBC complained that nuclear waste "can get into the ground water table and I can see the possibility of entire river basins that have to be essentially abandoned . . . it is dangerous and I'm not at all happy with what's being done about it."[70] Similarly, in a piece arguing that the nuclear industry "is plagued with safety questions," *Newsweek* quoted a Lehigh University scientist who admitted, "we simply don't have the technology to predict the safety of [reactor] vessels."[71]

It may be unfair to judge the media's presentation of expertise only on the basis of academic scientists and engineers. Many such scholars are highly reticent toward both journalistic inquiry and public policy matters. They prefer to stick to their intellectual lasts and shun public controversy. Indeed, our surveys revealed that anti-nuclear scientists were far more likely than others to seek out a public forum for their views.[72] Thus reporters might gain access to a minority viewpoint by default, since the pro-nuclear majority would be less likely to seek them out.

To gain a broader perspective on the media's use of experts, we widened the net to include all attributions of technical expertise. This entailed coding every direct and indirect citation of a scientist, engineer, or social scientist, regardless of affiliation, as well as every view attributed to unnamed scientists or experts. This resulted in a vast expansion of the expert category, which increased nearly threefold at the *New York Times,* fourfold at the newsweeklies, and sixfold at the networks. In other words, university-based scientists and engineers represented a small minority of the experts cited in the media. Most were associated with government, industry, or public interest groups.

The views expressed by this larger group were even further removed from those of the scientists and engineers we surveyed (see Table 12). Among all sources designated as experts, there was a further shift toward those who asked management questions and looked for political answers. In the pages of the *New York Times,* expert opinion shifted decisively into these categories, moving away from the more even distributions generated by unaffiliated academic experts. At the networks and newsweeklies, too, the number of those advocating political answers exceeded those proposing technical solutions.

What of their overall assessment of nuclear energy? At the *Times* the proportion of experts with pro-nuclear assessments slightly exceeded those on the anti-nuclear side, although most continued to offer a balanced or neutral view. At *Time* and *Newsweek* the media-designated experts remained strongly anti-nuclear, and at the networks the anti-nuclear margin increased to over five to one. In fact, at ABC, NBC, and *Newsweek,* there were over ten times as many stories citing anti-nuclear views as those with pro-nuclear assessments.

Newsweek, for example, ran a piece on allegations by three TMI engineers that the reactor operation and its major cleanup contractor "had overlooked safety checks and balances to meet cleanup schedules and were wasting millions of dollars—at times with the complicity of Nuclear Regulatory Commission staffers."[73] And a physicist interviewed by NBC concluded, "I think it will be necessary in the long run to abandon wide-scale use of

Table 12—Positions Taken by Experts Cited in Media Coverage

	New York Times	Magazines	Television
Questions			
Answered	20	1	3
Design	8	4	8
Impact	26	16	24
Management	46	78	65
	100%	99%*	101%*
Answers			
Technical	27	7	26
Political	73	31	27
Combination	—	62	47
	100%	100%	100%
Slant			
Pro-Nuclear	9	17	11
Anti-Nuclear	7	40	62
Neutral/Balanced	84	43	27
	100%	100%	100%
Number of Cases	154	253	133

*Totals reflect rounding error

nuclear energy for any purpose other than perhaps scientific research."[74]

Once again, *U.S. News* diverged sharply from the other newsmagazines. It produced an even split of pro- and anti-nuclear citations. For example, a 1979 *U.S. News* story discussed the scientific debate over the health risks of low-level radiation. It quoted the chairman of the National Academy of Sciences Committee on Biological Effects of Ionizing Radiation: "At low doses the risks are very small. There is a risk, but it's not the end of the world."[75] A few weeks earlier, *Newsweek* ran a similar story on radiation risks that asserted, "Some scientists think [current safety standards] underestimate the dangers of low-level radiation. Those fears are backed by recent studies of workers who have received doses well within government standards."[76]

The story cited a study of leukemia at Maine's Portsmouth Naval Shipyard, another of cancers at the Hanford nuclear facility in Washington state, and a British study linking X-ray therapy to cancer. All three studies were very controversial, as the article noted. But *Newsweek* included them in its story on radiation; *U.S. News* did not.

In sum, the major media rarely presented the views of academic scientists and engineers who were nonaligned in the nuclear debate. They were much more likely to rely on technical experts associated with government, industry, or public policy groups. By either definition, though, these sources reflected the media's perspectives on the nuclear debate rather than those of the energy community. Scientists and engineers cited in the media tended to frame questions in terms of management, to propose answers that demanded political resolutions, and to assess nuclear power negatively.

This picture contrasts strongly with results from our surveys of scientists and engineers, as well as the technical literature. Most energy specialists are more concerned with design and impact questions, regard most (though not all) uncertainties as capable of technical solution, and assess nuclear power in a positive light. Not only did experts cited in the media diverge markedly from the survey findings, their views varied from one outlet to another in ways that reflected each outlet's general treatment of the topic. Thus, the media seemed to rely on expert testimony more to confirm their presentation of the nuclear debate than to inform it.

Conclusion—The Experts and the Media

Most of the news stories analyzed were a far cry from the apocalyptic muckraking of "The Fire Unleashed." The major concern at all media outlets was to report the facts and interpret them in ways that made sense of a highly complex and controversial story. Even on a topic as hotly contested as nuclear energy, the national media are rarely given either to the "new" personalized journalism or old-fashioned advocacy journalism.

Nonetheless, this study of seven news organizations over fourteen years uncovered a gap between the way energy specialists conceive of this topic and the way the media report it. The differences occurred not only in how the media evaluated nuclear energy, but in how they structured the story—the questions they asked, the answers they sought, and the sources of information and expertise they used. One can recognize this divergence without regarding the energy community's perspective as definitive for social policy. Technical expertise is only one component of decisions on science policy. Safety assessments must be fit into a decision calculus that includes political and philosophical judgments, including such questions as the desirability of economic growth and the acceptability of risk.

We conducted extensive polling of leading scientists and engineers, as well as surveying the scientific and social scientific literature in the field. The results showed that most energy specialists support nuclear development and regard current nuclear reactors as safe. They see some serious problems, in areas such as waste disposal, reactor maintenance, and proliferation. At the same time, most are confident they possess the knowledge to solve such problems, most of which they regard as mainly technical matters.

In sharp contrast, major media coverage highlighted the uncertainties attending nuclear power, even in areas where scientists and engineers felt most secure in their problem-solving abilities. In framing questions, the media dealt mainly with management uncertainties, often ignoring the design and impact questions that engaged the expert communities. Whereas the energy specialists believe most problems are amenable to technical solutions, the media concentrated on political resolutions, with their inherently greater uncertainties.

These differences might be attributed to functional differences in the roles of scientists and engineers, on one hand, and journalists, on the other. That is, their professional responsibilities and mind-sets might be expected to lead them, more or less automatically, to perceive different aspects of the same phenomenon. There is doubtless some truth in this. But it cannot be the whole answer, because there were significant differences in coverage over time and among different outlets during the same time period. The latter is especially significant, because it cannot be attributed to events alone. If various news organizations report the same events differently, this suggests that different news judgments are taking place.

A major finding is the predominantly negative spin at most outlets. When journalists' interpretations, use of language, or choice of sources were skewed in one direction, they usually favored the anti-nuclear side. We found only a slight anti-nuclear tilt, and little spin overall, at the *New York Times,* while *U.S. News* actually favored the pro-nuclear side. At all other outlets coverage was tilted toward the anti-nuclear perspective by a wide margin. In the print media this slant seemed a response to the shock of TMI. On television it was there from the start.

The major media's emphasis on uncertainty in framing nuclear issues was consistent with the skepticism leading journalists professed in our survey. The preponderance of anti-nuclear spin may also correspond to similar attitudes in the newsroom. For example, we compared the attitudes at different media outlets and found the greatest skepticism toward nuclear energy among television reporters and producers. It was at the television networks that anti-nuclear coverage proved the most pervasive and lasting.

None of this proves that journalists consciously set out to slant their reportage against nuclear energy. As we have argued throughout this book, the influence of perspectives and paradigms is less direct than conservatives' conspiracy theories often suggest. Moreover, the contours of news stories are doubtless overdetermined by the simultaneous influence of external events, structural and organizational factors, and professional norms, as well as personal attitudes.

It is probably impossible to separate out the impact of each factor on the coverage. Consider the allegation on "The Fire Unleashed" that the TMI accident has already resulted in many cancer fatalities. In a gripping vignette, a local resident was shown recounting a lengthy list of neighbors who had died of cancer, as an on-screen graphic announced "20 cancer deaths, 19 current cases." Any such outcome is scientifically implausible, even apart from the conclusions of bodies as diverse as the Presidential Commission on TMI ("Kemeny Commission"), National Center for

Disease Control, General Accounting Office, and Pennsylvania Governor's Commission, which agreed that radiation damage was negligible.[77] The type and amount of radiation released during the TMI accident could not have caused cancer deaths so rapidly. The scientific debate on this issue concerned the possibility that cancers might appear many years after the event.

In light of such information, there are several possible explanations for ABC's airing of this charge. One is simple scientific ignorance. Since there was a debate about whether radiation from TMI *caused* cancer, the production team may not have realized that this referred to the statistical probability of a future increase in cancer incidence. A second factor concerns the demands of the medium. Television journalism works best with good visual material, dramatic situations, and a personalizing element that makes viewers feel involved with an individual shown on-screen. The resident listing cancer deaths filled all these requirements, while statistical probability estimates fulfill none of them.

There is also the possibility that the documentary team was psychologically prepared to believe such charges by their own attitudes toward nuclear energy. The television personnel in the media elite survey were even more critical of nuclear power than print journalists, and the content analysis recorded a "spin factor" of −25 for ABC News, representing a predominance of anti-nuclear over pro-nuclear stories there by a margin greater than two to one.

One other finding highlights the differences between journalists and energy specialists and also illustrates how newsmen's perspectives may subtly color their coverage. When the media's use of expert opinion was examined, the results reflected the views of journalists better than those of the experts. Scientists, engineers, and others designated as experts cited in news stories tended to reflect the overall tenor of media coverage, even though this clashed with the survey findings on the actual attitudes of energy scientists and engineers.

Part of this discrepancy might be attributed to the exigencies of news gathering. Reporters working on deadline cannot telephone a random sample of scientists for information. They need sources who are readily available to provide background information and quotable statements. Such sources are found more often in government, industry, and public interest groups than in the halls of academe. The relevance of this explanation is limited, however, since the findings held true for academic scientists and engineers who were cited.

If we return to the responses of leading journalists to the survey question about reliable sources, as reported in Chapter Three, we see that, given the opportunity to pick as many as they wished, journalists selected anti-nuclear groups and individuals over their pro-nuclear counterparts by nearly a two to one margin. So the major media's actual use of sources presumably reflects the choices the journalists themselves said they would make in covering the nuclear story. These choices, in turn, were presumably influenced by the mainly skeptical attitudes they held toward nuclear energy.

Let us recap the structure of the argument. Surveys revealed sharp differences between the energy group and journalists on nuclear safety. America's energy scientists and engineers largely viewed this technology favorably and downplayed the uncertainties involved in solving its problems. Major media journalists (including key science journalists) were more skeptical toward nuclear power and emphasized the uncertainties involved. When asked where they would turn for reliable information on nuclear power, the journalists picked mainly anti-nuclear sources, in line with their own attitudes.

Finally, the content analysis of major media news stories from 1970 through 1983 showed that the coverage accords with the perspectives of the journalists rather than those of the scientists and engineers. Particularly telling was the media's own use of sources. In the aggregate, experts cited in news stories tended to reflect the perspectives held by journalists, even when these conflicted with the perspectives revealed by our surveys. Moreover, experts cited by the different media outlets presented perspectives which varied according to each outlet's general treatment of the nuclear debate. Taken as a whole, this sequence of findings suggests that media coverage of the nuclear debate was not unrelated to journalists' own attitudes toward nuclear energy.[78]

This is not a matter of partisan bias or anti-nuclear crusading. It reflects a series of routine news judgments, of daily decisions repeated over the course of several years. It is not conscious intentions but common assumptions that quietly direct news coverage toward the dominant perspectives of the newsroom. Whatever the reasons, though, some crucial links seem to be missing in the chain of information leading from scientists and engineers to the general public. And over the years, the public increasingly has come to share the media's perspective on the nuclear debate.

Postscript on Chernobyl

A comment should be added on the recent accident at the Soviet nuclear plant at Chernobyl. The information available is still sketchy, but despite reports in the American press, we do not really know the magnitude of the accident. Chernobyl may not turn out to be as costly to human life as the non-nuclear disaster at Bhopal.

Western scientists and engineers have long been critical of the casualness with which the Soviets have dealt with nuclear safety issues. Most Soviet nuclear plants, for example, are not protected by massive containment structures. While the Chernobyl plant may have included such a structure, we do not know the effectiveness of its specifications.

Clearly, Chernobyl has raised new questions about nuclear energy. However, this does not affect our analysis of media coverage of the issues. It is possible that the media (and anti-nuclear energy groups) *have* been more correct in their assessments than have the experts. But our contention is that journalists' skepticism, which is related to their broader social perspectives, has resulted in a portrayal of nuclear safety issues which often differs from that of most energy experts. That conclusion still stands.

READIN', WRITIN', AND RIGHTS

[Busing] is social therapy, and like personal
therapy, it is not easy."
—Psychologist Kenneth Clark, quoted in *Time*

"Bus Teddy"
—Boston graffiti

THE BUSING controversy never grew too bitter for Johnny Carson
to joke about it. Columnist William Raspberry summarized one
"Tonight Show" routine to make his own point about the debate:

> The turbaned wonder puts the sealed envelope against the side
> of his head, ponders briefly, then intones: "The answer is: bus-
> ing."
> Unlike Johnny Carson's "Carnack the Magnificent," how-
> ever, there is no need to open the envelope to see what the
> question was. When it comes to race and public education, the
> answer is always: busing.[1]

After fifteen years of controversy, everyone knows the Supreme Court's answer to school segregation is busing. Yet we may
have forgotten what the questions surrounding this issue were
initially. We may recall the catchwords of the busing debate—

racism, white flight, quality education, neighborhood schools. But behind the catchwords lay an often technical and sometimes heated scholarly debate about the assumptions and implications of busing. Reviewing this debate is a prerequisite for judging media coverage of this long-running social and political controversy.

Busing: Goals and Outcomes

The Supreme Court's Role. In the first eighteen years after *Brown* v. *Board of Education,* every important Supreme Court opinion on race relations and education concerned school systems in southern or border states, where separation of the races previously had been required by law. The existence of predominantly black schools in the North was assumed to be a reflection only of residential patterns. Since there were few racially integrated neighborhoods in the North, there were few racially integrated urban schools. It was assumed that this *de facto* school segregation—segregation existing for reasons other than government policy—could not be affected by the courts. Courts cannot act where no violation of law exists.

In 1973, however, the Supreme Court ruled on *Keyes v. Denver School District No. 1,* its first desegregation case from a large northern city. The Keyes decision was a turning point in the evolution of the Court's involvement in race and education. It equated the segregative actions taken by officials in northern school districts with those imposed by the southern states after Reconstruction. This made the remedies approved in the rural South, like busing and redistricting, instruments that now could be used in Detroit, Chicago, or other northern cities.

Moreover, the legal requirement that the courts remedy deprivations of legal rights helped convert *desegregation,* a stance that laws separating the races must be blotted out, to *integration,* one holding that the law required racially mixed results. Until 1970, the Constitution had been interpreted as invalidating all legal distinctions based on race. For that reason, the courts were prohibited from relying on race-conscious remedies to rectify legal harm. But the Court, first in Charlotte, North Carolina, then in

Denver, focused on assuring integration as evidence that the results of wrongful actions had been undone.

Throughout the remainder of the 1970s, the Keyes decision was applied in many northern cities and its implications were spelled out, as desegregation plans were adopted and implemented. The Supreme Court refused, in 1974, to allow surburban Detroit districts to be included in desegregation plans in the absence of evidence that they also had practiced intentionally segregative policies.[2] The Court reaffirmed Keyes in the face of strong criticism when it upheld lower court desegregation orders in Columbus and Dayton, Ohio.[3] These court decisions and the earlier Civil Rights Act of 1964, which prohibited racial discrimination in public accommodations, were enforced by the Justice Department and the Department of Health, Education and Welfare. This alliance of institutions had helped achieve a social revolution in the South where, within a decade, virtually every aspect of daily life was desegregated.

In northern city schools, the task was far more complicated. In some cities, assignment procedures were adopted that set certain racial quotas for student bodies, integrated teaching staffs, and sometimes even revised school curricula. This was to ensure that each school had a distribution of blacks, whites, and (sometimes) other minorities reflecting the racial composition of the entire school system. But given the size of most urban neighborhoods, the principal device for complying with Keyes was busing children into different school districts.

This widespread reliance on busing quickly became controversial. In Boston and Louisville, especially from 1974 to 1976, violence accompanied the opening of school each September, as angry parents protested student reassignments. Many cities experienced busing without violence, but opponents attacked it as useless and even harmful to students. Many families moved out of cities subject to court order, apparently to avoid the inevitability of busing altogether. And throughout the decade, popular confidence in the schools eroded.

Yet not all the activity on busing took place the courtroom or on the streets. Busing opponents in Congress annually sought to prohibit its use as a tool of racial integration by means of laws or constitutional amendments. California voters passed a referendum that prohibited busing in desegregation cases. By the end of the decade, white exodus from school districts included in busing plans made goals for integrating schools increasingly difficult to achieve.

Having briefly surveyed the history of judicial attempts to desegregate the public schools, let us examine the debate over the results that busing achieved. School desegregation was undertaken primarily to ensure that all Americans enjoy equality of opportunity. Desegregation also focuses on educational outcomes. The 1954 Brown case asserted that segregated education had a "detrimental effect" on minority children, inhibiting the motivation of a child to learn, and thereby retarding educational and mental development. Finally, school busing was undertaken to achieve a society where social and legal distinctions based on race have no place.

White Flight. Perhaps the most important achievement of the courts since the Brown decision has been their success in eliminating southern dual school systems. But in the North, segregation often worsened in the 1970s, despite efforts of the federal government and the courts to eradicate it through busing programs. Segregation was especially pronounced in large northern cities.[4]

Throughout the latter 1970s, social scientists debated whether court-ordered desegregation actually encouraged the exodus of whites from the public schools, just the opposite of what the courts intended. The persistence of "white flight," an exodus that usually increased once busing plans were started, is especially important because it calls into question one major argument in support of school busing: that integrated schools create educational benefits for whites and blacks independent of the effect on minority achievement. Some scholars argued that policies intended to ensure that blacks and whites study and learn together may instead create majority black schools.

This conclusion was usually treated as an argument against large-scale busing plans, though some called for even more inclusive plans aimed at mostly white suburban school districts. The most heated controversy, however, concerned whether white migration was really a product of busing's adverse consequences on the schools.

The white flight issue came to prominence in April 1975, when sociologist James S. Coleman and two colleagues presented research concluding that school desegregation caused a decline in white enrollment in the public schools where busing was taking place.[5] In his famous 1966 report, *Equal Educational Opportunity,* Coleman had appeared to throw the weight of social science behind school integration. In this new research, he reached different conclusions about its efficacy.

This finding quickly became a focus of controversy among sociologists. Later the same year, Christine Rossell published a study that seemed to deal a severe blow to Coleman's white flight thesis.[6] Rossell found that the school districts with the highest degree of desegregation experienced at most "minimal" and "temporary" white flight. Moreover, the small white flight that did occur took place *before* school opened in the first year of the implementation of a desegregation plan. Thus, she concluded, white flight occurs not from problems accompanying school desegregation, but the *fear* of problems.

In 1978, however, Diane Ravitch published a damaging critique of Rossell's methods.[7] Ravitch's examination of twenty-nine large cities showed that absolute white exodus from inner-city public schools was substantial. Probably the most sophisticated study of white flight was completed by David Armor in 1979.[8] After reviewing several major busing studies, Armor concluded that substantial white flight did occur, especially during the first year after the implementation of a desegregation plan.

By the end of the 1970s, white exodus as a response to busing for racial balance had become a fact too obvious to deny. In Los Angeles, for example, 60 percent of the 20,000 students involved in a 1978 busing plan never showed up at the predominantly minority schools to which they were assigned. When a second desegregation plan was implemented in 1980, 40,000 fled the system. At least half the total decline in Los Angeles' enrollment during that period has been attributed to court-ordered busing.[9]

New York, Philadelphia, Chicago, Detroit, Boston, and many other cities all lost at least 30 percent of their white students in the 1970s.

At the same time, political support for large-scale northern busing began to erode. The Department of Justice under the Reagan administration reversed its past stand in favor of school desegregation and sided with the states of California and Washington to defend state anti-busing laws. The Justice Department also refused to pursue busing as a remedy in St. Louis and Chicago. In 1981, it refused to appeal a court dismissal of a Carter administration plan to desegregate the public schools in Houston by busing children from mostly white suburbs to schools in the central cities.

Racism vs. Rational Concerns. In view of the evidence supporting white flight, we must inevitably ask why so many whites abandoned cities where busing was implemented. One explanation may be white racism. Supporters of busing argue that large numbers of white children have always lived far enough from their schools to require bus transportation each day, so white racism must be at the root of parents' objections. Some studies support this explanation. In their 1979 study of white attitudes toward busing, David Sears and his colleagues concluded that racism played a strong role in white opposition.[10]

Other scholars point to evidence suggesting that racism is not the primary factor in explaining this opposition. First, surveys show that since 1954, racial tolerance and support for integration have markedly increased among white Americans. Racial tolerance among whites has grown despite their consistent opposition to busing. This opposition is strong even among white college graduates, young people, and others expressing the highest levels of racial tolerance. Although opposition to busing is not the predominant view of American blacks, it is still strong among members of that group.[11]

But public opinion polls may be a poor indicator of racism. Whites may say that they favor integration, but act differently when integration takes place in their community and involves their children. Sears adopted this point of view, suggesting that white attitudes on racial matters vary by issue. Whites may be tolerant on issues involving equal opportunity for blacks and formal relationships, such as access to public accommodations, but much less tolerant on more intimate types of interracial associations concerning marriage or close friendships. Sears and his colleagues used several measures for determining "symbolic racism," including a belief in the intellectual superiority of whites and opinions regarding racial protest. They found that symbolic racism is the most important determinant of white opposition to busing.

Critics of the symbolic racism argument assert that not all the supposed indicators of white racism actually measure racist attitudes. For example, widely held white beliefs that the civil rights movement was moving too fast, or that racial protest was hurting the black cause, could be considered nonracist opinions about the desirable pace of social change.

Another school of thought holds that white opposition to busing mainly reflects rational concerns about its costs and benefits. Scholars like David Armor argue that white parents do not object to racially integrated schools but to perceived social costs, such as the loss of local schools and, especially, fear of exposing their children to crime.[12]

Studies have shown that crime is a serious problem in American public schools.[13] The problem is most acute in those schools that are likely to be included in busing plans (urban public schools located in high crime neighborhoods, with large numbers of minority students).[14] Therefore, according to this argument, parents' perceptions that court-ordered busing to ghetto schools might harm their children may reflect this concern for safety rather than racist attitudes.

An advantage of the rational concerns argument is that it may help explain opposition to busing among blacks. To explain white opposition, moreover, it is not necessary to treat these two positions as mutually exclusive. The question is not whether racism or rational concerns account solely for negative attitudes, but the relative explanatory power of each. Even today, however, no consensus has emerged among social scientists as to their relative importance.[15]

Improving Minority School Achievement. Another goal of busing is to improve educational outcomes for minority students. The Supreme Court stated in its Brown decision that segregation gave black pupils a sense of inferiority about themselves, thereby affecting their performance in school. The Court cited social science research in support of that conclusion.[16] Works by Samuel Stouffer,[17] Morton Deutsch, and Mary Evans Collins[18] concluded that interracial contact diminished white prejudice. These findings provided the basis for an assumption by supporters of integration that has continued until very recently: racial integration would lead to improved black educational achievement and an improvement in the inferior social status of blacks. It was an assumption that went almost unquestioned in the North until the mid-1960s, when these conclusions were cast into doubt. However, it provided much of the theoretical justification for the Brown case and its progeny.

In 1966, a major survey of education was directed by James S. Coleman. The Coleman report found that black students performed at lower levels than white students in reading and mathematics, in all regions and in all grades, and that black students had lower aspirations, lower self-esteem about their academic ability, and a more fatalistic attitude about their ability to change their social and economic environment.

The report also noted that disadvantaged children of all races performed slightly better on standardized tests when they attended predominantly middle-class schools, and that middle-class children did not perform worse in schools with large numbers of poor students. These conclusions have often been cited in support of school integration. A report of the United States Commission on Civil Rights, *Racial Isolation in the Public Schools,*[19] was premised on the Coleman report. The commission found that educational outcomes for black students were influenced by several socioeconomic factors—their home backgrounds, the quality of education provided in the schools, and the social class of their classmates.[20] These findings became a cornerstone of educational policy in the following decade, as many educators sought to encourage school integration in order to improve black pupil achievement.

As the focus of school desegregation shifted northward after Keyes, however, some social scientists began to question the benefits of school integration. In 1972, a study by David Armor found that busing resulted in a decline in the grades received by black students and no increase in achievement scores, compared to non-bused control groups. Busing did not seem to affect the self-esteem of black students, and it resulted in an overall decrease in black support for integration. Armor concluded that large-scale court-ordered busing programs were ineffective means of improving either student achievement or interracial harmony.[21]

Thomas Pettigrew responded that Armor relied on an incomplete group of desegregation studies and that the resulting conclusions were "selectively negative." Moreover, Pettigrew pointed out that the "critical conditions" under which busing and integration have taken place are so rarely present that it is impossible to judge such programs on their own terms.[22]

Also in 1972, a large-scale study by Christopher Jencks and others argued that income redistribution, not school reform, was most likely to improve the lives of the poor.[23] Other attempts to study the effects of race and ethnicity on learning soon followed these early efforts.[24]

In 1975, Nancy St. John published the most comprehensive review of school integration studies to that time.[25] She found that, after more than a decade of research, there were no conclusive results on the disputed relationship between school racial composition and academic achievement. Most studies concluded that black educational and job aspirations were higher when the percentage of whites in the school was small, indicating that black self-concept and black aspirations tended to be higher in segregated schools. St. John concluded, "It seems as though desegregation must be dysfunctional in some ways for minority youth."[26]

St. John's analysis of the research concerning the effects of integration on racial prejudice produced perhaps the most ambiguous conclusions of all. Her studies indicated that "desegregation sometimes reduces prejudice and promotes interracial friendship and sometimes promotes, instead, stereotyping and interracial cleavage and conflict."[27] Whether such prejudice would diminish or grow following integration depended on situational factors, such as the nature of interracial contact and the black pupils' sense of cultural marginality.

In 1978, Walter Stephan did another survey of the literature on the effects of integration on student achievement.[28] He tested the conclusion, used in social science testimony in the Brown case, that desegregation would lead to more positive interracial attitudes among both blacks and whites, would raise black self-esteem, and would promote scholastic achievement. Stephan found that over two-thirds of the studies showed that desegregation failed to produce unqualified positive results. His summary agreed with St. John's overall finding that desegregation rarely harms black students, occasionally improves their scholastic achievement, but generally has mixed outcomes.

The effects of desegregation on race relations are also ambiguous. One survey of studies on this topic found that the process promotes more amicable interracial contacts than under segregation,[29] but others disagree.[30] Finally, test results from cities around the country lead to no firm conclusions about the relationship between desegregation and achievement.[31] Perhaps the most concise summary of the effects of school desegregation on black achievement, self-esteem, and aspirations was given by Coleman in 1976. He concluded that, ". . . school desegregation is seldom harmful . . . sometimes beneficial, but not sufficiently so that school desegregation can be a major policy instrument for increasing black achievement and self-esteem."[32]

Such conclusions have produced important changes in the form of remedial decrees that many judges have used in desegregation cases in the past few years. Some busing plans now contain provisions for changing educational services offered in the schools, as well as provisions for the reassignment and busing of students.

For example, the remedial plan in Boston required that educationally outstanding "magnet" schools be established. It paired Boston public schools with universities in the area in the hope that these institutions of higher learning could help improve the programs offered.

This concern with educational reform is characteristic of other cities currently undergoing court-ordered busing. But the emphasis on educational excellence reveals an important shift in the judiciary's thinking about desegregation. Twenty years earlier it was assumed that integration improved the education offered minority children and cured the "condition that offends the Constitution."

Busing in Retrospect. Busing was one of the great domestic controversies of the 1970s, especially after the Supreme Court's 1973 Keyes decision broadened a regional struggle into a nationwide conflict. By the end of the 1970s, the bulk of scholarly studies had concluded that busing was a key factor in white exodus from the cities. Busing supporters often pointed to racism as the principal motive for white flight. Some studies concluded that racism was the most important determinant of white opposition to busing. Other scholars argued that white opposition to busing was mainly based on beliefs that mostly black schools have serious problems, such as crime and poor student achievement rates. Busing also violated strong attachments to neighborhood schools.

Another major goal of busing was to improve educational achievement among minority children. As the focus of school desegregation shifted northward in the 1970s, researchers could find no consistent link between desegregation and improved educational achievement among minority children.

In brief, busing for school desegregation involved a myriad of complexities that divided social scientists as well as parents and children. Most researchers now agree that persistent white flight at least partly defeated the intended goal of increased educational equality. On other issues, the evidence is ambiguous and sometimes contradictory, and disagreements persist on the interpretation and implications of relevant data. Even today there is no scholarly consensus on the primary motives of busing's opponents or the effects of busing on minority achievement.

Busing: The Coverage

Our study looked at coverage in four major media outlets from 1970 through 1979: The *New York Times, Time,* the CBS evening news, and the *Washington Post.* The *Times* is the nation's most respected newspaper; *Time* has the highest circulation among the newsweeklies; and CBS enjoys the greatest viewership of the television networks. The *Post,* a highly influential paper among Washington elites, was included because the busing issue generated so much policy-oriented coverage in the nation's capital.

Coverage of busing was so heavy that we could examine only samples at all outlets except *Time,* where every article was coded. At CBS one-third of all relevant broadcasts were selected randomly. At the newspapers, which generated the most coverage, twelve weeks were selected randomly from each two-year period from 1970–71 through 1978–79. All articles appearing during those weeks were coded. (Analysis of *Post* coverage began in 1972, because no index existed for earlier articles.) This procedure permits analysis of changes in the coverage over time. To ensure that the sample did not miss coverage of important occurrences, it was augmented by eleven key weeks representing such events as President Nixon's 1972 anti-busing statement and the Denver and Detroit Supreme Court decisions.

Even this partial sample yielded a massive amount of coverage. We coded busing-related arguments and activities mentioned in over 5,000 column inches of the *New York Times,* 1,500 inches each from the *Washington Post* and *Time,* and seven hours of CBS newscasts. Most of the news was concentrated in the early years of the decade, before the busing story faded from view after 1975.

Arguments

We coded the major pro- and anti-busing arguments that dominated the debate. The pro-busing arguments were grouped under three major headings. First, proponents of the "equal education"

231

argument asserted that busing is necessary to realize the constitutional rights of minorities to have an equal education, or to counter the effects of segregation and racism.

The second major pro-busing argument claimed that busing would promote racial harmony, both in school and in the wider society. Thus, as contact between the races increased, interracial tension and white prejudice would eventually decrease. The third argument centered on improving minority performance in desegregated schools. This argument might include evidence that busing resulted in higher grades and test scores or better job and college prospects for minority students.

Opponents to busing used four major arguments to make their case. The first asserted that mandatory busing plans would cause white parents to withdraw their children from the affected public schools and place them in private schools or move to another, unaffected school district. The second claimed that busing would cause a general decline in the quality of education. This category included assertions of falling grades or test scores or a deterioration of the learning environment.

A third anti-busing argument held that busing would weaken the connection between community participation and the operation of the local school. This argument focused on the importance of neighborhood or ethnic ties to local schools. It also included claims about hardships, such as long bus rides, produced by sending children to schools outside their community. The last argument asserted that busing would trigger increased racial tension and violence in schools, or subject children to unsafe school environments. This category included fears expressed by white parents for the safety of their children in urban schools.

We coded both the frequency with which each argument was presented and how it was evaluated—whether it was affirmed, refuted, or no clear judgment was made concerning its validity. The degree of support for each argument was measured by subtracting the percentage of refutations (negative spin) from affirmations (positive spin). For example, if an argument was affirmed 60 percent of the time and refuted 30 percent, with the remainder unclear, the resulting index of support would be +30 (60 minus

30). Scores could range from +100, when the argument was always affirmed, to −100, when it was always refuted. If an argument was refuted equally as often as it was affirmed, the result would be a score of zero.

This procedure revealed that the media usually presented arguments without refutation. If they wanted to present both sides of the busing debate, they usually did so by presenting a pro-busing argument and balancing it with a different anti-busing argument. Thus, with rare exceptions noted below, scores on the "spin index" were strongly positive.

We found that coverage of the busing debate produced a slight but consistent tilt in favor of pro-busing arguments. At all four media outlets, the majority of arguments coded presented busing in a favorable light. Overall, as Table 13 shows, pro-busing coverage accounted for 60 percent of the arguments at CBS, 59 percent at *Time*, 58 percent at the *New York Times*, and 54 percent at the *Washington Post*. [33]

Table 13—Media Coverage of Busing Arguments

Arguments	New York Times	Time	Washington Post	CBS
Pro-busing				
Equal Education	34%	30%	24%	43%
Racial Harmony	12	19	14	17
Minority Performance	12	10	16	0
Pro-Total:	58%	59%	54%	60%
Anti-busing				
White Flight	12	17	27	11
Quality Education	5	6	9	8
Local Schools	13	11	10	17
Violence/Discipline	13	7	0	5
Anti-Total:	43%	41%	46%	41%
Amount Coded	1,419″	582″	267″	84

Note: *New York Times* and CBS percentage totals reflect 1 percent rounding error. Raw totals represent column inches for print sources and number of arguments for television.

The anti-busing arguments were somewhat more likely to be criticized when they did appear. As Table 14 shows, they averaged +35 on the spin index measuring argument support, compared with +48 for their pro-busing counterparts. This difference reflects the media's rejection of the argument that busing was associated with violence or discipline problems in desegregated schools. This was the only argument to receive a negative overall score, indicating that it was refuted more often than affirmed.

The most coverage went to the equal education argument, although claims of increased racial harmony and improved minority performance also received considerable attention. Among the anti-busing arguments, the white flight phenomenon was the most heavily covered, followed by concerns that local schools would be undermined. The two other anti-busing arguments, which claimed that busing would expose children to violence or impair educational quality, received scant attention.

Equal education. The argument that busing was necessary for minorities to achieve equal educational opportunities claimed by far the most attention. It received at least twice the coverage of

Table 14—Busing Coverage Argument Support Index	
Arguments	Mean Score*
Pro-busing	
Equal Education	+48%
Racial Harmony	+68
Minority Performance	+27
Total:	+48
Anti-busing	
White Flight	+57%
Quality Education	+52
Local Schools	+36
Violence/Discipline	−4
Total:	+35

*Average score on argument support index across all four media outlets, weighted equally. Index is constructed by subtracting percent of negative coverage from percent of positive coverage.

any other argument presented by CBS or the *New York Times* and nearly twice the coverage that *Time* gave any other argument. Only at the *Post* was coverage of the equal education argument slightly exceeded by the space accorded to white flight.[34]

The equal education argument was presented in its purest form in a 1972 *Post* article quoting U.S. Civil Rights Commission Chairman Theodore Herburgh. He argued that efforts to end busing would "strip away the constitutional right of all children to equal educational opportunity."[35] The implication was that busing was the necessary means to the constitutionally mandated goal of racial integration. Sometimes the notion of equal opportunity was conveyed in very concrete terms, like those used by busing advocates in Pontiac, Michigan, cited in *Time:*

> School Superintendent Odell Nails is convinced that busing was necessary to produce equal educational opportunities because it focused the clout of concerned white parents on the condition and equipment in schools that had been all black and largely neglected. "In the old days," he says, "black schools had to borrow microscopes for two weeks a year." Adds Principal Daryl Lee of Jefferson Junior High: "Now, everyone shares in the wealth and the poverty."[36]

The defense of busing as a means to educational equality also included the idea that it was necessary because of our society's racism. For example, CBS broadcast a Louisville NAACP official's charge that opposition to busing there came from "racist elements in the community who don't want to see quality education" for blacks.[37]

The core of the equal education argument was that busing would fulfill the promise of the historic 1954 Brown decision, which proclaimed that "separate but equal" is inherently unequal. In 1975, *Time* even interviewed Brown's daughter Linda, now an adult with children of her own. She made the link explicit: "To get racial balance in the school system I would have my children bused. This is what my father was fighting about 20 years ago."[38]

Racial Harmony. The claim that busing would increase racial harmony received about the same amount of attention at all four outlets. It ranked second to the equal education argument everywhere except at the *Washington Post,* where it placed fourth. The amount of coverage devoted to this argument varied only from 12 percent at the *New York Times* to 18 percent at *Time.*

Television proved an excellent medium for illustrating racial harmony in the schools. For example, a 1972 CBS broadcast showed a group of black and white school children in Pontiac, Michigan, the scene of earlier anti-busing violence, giving a school concert. The words they sang were, "Put a little love in your heart."[39]

In a similar vein, *Time* ran a story on a visit by Boston students to a peacefully desegregated school in Charlotte, North Carolina. It quoted a local high school student, "We want you to know we've learned a lot about judging anybody, black or white, as an individual. It just took time."[40]

One *New York Times* story supplemented such examples of harmonious relations with a statement of the argument that underlay them. It quoted a Chicago mother, "I think busing is a healthy idea. It's about time that blacks and whites started getting together and a good way to start is through children."[41] Another *Times* piece nicely combined this rationale with an illustration from Central High School in Little Rock, Arkansas, the scene of a famous struggle over integration in the 1950s:

> But why has Central High, after years of tumult, gone so far toward racial harmony? . . ., today's black and white students have been going to school together since the early grades. Little Rock abandoned tokenism in 1971 and began massive desegregation with busing amid relatively minor disturbance. . . . "When the Central High Tigers are on the field" [a black senior said], "everybody sitting on our side of the stadium is a Tiger, regardless of what color they are."[42]

Minority Achievement. The remaining pro-busing argument, which stresses improved academic skills for minorities, received about as much attention from the print media as the racial harmony argument. However, we couldn't find a single CBS broadcast on this topic. This surprising disparity might be attributed to the difficulty of portraying this argument visually. Racial harmony and equal access to educational opportunities are topics that lend themselves to visual treatment, such as pictures of black and white children attending school together. The controversy over minority academic performance was more technical, often revolving around interpretations of test scores. In any event, it was not covered by CBS in the stories sampled.

Press coverage of this argument was exemplified by a 1972 summary in *Time:* "School integration can accomplish a great deal . . . researchers have verified that poor black children do at least marginally better in white-majority classrooms, presumably because they pick up their middle-class white schoolmates' learning skills and attitudes toward education."[43] A later *Time* article extended this argument to allay concerns about declining performance among whites. It quoted a Jacksonville, Florida, school official: "According to Associate Superintendent Don Johnson, national test scores indicate that [busing for] desegregation has resulted in 'significant benefits for the black students and no loss of achievement for the white student.' "[44] The *New York Times* reported similar positive findings in Little Rock, Arkansas:

> [The School Superintendent] said that much progress had been made in closing the academic gap between white and black students. Blacks now score considerably higher on tests and whites score slightly better, he said. Desegregation has made these gains come easier, he said.[45]

White Flight. Among anti-busing arguments, claims of white flight and threats to neighborhood schools each garnered considerable media notice. (Neither could approach the attention given the equal education argument in overall coverage.) Of the two, the white migration argument occupied the greater share of the news, largely on the basis of heavy coverage by the *Washington Post.* It accounted for 27 percent of all argument coverage in that category, edging out the equal education argument by 3 percent. It finished no higher than third at the other outlets but never fell below 11 percent of total coverage at any of them.

Especially during the mid-1970s, readers encountered regular recitations of dismal statistics detailing the resegregation of public school systems, after busing plans triggered white migration. A 1975 *Time* article was typical of many:

> Yet even in communities that have fully obeyed the courts, the fear of busing often precipitates the flight of whites, who move to the suburbs or take their children out of public schools to escape desegregation. During the three years busing has been used to desegregate the Atlanta schools, 40,000 white students have fled the system and city schools have gone from 56% to 87% black. In Memphis, enrollment in private academies increased from 13,000 in 1973, when a federal court ordered the city schools to desegregate, to 35,000 today, while the public school enrollment tipped from 50% black to 70% black. Even in Charlotte, home of the most successful and widely acclaimed busing plan in the U.S., enrollment in private academies has more than doubled in the past five years of court-ordered busing.[46]

This was one topic on which the media presented an alleged social cost of busing with little notice of the heated scholarly debate. While the sociologists fought over statistical interpretations and research methods, the media took it for granted that busing was a major cause of white migration from inner city areas. Toward the end of the decade, *Time* even took a swipe at the scholars for not believing the evidence before their own eyes: "There is now considerable academic consensus that in large cities a significant linkage exists between white flight and forced busing. The fact that sociologists show signs of catching up with everyone else's common sense observation should be reassuring."[47]

Nonetheless, a funny thing happened between the occurrence of white flight and its reportage. Although we have treated this phenomenon as an argument against busing, it was not always portrayed in that light. Instead, it was often seen as a problem to be overcome, or as evidence of white racism, rather than a reason to change policies. Thus the *Washington Post* quoted an NAACP representative, "So we must halt the white flight and reverse it. We want to attract middle-class whites and blacks in the suburbs and those whose children are in private schools back to our public schools. I think an enlightened school administration can bring them back."[48] And a CBS reporter drew attention to alleged northern hypocrisy over busing. He noted that, in Illinois, where the first northern school districts were ordered to desegregate, many whites took their children out of public schools. He called this an "irony," since a recent Illinois survey said that most whites wanted racial equality, but opposed busing.[49]

Neighborhood Schools. Concern over neighborhood schools was the other anti-busing argument that received widespread attention. Although never a dominant argument, neither was it ever ignored. Coverage ranged from a high of 17 percent at CBS to a low of 10 percent at the *Washington Post.* For example, the *New York Times* quoted the black chairman of a parents' advisory board in Boston, "I believe in neighborhood schools—[children] should be able to get a good education anywhere. They should not be forced to go elsewhere."[50] The *Post* presented a similar sentiment, more bitterly expressed, from a white mother in suburban Chevy Chase, Maryland: "They have destroyed the fabric of our schools. . . . I don't care what color the school is. I want my child close by."[51]

Two quotations from *Time* illustrate the other facet of this argument—anger over disruption of a neighborhood's ethnic solidarity. As a white community leader in Boston put it, "We are not violent and racist. But we are fiercely loyal to our community. . . . Now we've got to give it all up, everything we've worked years for."[52] A Chicago parent was even pithier: "Busing means the destruction of our neighborhoods, and we're going to fight for our survival."[53]

Quality Education. The argument that busing would impair educational quality received scant attention. It ranked last in coverage at the *New York Times,* sixth at the *Washington Post,* and fifth at CBS. Its share ranged from a low of 5 percent at the *Times* to a high of only 9 percent at the *Post.* The latter reported that two white parents were transferring their child to a private school in the face of a busing plan, because "they are afraid the quality of education may deteriorate at Chevy Chase."[54] Similarly, CBS gave an angry Florida parent the opportunity to say that, because of busing, "the quality of education has gone right out the window."[55] To cite one more exception to the generally low coverage, *Time* provided a more detailed portrait of educational problems in one city:

> Horror stories about life in the city's public schools have increased since 1974, when a local commission announced that deteriorating schools were "the most serious problem facing the city." While attempting to measure the abilities of students, Stanford University sociologist Sanford Dornbusch reported that he found 62% of the black male students four years behind whites in reading ability by the tenth grade. Many students were unable to read Dornbusch's questionnaire. Fearing that busing their children will only bring them more poor education, some blacks and many Chinese have joined whites in bitter resistance to busing.[56]

This argument also produced a rare instance of negative spin, a score of −17 at *Time*. For example, a 1974 article on Boston argued that busing's negative impact paled before the general inadequacy of the school system. Even without busing, the article concluded, "quality education" was a misnomer for what passed for schooling in South Boston: "As long as [substandard schools like South Boston High] exist, neither blacks bused in to them from the ghettos nor the whites who already attend them will have a chance for a decent education."[57]

Violence. Of all seven arguments coded, concern about crime and violence in the schools ranked last in coverage at the *Post* and sixth at *Time* and CBS. At the *New York Times,* it was clustered with four other arguments receiving about equal attention. The amount of coverage accorded this argument ranged from a high of 13 percent at the *New York Times,* to half that amount at *Time* and CBS, and less than 1 percent at the *Washington Post.*

One of the few *Post* stories that raised this issue concerned a suburban Louisville mother who refused to allow her daughter to be bused to an inner city school. The article quoted her as saying, "Our two kids went to Parkland Jr. High School when we lived in the city. We had plenty of trouble there, trouble with discipline, trouble with fights. . . . I wasn't going to have my kids go to a school like that so we moved out here."[58]

Two brief segments from *Time* stories illustrate other ways in which this argument was voiced. One reported on a 1976 U.S. Civil Rights Commission study that "frankly conceded that disciplinary problems have markedly increased in many of the desegregated schools, with a disproportionate number of minority youngsters subject to disciplinary measures, often suspensions and expulsion."[59] Another let a white Boston student speak for himself: "How can you learn anything if you're afraid of being stabbed?"[60]

Overall, though, such assertions occurred infrequently. Moreover, this argument was notable as the only one the media consistently failed to present as believable. On the spin index, it scored —17 at the *New York Times,* zero at both the *Washington Post* and CBS, and +5 at *Time.* For example, a CBS story focused on anti-busing sentiment in Pontiac, Michigan. First, the leader of a parents' anti-busing group said busing was promoting violence in the schools. The reporter then rebutted this argument by citing school statistics attesting to a dramatic drop in violent incidents. The reporter concluded, "The kids have learned to forget racial hatred."[61] The broadcast not only refuted the school violence argument, but also implied that racial hatred was the real reason behind anti-busing sentiment.

A *New York Times* report on Boston illustrates a different type of refutation. Rather than citing statistics, the reporter adopted an anecdotal approach:

Over the back fences these days, Hyde Park mothers are trading tales of crime and rape in black Mattapan, although there is plenty of crime in Hyde Park. "I wouldn't even drive through that section," said [Fran Onishuk]. . . . If Mrs. Onishuk visited

Mattapan, she would probably be surprised to find that much
of the area is not unlike her own neighborhood. She would see
young black fathers trimming hedges and painting the shutters
of small shingled houses and happy black children cycling and
rushing off to Boy Scout meetings.[62]

Coverage Over Time. There were three distinct periods in the
coverage of pro- and anti-busing arguments. The first period,
1970–73, was dominated by pro-busing arguments generally and
especially concern over equal education. The second period, 1974–
75, showed an increasing number of anti-busing themes, particularly that of white flight. The decade's latter years, 1976–79,
showed both a general drop-off in coverage and a resurgence of
pro-busing themes. Of themes that persisted throughout the decade, the equal education argument almost continually dominated
coverage, followed by images of racial harmony. The only anti-
busing theme to emerge in more than one medium and time period
was white flight.

From 1970 to 1973, equal education was the major concern at
every media outlet. During these early years, the theme of racial
harmony placed second among arguments reported at *Time* and
the *New York Times.* Anti-busing arguments broke into the top
ranks only sporadically, at the *Washington Post* and CBS. At the
Post, white flight emerged as the second most heavily covered
theme during 1972–73. At CBS, the argument favoring local
schools was the second most heavily covered during 1970–71.
Many parents were shown objecting to busing not because of race
but because they wanted their children to attend neighborhood
schools.

It was not until the middle 1970s that anti-busing themes
threatened to dominate major media coverage. During 1974–75,
coverage of white flight surged ahead of equal education themes
at the *Washington Post.* Meanwhile, the fear of crime or violence
in the schools became the number one argument at the *New York
Times,* followed by coverage of white flight. Even during this
turbulent period, however, equal education and racial harmony
remained the themes most often covered by *Time* and CBS. During

the latter half of the decade, these pro-busing themes reasserted themselves everywhere, even as total coverage dropped sharply.

Thus, the upsurge of anti-busing arguments proved brief and partial. The predominant argument was always the portrayal of busing as the only means of assuring educational equality. Coverage of the claim that busing would eventually yield racial harmony was nearly as pervasive. None of the anti-busing arguments attained such consistent media attention. Concern over white flight came closest, but busing began to fade from the media agenda soon after this argument became newsworthy. Moreover, the decline of pro-busing themes in 1974 and 1975 proved a temporary hiatus. They dominated the discussion at all outlets at the decade's end, as they had at the outset.

Summary. Our examination of busing arguments focused on the main ideas that pro- and anti-busing advocates used to make their case. The case for busing centered on arguments that it was necessary to give minority students equal educational opportunity, to promote racial harmony, and to improve the achievement levels of minority students. Opponents claimed that busing would cause a decline in the quality of education, weaken neighborhood solidarity and community schools, and promote racial tension or violence, jeopardizing the safety of school children. Later, they argued that busing was causing whites to abandon the public school system, leading to resegregation.

All four media outlets gave somewhat more coverage to the pro-busing arguments, especially the theme of educational equality. Among anti-busing arguments, white flight received the most attention. By contrast, claims of increased tension and violence received the least coverage of all arguments. Moreover, the violence argument was the only one with a predominantly negative spin. Thus, anti-busing arguments received not only less coverage but also less credence than pro-busing ones.

The findings also argue against one fashionable interpretation of media coverage—the "bad news bias," or the notion that news coverage of any public policy issue will be predominantly critical, negative, or anti-establishment in tone. The media not only tended to affirm the value of busing, despite widespread public opposition to it, they also tended to affirm any argument they presented. So we did not find much negativity, either with regard to busing policy or as a general structural principle. When it came to busing, the media were anything but nattering nabobs of negativism. Instead, our studies show they tended to accentuate the positive and eliminate the negative.

Activities

Important as they are, the arguments are only one part of the busing story. Much of the coverage described not the debates but the activities associated with busing. The activities that were described provided a framework for understanding and evaluating the causes, implementation, and outcomes of busing plans. Therefore, we examined the descriptive side of media coverage as well.

Most activities related to busing could be catalogued into three major groups—legal, political, and school related. Legal activities referred to any court decisions, orders, or other litigation procedures. We distinguished among four types of political action: official, grassroots, nonviolent protest, and violent protest.[63] The third major group of activities concerned the functioning or disruption of school operations. Under this major heading were three categories—normal school routine, disruptive incidents, and police security.[64] Finally, other material such as descriptions of city life or historical backgrounds were grouped together in a residual category.

As Table 15 shows, the media treated busing primarily as a political story and only secondarily as a legal story. Their coverage belied traditional criticism of the news for emphasizing conflict, disruption, and violence. Instead, they stressed the "establishment" side of the story, focusing on official political and legal activity, rather than populist dissent or violence. Coverage of school activities also stressed normalcy rather than disruption.

The media by no means ignored the violence that erupted in such major trouble spots as Boston and Louisville. As a proportion of overall coverage, however, violence and protest received relatively little attention. The one exception to this pattern was

Table 15—Media Coverage of Busing Activities

Activity	New York Times	Time	Washington Post	CBS
Political				
Official	42%	15%	41%	36%
Grassroots	3	*	5	4
Nonviolent Protest	4	17	5	10
Violent Protest	*	6	1	7
School				
School Routine	9	18	3	20
Racial/Violent Incidents	*	3	2	0
Police/Security	5	14	1	5
Legal	21	15	17	17
Other	16	12	25	1
Total:	100%	100%	100%	100%
Amount Coded	3,691"	1,004"	1,209"	282

*less than 1 percent

Time, which emphasized protest, school disruption, and police security activities more than the other outlets.

Legal. Legal activities, such as court decisions, laid the groundwork for the busing controversy. Yet, most legal reporting focused on the impact of court decisions rather than the reasoning behind legal debates. The media had difficulty explaining the subtleties and technical details of legal behavior. Instead, court decisions usually were portrayed as stimuli that produced significant consequences. Ironically, the arena where busing arguments developed generated the most formulaic and least diversified coverage.

Given their importance, legal activities claimed a modest amount of space at all four outlets, ranging from only 15 percent at *Time* to 21 percent at the *New York Times*. Even the types of legal activities described had similar proportions of coverage at the various outlets, e.g., court findings of segregation, busing remedies proposed, appellate decisions promoting or limiting busing, administrative actions, and so forth. Coverage of legal activities often focused on major court decisions involving busing. On television such stories were often restricted to brief summaries read by anchors. They focused narrowly on the decision itself with little or no attention to the legal reasoning behind a given ruling. **Political.** By far the most coverage of busing focused on official political activities. This facet of the busing story predominated at every outlet except *Time*, where several activities received about equal attention. Elsewhere it dwarfed coverage of every other activity, receiving about twice as much attention as all legal issues. Coverage often focused on federal legislation to ban busing or diminish its impact, as well as official pronouncements and reactions to busing controversies in particular locales. State and local officials also received extensive coverage, as politicians, state agencies, and local school boards grappled over court-ordered busing plans.

Other political activities received surprisingly little coverage. Grassroots activities, such as petitions and referenda, received from 1 to 5 percent of the coverage at these outlets. Protest also attracted scant attention, especially at the newspapers. The *New York Times* gave only 4 percent of its coverage to nonviolent protest, and less than 1 percent to violent protest. At the *Washington Post*, the figures were 5 and 1 percent, respectively. It is almost a truism that television emphasizes conflict and violence more than print media, and CBS did give proportionately about twice as much attention as the newspapers to nonviolent protest, 10 percent of its total activity coverage. The network also devoted the most attention of all outlets to violent protest. Yet that amounted to only 7 percent of its coverage.

Nonetheless, CBS was not the most protest-oriented outlet in our study. That distinction belonged to *Time*, which devoted fully one-sixth of its coverage to nonviolent protest, and an additional 6 percent to violent protest. The magazine was the only outlet that gave more coverage to protest than to official political activity.

Indeed, no other outlet devoted even half as much coverage to grassroots protest as to official activity.

Especially interesting in light of *Time*'s relatively heavy coverage of violence was its criticism of other media for playing down violent activities associated with busing. In a 1975 story, *Time* rebuked the Louisville, Kentucky, media for ignoring an incident when police fired on a motorist, because they "had adopted a set of voluntary guidelines . . . to prevent an exacerbation of tension." The article noted that one local paper "finally printed the story last week only after *Time* started checking on it."[65]

In sum, media coverage stressed official political activities over grassroots actions and the disruptions of both violent and nonviolent protest. The total of all these extra-institutional political activities accounted for only one-sixth as much space as official activity reported in the *New York Times,* one-fourth of that in the *Post,* and just over one-half at CBS. *Time*'s coverage was a notable exception to this trend.

School Activities. The media focused on the least disruptive elements of busing not only in the political realm, but also in describing school activities. School routine predominated, very few violent or racial incidents at school were reported, and only *Time* gave much coverage to police security activities. CBS did not have a single story among those coded on disruptive school incidents, and the *New York Times* gave it little more—less than 1 percent of its total activity coverage. Such incidents accounted for only 2 percent of the coverage at the *Post* and 3 percent at *Time.*

In contrast, all media outlets gave heavy emphasis to routine school activities. CBS devoted one-fifth of its coverage to school routine, four times the coverage given to all reminders of disruptive incidents and security measures. For example, in 1975 a CBS correspondent reported that, after a year of busing in Denver, fears of disruption were "unfounded," while pictures of children doing lessons in the classroom were flashed on the screen.[66]

Eighteen percent of *Time*'s coverage was devoted to routine school activities. At the *New York Times,* it was half that, but still almost twice as much as the coverage given school incidents and police security. At the *Post,* only 3 percent of the coverage was of school routine, but the amount given to incidents and security was a fraction lower still. So the dominant impression was one of normalcy, with less attention given to the negative impact of busing on the everyday functioning of the schools.

A 1976 *Washington Post* vignette illustrates how routine school activities can provide a framework for showing just how well busing could work:

> Last Thursday morning on the Silver Spring streets around Rosemary Hills Elementary School, two Montgomery County school buses rumbled by in opposite directions.
>
> In one bus sat Kevin Washington, a wary Rosemary Hills fourth grader who had joined 15 others to visit Larchmont Elementary . . . as part of a desegregation plan . . . Kevin began to smile as his future classmates jovially pummelled each other and asked him about Rosemary Hills sports.
>
> In the other bus Stephen Berkeley . . . who will be sent to Rosemary Hills this fall, spent most of the bus trip laughing uproariously and sitting on a classmate.
>
> Two months after the Montgomery County school board approved its controversial grade level reorganization to desegregate mostly black Rosemary Hills, these two boys are taking it in stride. Kevin . . . said of Larchmont afterward: "I think it was nice." Stephen . . . had announced to his mother the day before: "I'm going to like it when I get there."[67]

Coverage Over Time. In both its early and later phases, coverage at all outlets except *Time* was dominated by reports of official political activities and, secondarily, school routine. The *New York Times* and CBS gave the most coverage to these two types of activities throughout the decade. At the *Post,* official political activities always predominated, though the second-ranked story changed from year to year.

Time started out in lockstep with the other outlets, covering primarily the doings of officialdom and school routine. But then the disruptive activities associated with busing became more of a factor. From 1972 to 1973, nonviolent protest became the second most heavily covered topic there. During 1974 and 1975, nonviolent protest took the top spot, followed by police security. Only at this single media outlet, for this brief period, did the negative side of the busing controversy dominate the coverage. After 1975, coverage of nonviolent protest dropped off at *Time,* while school routine became the top story.[68]

Thus, the media's emphasis on normalcy and official channels hardly varied throughout the decade, despite the rapid changes and jagged discontinuities in the events surrounding the busing controversy. Only *Time* gave more or less continuously heavy coverage to protests against busing. Violence and protest were not ignored, but they never dominated the news agenda.

Conclusion: The Media and Busing

The busing story began in the courts and ended in the schools and the streets, with some detours through the corridors of power. For all the weighty constitutional issues that were raised, however, the judicial rationales generally took a back seat to their political implications and their practical impact. There was substantial coverage of court decisions, but the media had difficulty explaining the subtleties and technical details of legal behavior. Typically, the public learned much about the results of a judge's decisions, but far less about the reasoning behind it.

In covering the political side of the story, the media were more at home with the familiar routines of hearings and press conferences than with the grassroots clamor and chaos that often accompanied busing plans. Eruptions of protest and violence were certainly not ignored, but neither did they take over the coverage or set its overall tone. Instead, the disruptive side of the story usually bowed to the "establishment" side represented by official political activities. Inside the schools, the coverage emphasized normalcy and the daily routine rather than the fear or the actuality of disruption and racial incidents. The major newspapers gave especially sparse coverage to protest activities. The most protest-oriented outlet was not a television network, as one might expect, but a weekly newsmagazine. *Time* devoted proportionally four to five times as much of its coverage to protest activities as did the *New York Times* and *Washington Post.*

This discrepancy illustrates a more general point. News organizations had considerable discretion in covering such a long-running and multifaceted story. By focusing on conflict and protest, *Time* broke the mold of coverage that usually emphasized established procedures and the orderly implementation of busing plans. Even during the middle of the 1970s, when ugly conflicts erupted in Boston, Louisville, and elsewhere, only *Time* featured protest ahead of official political activities.

Time's coverage was more than an exception that proved the rule. It was also the exception that disproved the "mirror" theory of media coverage. If events dictated the coverage, if protest got short shrift because it was in short supply, then how do we explain *Time*'s continual emphasis on this side of the story? The answer, of course, is a difference in news agendas, whatever the reasons behind it.

In addition, the busing story did not lend support to the notion that the press follows public opinion. Busing was rejected by overwhelming majorities of whites, as well as substantial minorities of blacks.[69] Yet every media outlet we studied gave a majority of its coverage to arguments in favor of busing. Moreover, anti-busing arguments were the only ones that were ever refuted a majority of the time they appeared.

News media gave particular attention to the argument that busing was necessary to provide equal educational opportunities for minority children. They also gave moderate coverage to claims that busing would improve minority achievement levels and contribute to racial harmony in the long run. Of the major anti-busing arguments, claims of white flight and neighborhood disruption received substantial coverage. Arguments that busing would impair quality education or contribute to school crime and violence largely were ignored.

A separate issue is the credence the media attached to these assertions. As a rule, arguments rarely were refuted. Balanced stories tended to provide arguments from both camps rather than presenting two sides of one argument. Nevertheless, the only arguments to be primarily refuted were those that blamed busing for declining educational quality and rising school crime and violence. These anti-busing arguments, especially the latter, thus received not only the least coverage but the most negative coverage.

The media's presentation of these arguments can also be measured against the scholarly literature on them. The evidence on busing's contribution to racial harmony and improved minority performance is mixed, with substantial data both supporting and contradicting these claims. The equal education argument is a bit more complex. Scholars like Armor and Coleman argued that this theoretical benefit was vitiated by white flight and subsequent resegregation. Yet the media affirmed both the equal education and white flight arguments, despite substantial (if temporary) scholarly controversy over the latter. An explanation for this apparent paradox lies in the media's treatment of white migration as an obstacle but not necessarily an argument against busing. Many stories acknowledged the fact of white flight but not the implication that it undermined the educational equality busing was supposed to provide.

Finally, the unique skepticism attached to warnings of school crime and violence appears unwarranted in light of the scholarly literature. This is a controversial topic, which is attributed to symbolic racism by some scholars but to rational fears and accurate perceptions by others. Although it is no more heated than disputes over minority performance or the implications of white flight for educational equality, the violence argument was unmatched in its negative reception by the media. The implication was that parental opposition to busing on these grounds expressed underlying racist sentiments rather than rational fears for their children's safety. This facet of the coverage was in keeping with a more general tendency to downplay fears or threats of school violence or disruption. Both in the activities covered and the arguments presented, this angle consistently was overshadowed by more positive themes.

This pattern of coverage runs counter to another widespread explanation of media behavior—the bad news bias. We found that the major media often dismissed or reinterpreted the so-called bad news about busing. In both the political arena and the classroom, they emphasized order rather than disorder, established channels for protest rather than spontaneous outbursts, and the importance of the end goal (integration) rather than the weakness of the means (busing). When busing moved north in the mid-1970s, the ensuing social conflict was duly chronicled, though often from the perspective of new obstacles that needed to be overcome. As the adverse consequences of busing continued to escalate, however, the coverage fell off dramatically, and what was left returned to the early themes of official political activities and school routine, equal education and racial harmony.

On the surface, this coverage seems anything but adversarial. On the contrary, it reminds us of the leftist "hegemony" theorists who argue that the American media reinforce the established order and play down the conflict and the discontent that might threaten it. Unfortunately for this line of criticism, the "establishment" being upheld here had itself ordered massive social dislocation in the name of racial justice. Insofar as they supported this effort, the media aligned themselves with the forces of change and against more traditional or conservative elements in American society.

In short, media coverage of busing cannot be explained as either a mirror of reality or a reflection of public opinion. Journalists were neither the purveyors of a bad news bias nor the handmaidens of the conservative establishment. Our impression is that they attempted to act as responsible citizens in helping their country adapt to reforms that were, in their view, necessary and long overdue, despite the short-term conflict and disruption. Thus, their coverage may reflect not mass opinion but the enlightened opinion of liberal intellectuals in universities, think tanks, and federal courtrooms.

The history of major media involvement in racial issues should also be considered. A decade earlier, many leading journalists cut their teeth on the long-running story of the civil rights movement. They brought tales of racial injustice in the South to the attention of the nation and helped speed social reform. Is it any wonder that

252

they should treat busing as an extension of the same story, to be covered from the same angle, as a struggle for justice against entrenched forces of racism and ignorance?

This was less a matter of advocacy journalism than an accumulation of ordinary daily decisions—what events to cover and how to explain them, what arguments to present and when to seek out the other side. Such decisions, as we have seen, are filtered through the perspectives and motivations of even the most professional journalist. Perhaps without anyone's conscious intention, the collective result was to emphasize the benefits of busing a bit more than the costs, to focus on the successes a bit more than the failures. Eventually, as the problems multiplied and the answers seemed less and less certain, the response was to move on to other, less troubling stories.

LOOKING FOR J.R.

"GAO Study Asserts That Oil Companies
Worsened Shortage"

—*New York Times,* September 14, 1979

"GAO Says Oil Firms Aren't To Be Blamed for
Recent Shortage"

—*Wall Street Journal,* September 14, 1979

THE GUEST speaker was a former network correspondent now working for a multinational oil company. The audience of college students, familiar with his previous occupation, could only be disillusioned by his current job. So he took the bull by the horns. He began, "I want to tell you right up front that I work for an oil company now." He capitalized the next words with his hands and eyebrows: "That's BIG OIL. As in ORGANIZED CRIME."

Such defensiveness is understandable, in light of public attitudes toward the oil business. Since the energy crises of the 1970s, suspicion and hostility toward the oil industry have far outweighed any antipathy Americans feel toward big business in general. One study found that, out of twenty-three national polls comparing various industries since 1976, the oil industry drew the most negative ratings fifteen times. In several other polls, petroleum finished barely ahead of tobacco as the public's least favorite industry. The oil industry was chosen most often as too big and powerful, having high profits, not open and frank, uninterested in its customers' well-being, and unwilling to balance profits with the public interest.[1]

The view of the oil companies as a monopolistic and profit-rich industry dates from the days of John D. Rockefeller's Standard Oil Trust. Despite increasing government regulation and the new power of the OPEC countries, criticism and distrust of the industry became more widespread than ever during the 1970s. As oil prices and profits rose dramatically, the case against the oil companies was strengthened in the eyes of the public.

The populist tradition in American politics, in part a reaction to the Standard Trust, was bolstered by the experiences of the late 1960s and early 1970s. Distrust of both government and business became commonplace with the revelations of Watergate, illegal campaign contributions, and corporate bribery abroad. Following the oil embargo of 1973, news stories on the industry, which previously had been confined to newspapers' financial sections, began to appear on front pages and nightly broadcasts. In this climate, the oil companies became a natural focus of public and media scrutiny.

Public concern has focused on three major topics: the high degree of industry concentration or monopoly, the level of profits, and the manipulation of supply to maintain high prices. These three issues are closely linked in economic theory. For example, monopolistic control of a market allows a single producer to manipulate supply to maintain artificially high prices. This creates "excess" profits beyond those obtained in a competitive market.

This study will first examine each of these topics, in light of the evidence provided by academic and other technical studies. Then it will look at how the national media have covered the same issues.

"Obscene" Profits

Critics have long held that the oil industry's high degree of concentration earned companies excess profits. This charge did not evoke popular concern or attention prior to the 1973 oil embargo. Throughout the 1950s and 1960s, oil prices remained low and relatively stable in the United States. For example, in 1950 the average retail price for regular gasoline was twenty cents per gallon. By 1972, the price had risen to only twenty-five cents per gallon. Corrected for inflation, this actually represents a decline of nearly 30 percent. Crude oil prices followed similar trends during this period.[2]

Throughout the 1950s and 1960s, production of domestic oil was increasing, and supplies were viewed as ample for the foreseeable future. By the early 1970s, however, the trends in supply and demand began to move in the opposite direction. Demand increased as a result of economic expansion following the Vietnam War, increasing gasoline use, and new environmental regulations that encouraged a shift from coal to oil. At the same time, oil production in both the United States and Canada peaked and then declined. By 1972, most people involved in the oil industry realized that shortages were a real possibility. The United States had become a net importer of oil, relying on the Arab countries for 1.2 million barrels per day by 1973.

Then, between October 1973 and January 1974, the OPEC countries raised the price of crude oil almost fourfold, from $3.00 to $11.65 per barrel. A simultaneous embargo on shipments to the United States reduced OPEC-supplied oil by 98 percent. This amounted to a 7.4 percent drop in total U.S. supply, which exacerbated the price increases still further.[3]

The public had just recovered from this onslaught when the oil companies' 1973 earnings reports were released. During the third quarter of 1973, Exxon's profits increased 80 percent over the same quarter of 1972, Gulf's earnings rose 91 percent, and other companies posted increases of similar magnitudes.[4] Faced with a public uproar, industry spokesmen argued that the high profits were deceptive. They asserted that, first, 1972 had been a particularly bad year for them, so that 1973 profits appeared large by comparison. Second, the dollar was devalued in 1973, increasing the value of foreign investments denominated in other currencies. Third, rapid inflation had artificially boosted profit reports. Finally,

OPEC's quadrupling of oil prices sharply increased the value of oil company inventories and reserves.

Industry explanations fell largely on deaf ears, as continuing increases of prices and profits stirred public ire and congressional investigations. Yet the issue is by no means clear-cut. Financial analysts have long regarded the oil industry as one of the more complex segments of the economy. To assess the arguments over "obscene" profits, we will review some major studies of industry profits.

To understand the issues involved, we must first discuss the concept and measurement of profitability. In accounting terms, profits are the net income of a business after operating expenses, capital costs, and taxes have been subtracted. Net income is an absolute amount. However, profits can also be measured as a relative amount. A reported increase in profits gains new meaning with reference to the investment, sales, or asset base necessary to produce the profit. A firm may enjoy an increase in profits while retaining a profit *rate* equal to or lower than that of the previous year, due to changes in the firm's net worth. Therefore, in our discussion, the profit rate will be variously referred to as the return on owner's equity, net assets, or net worth.

One element of the industry's defense concerned the effects of inflation on profits. The rapid inflation of the 1970s resulted in dramatic increases in the profit rates of most industries. To some extent, however, these increases were illusory, due to the effects of inflation on traditional accounting methods. Goods valued at lower "historical" or original costs were sold at higher inflated prices. This created the appearance of a substantial increase in earnings. However, this profit was only temporary, for the inventory had to be replaced at the higher current and future costs. Inflation also distorts the calculation of depreciation allowances and the estimation of net worth.[5] Moreover, like consumer incomes, corporate earnings suffer a loss of real purchasing power due to inflation.

The dramatic impact of inflation on profits is illustrated by Commerce Department studies.[6] Corporate earnings in 1978, for example, indicated an average increase of 17 percent from the 1977 figures. The Commerce Department's adjustments for inventory gains reduced this increase to less than 3 percent. Yet even this gain was expressed in current dollars. Expressed in constant dollars this 3 percent increase actually became a 4 percent decrease. Finally, the increased business volume in 1978 masked what First National City Bank (FNCB) estimated as a real per-unit decrease of 9 percent.[7] Similar results were obtained by economist George Terborgh in a study of 1976 corporate profits.[8] For the oil companies these findings have a special significance. The OPEC price increases distorted inventory holdings in the same way as inflation. The increases clearly represented a windfall for the companies. On the other hand, their stocks had to be replenished at higher prices.[9]

Although charges of excess profits first attracted widespread attention in the early 1970s, it is useful to evaluate the industry's performance over a longer period to capture the long-term trends. If oil companies enjoy excess profits by virtue of their market control, their profits should be consistently higher than those for other industries. One of the most reliable sources of information on oil company profitability is the annual corporate earnings survey prepared by the FNCB.[10] These data reveal that oil industry profit rates are comparable to the so-called normal rate of profit for industry since 1950, as expressed by the average rate for all U.S. manufacturing industries. The profit rate for the petroleum industry was just over 1 percent above the average for all manufacturing industries during the early 1950s. From 1955 through 1969, however, it was usually less than the overall average. The oil industry recovered in the 1970s, with an average profit of less than 1 percent above that of all manufacturing industries. During the thirty-year period from 1950 through 1979, yearly profits of the petroleum companies finished above the average for manufacturing industries fifteen times and below average fifteen times.

One can also compare profitability in a somewhat different fashion, by ranking the oil industry's profit margin against that of other major industries. A Senate Finance Committee report ranked the profitability of twenty-five industries from 1963 through 1972, based on FNCB data.[11] During that entire decade just prior to the energy crisis, the oil industry averaged fourteenth in profits out of the twenty-five. It dropped as low as eighteenth in the yearly ratings and rose as high as eighth place.

Comparable data from FNCB reports for the 1973 through 1979 period show that the first oil shock in 1974 rocketed petroleum to the second-best profit margin of all industries listed. Then, in 1979, for the only time in the seventeen-year period, the oil industry claimed the top position, with profits reaching a postwar high of nearly 23 percent. Those two years, however, were the exception. In three of the four years between the two oil crises, the industry ranked sixteenth or lower. As a result, its average profit ranking for the 1973–79 period rose to ninth place among the twenty-five industries cited.

The Senate Finance Committee also contrasted the profitability of oil and gas producers (i.e., crude production only) with that of the integrated companies (i.e., those dealing with all aspects of production). The integrated firms (both international and domestic), such as Mobil and Exxon, had consistently lower profit rates than the crude producers.[12] The four largest integrated companies, however, have been consistently more profitable than their smaller integrated competitors. The difference was usually 2 or 3 percent and never exceeded 4 percent prior to 1974.

Why were the largest integrated companies more profitable? Several factors may come into play. First, the four largest companies are international firms, while many of the others are domestic. International companies have historically earned a higher rate of profit due to the lower cost of foreign oil (prior to 1973) and price controls on the domestically drilled product. Second, they also enjoy certain tax advantages. Third, the larger firms in any industry should exhibit higher profit rates due to economies of scale resulting from the size of their operations and their greater efficiency in production. Thus, they are better able to utilize the advantages enjoyed by all integrated companies.[13]

A second source of information on oil company earnings is provided by Shyam Sunder's survey of industry profits from 1961 to 1975.[14] Sunder used both equity- and value-weighted measures of profitability. An equity-weighted measure gives equal statistical weight to each firm, regardless of size. A value-weighted measure weighs the data from each firm in proportion to its relative importance in the industry. In his survey, the true measure of profitability for the entire industry lies somewhere between the two.

As with the FNCB study, Sunder's data indicate that petroleum industry profitability was below average from 1962 to 1969. From 1970 to 1971, it was above average, only to fall again in 1972 to 1973. In 1973, the rate of profit increased sharply, peaking in 1974 and then dropping just as sharply in 1975, although remaining above the average for other industries. The overall 1961 to 1975 average profit rates for oil vs. all other industries were 10.3 percent vs. 10.4 percent (equity-weighted) and 11.9 percent vs. 12.0 percent (value-weighted). The similarity between the figures suggests, again, that profitability for the oil companies was no greater than that of other industries. Sunder concluded that the sharp increase in profits occasioned by OPEC price increases permitted the oil companies to make up for nearly a decade of lower than average profits during the 1960s.

Several economists have commented on the problems of comparing the accounting data of different companies.[15] As an alternative to accounting calculations, Sunder examined a variety of stock market–based measures of profit. Although not without problems, market-based measures permit adjustments for risk differentials and eliminate some difficulties of data interpretation. The element of risk is reflected in the market price of a stock. The price changes in response to how investors perceive the industry's performance and future prospects. Sunder concluded that the oil industry's performance was better than average for firms listed in the New York Stock Exchange. However, he cautioned against "placing too much confidence" in these results because of the industry's "high volatility."[16]

Edward J. Mitchell also examined oil industry profits using a stock market–based measure.[17] He calculated the profits of oil company common stockholders and compared this rate of return with that of the *Standard and Poor 500 Stock Composite Index.* During the 1953–72 period, Mitchell found that none of the twenty-one domestic oil companies equalled the *Standard and*

Poor 500's rate of return. In fact, after 1960, these producers earned less than half that. Finally, the eight internationals earned an average return of more than 20 percent below the Standard and Poor index for 1953–72.

Overall, these data on oil industry profitability show no evidence of a sustained high rate of profit above the average level for United States manufacturing industries. They do indicate, however, that the profitability of the integrated international companies has at times exceeded that of other types of oil companies. Whether a certain level of profit is appropriate or "obscene" is a political judgment, not an economic one. Economic analysis shows only that oil industry profitability has not been unusually high over the long term, despite windfall profits from the energy crisis.

The "Oilogopoly"

Is the oil industry an oligopoly, in which a few large firms control the production, refining, transport, or marketing of oil?[18] Without question, the large multinational, integrated firms have long wielded great power in the world oil market. By the same token, however, their power is not as extensive as it once was. These "Seven Sisters" did control the world market for oil in the pre–World War II period. In 1953, the Justice Department filed the International Petroleum Cartel suit against five companies for allegedly conspiring to fix prices and withhold supply. It took no further action until 1968, when the suit against one of the companies was dismissed. Eventually, the government decided not to prosecute. This decision reflected the international expansion of independent producers and refiners and the imposition of import quotas for foreign oil in 1959. But such decisions inevitably reflect political concerns. What do the economic analyses show?

The degree of oil industry concentration can be measured in terms of either the ease of market entry or the percentage of market shares controlled by the leading firms. Market entry may be hindered by a variety of barriers. These include structural barriers, such as the special technical knowledge needed for production, high entry costs, and large economies of scale. Other barriers can result from government policies, international politics, circumstances of the time, or anticompetitive industry practices. The oil industry exhibits each of these potential barriers to some degree. In practice, though, they may not prohibit the entry of new firms.

Thus, a House Committee on Banking and Currency staff report found that the number of companies operating in the Middle East grew steadily from eight in 1940 to nearly a hundred in 1974.[19] These figures refer only to the increase in producing companies. In other areas of the industry, the entrance of new firms was equally pronounced. Economist Neil Jacoby reports that between 1953 and 1972 ". . . more than three hundred private companies and more than fifty different government owned companies entered the foreign oil industry *de novo* or significantly expanded their participation in it."[20]

John Blair, one of the industry's foremost critics, rejects the view that entrance opportunities for independents expanded over the years. According to Blair, "Opportunities for the entrance of newcomers have from time to time made their appearance. But, generally speaking, the efforts of newcomers to gain a viable foothold have either been frustrated, or, if initially successful, short-lived."[21]

Blair supports his argument with numerous case studies. Nonetheless, the overall industry trend seems to suggest increased participation by additional firms.[22] After World War II, the number of firms increased in all segments of the industry (i.e., production, refining, transport, and marketing/distribution). The new firms did not specialize in any particular segment. The largest increase, however, was in the area of production and exploration.

These changes reflect the emerging preference of host governments for a variety of concessionaires. Producing countries became reluctant to award oil development rights to a few large firms, as they sought a more influential role in developing their natural resources. The original practice of granting long-term concessions to the Seven Sisters had political origins. It reflected their entry into the Middle East when European countries still maintained colonial relationships with the host governments.

Advances in petroleum technology also encouraged competition. Innovations such as catalytic reforming made it possible for small-scale companies to compete with the larger firms.[23] Finally, postwar increases in demand, as Europe rebuilt and the developing nations embarked on ambitious modernization programs, made investment opportunities brighter.

A second measure of industrial concentration is the degree of the market controlled by the largest firms. Jacoby found that the combined market share for the four largest firms (the usual measure) averaged 40 percent for all U.S. manufacturing industries in 1970. In the oil industry, the top four firms had 27 percent of crude oil production, 35 percent of crude oil sales, 34 percent of gasoline-refining capacity, and 30 percent of gasoline sales. Nor did any one firm hover over the others. The largest was Exxon, which accounted for 12 percent of crude oil reserves and about 9 percent of both crude production and refining capacity.[24] Jacoby rated oil industry concentration "low" at the four-firm level and "moderately low" at the eight-firm level.[25]

The level of concentration had declined significantly in the years preceding the energy crisis. During 1953–72, Seven Sisters on-paper control of concession areas declined from 64 percent to only 24 percent of the market. Their control of proven reserves dropped from 92 to 67 percent, and their refining capacity was cut from 73 to 49 percent.[26] In the domestic oil industry during this period, the degree of concentration remained relatively stable. For example, in 1965 the eight largest firms accounted for 39 percent of total production. Their share rose to 42 percent by 1974. Their refining capacity constituted 53 percent of the total in both years.[27]

The largest firms did increase or maintain their shares in both production and refining from 1965 to 1974. Equally significant, though, was the emergence of the independent refiner after 1965. Independents are absent from domestic production partly because there are few new areas suitable for production in the United States. The newly leased areas tend to be offshore or in such inhospitable environments as Alaska's North Slope. Smaller companies often lack the financial and technical resources for these operations. It was in crude production that the independents made their greatest inroads into the foreign market. In the international market there was a decline in concentration of crude production during this period.

Many oil industry analysts support the view that concentration ratios have declined over the past thirty years.[28] However, some critics, notably Walter Adams, Joel Dirlam, and Walter Measday, contend that the ratios are increasing. The apparent contradiction stems from the specific ratios used by each group. The critics base their argument on a Federal Trade Commission (FTC) report indicating that the eight largest companies accounted for almost as large a share of North American crude production in 1973 as did the largest twenty firms in 1955.[29] Other analysts argue that concentration ratios have increased in the domestic market because producers have given up concessions that are no longer profitable. Domestic production has been declining since the early 1970s, as have reserves since the early 1960s. Concentration will increase as fewer companies are left with profitable holdings.

Finally, economic opinion on this issue has been examined systematically. In 1975, Barbara Hobbie polled academic economists and journalists on their attitudes toward charges of oil industry monopoly and proposals for divestiture.[30] The economists she surveyed had testified before congressional committees or published extensively on oil economics; the journalists were mostly editors from large-circulation newspapers and periodicals.

Hobbie found that 76 percent of these economists rejected the charge that the major oil companies possess monopoly power in any stage of the oil business. By contrast, 54 percent of the journalists agreed with this allegation. As to specific operations, Hobbie concluded, "in all cases—production, refining, marketing, tankers, pipelines, and other energy areas—the economists perceived fewer monopoly problems than did the journalists."[31]

On the broader question of whether the major integrated companies "make it difficult" for independent companies to compete, two out of three economists (67 percent) disagreed, while two out of three journalists (68 percent) agreed. Finally, a majority of economists agreed that there was a "consensus among economic experts" against divestiture. Only a third of the journalists saw it that way.

Overall, this survey of economists, like the concentration comparisons over time and across industries, offers little support for the current portrayal of petroleum as a monopolistic or oligopolistic industry. On the other hand, this image was more appropriate in the pre–World War II era, and case studies demonstrate that anticompetitive structures and practices have existed in particular instances.

We have not evaluated the argument that the vital nature of the oil industry demands stricter criteria in deciding what level of concentration harms the public interest. This is a matter of social philosophy rather than purely economic analysis. We conclude only that current concentration rates in the oil industry do not diverge markedly from those in other manufacturing industries.

Manipulating Supply

Of all charges levied against the oil companies, that of manipulating supply is the most defensible. Throughout the industry's history, the companies have always tried to control the supply of oil on the market at any given time. In response, it may be argued that their efforts partly stem from the technical nature of production, the uncertainty of supply over the long term, and the disruptive effects of new and unexpected sources for oil on its price.

Although the cost of drilling oil is low compared to its historical selling price, the industry must always search for new sources of supply. Since oil is an exhaustible resource, the risk of an unsuccessful search increases over time. In addition, costs of drilling are initially high, drop after pumping begins, but then increase along with output. As each barrel is pumped from a well, declining well pressure makes the recovery of the next barrel more expensive. The rate of pumping the oil also affects the cost. The faster the rate of exploitation, the quicker costs increase. The storage costs of excess supplies are also quite high. Thus, any new supplies are generally put on the market. Each company must be constantly on the lookout for new sources of supply lest its competitors get the jump on it. So each company also runs the risk that new supplies will be found before the market has expanded sufficiently to absorb them.[32]

One solution to these problems would be for each company to produce only enough to meet its current needs. This was made impossible, however, by the property rights in the original major producing country, the United States. Here the right to exploit underground resources belongs to the owner of the surface land. Oil pools, unfortunately, do not conform to the shape of individual ownership plots. By the time the oil boom hit the lucrative Texas oil fields in the early twentieth century, the land had already been divided among individual owners. Since large pools could be drilled successfully with only one well, producers sought to economize on land costs by leasing the smallest plot possible.

The law of capture ruled that the oil in any given field (often several hundred square miles) belonged to the individual who pumped it out. Therefore, each producer sought to pump as much oil as possible from a common pool shared with rivals. Rational pumping by an individual only ensured that oil would be drained off by competitors. As new supplies flooded the market, each producer tried to dispose of his portion as quickly as possible in order to pump more. Prices dropped drastically, forcing many producers into bankruptcy. This is what gave the industry its early boom-or-bust character. Federal antitrust regulations prevented producers from banding together to control supply.

In the 1920s, after the discoveries of vast oil resources in the Middle East, the host governments retained the right to lease all underground resources. Fearful of overproduction, the Middle East producing companies formed a cartel to control the potential surplus. Each agreed to refrain from competition in markets already supplied by another cartel partner. Excess supplies, beyond those needed in existing markets, were pumped only for new markets or those supplied by noncartel companies. By 1932, all future Seven Sisters companies except one had become participants in this cartel. They engaged in various anticompetitive practices aimed at maintaining their market domination and controlling independent companies' access to refiners and marketers.[33]

The specter of cheap Middle East oil flooding the U.S. market prompted domestic producers to seek a solution to their own problems of supply. Thus, producing states of the Southwest formed an interstate compact that limited each state to producing no more oil than it had in 1928. The individual states would then ration their allotments among producers operating within their borders. In time, this so-called pro-rationing scheme came to focus solely on maintaining prices.

These practices severely restricted free competition. The operation of the cartel during the 1930s enabled the Seven Sisters to maintain higher than average profit rates, since the price of oil always far exceeded its true costs. However, it can also be argued that production restrictions served consumer interests as well. If a well is drilled too quickly, the ultimate amount of recoverable reserves decreases. The production quotas thus encouraged rational exploitation of the well and kept costs down.

The international cartel operated throughout the 1930s. It was informally abandoned with the approach of World War II and never re-established. After the war, the international companies did not need the cartel, for its provisions had become internalized by each company as customary operating procedures. In addition, successful national cartels had developed. There was tacit acceptance of the companies' common interest in controlling supply.

Throughout the 1950s and 1960s, the increase in world demand for oil laid to rest most fears of overproduction. The old fears were raised again by increased competition from the independents and demands of the host countries for more rapid production to increase their tax and royalty payments. But the changing structure of the world oil market in the late 1960s prevented new supply problems.

After 1965, growth of demand for oil exceeded growth of supply. The Texas oilfields were reaching their productive peaks and would soon begin to decline. Thus, the pro-rationing scheme ceased to have any meaning for price maintenance. Instead, price controls on domestic oil were used to keep expensive Texas oil competitive with Middle East oil. Oil import quotas, in effect from 1959 until April 1973, were also partly designed to protect the domestic oil industry. By limiting the amount of foreign oil that could be imported into the United States, the government ensured the market shares of the domestic producers. Had foreign oil been freely imported during this period, prices for oil products would have been lower.

Thus, until 1973, domestic and international producers did actively manipulate the supply of oil, in order to increase and stabilize its price. Critics point to such practices as price squeezing, denial of supplies, and production manipulation. Since the OPEC oil embargo of 1973, however, control of supply has mostly passed from the oil companies to the producing countries.

Nonetheless, concerns over industry manipulation persist. The simultaneous shocks of supply shortages and price increases led to charges that the companies withheld supplies in order to justify planned price increases. Conversely, industry supporters argue that the shortages led to higher prices, particularly since OPEC tended to combine production cutbacks with price increases. It is also unclear how much control the oil companies had over the OPEC price increases of October 1973. The bulk of the OPEC oil was produced by the major international oil companies,[34] and the magnitude of the October increase was in part due to the companies' reluctance to meet earlier government demands for a somewhat smaller increase.[35]

During the past decade, the federal government has subjected industry performance to close and periodic scrutiny. Price increases and supply shortages are investigated routinely by the Department of Energy, the General Accounting Office (GAO), the Congress, and the Federal Trade Commission. The government has also taken a more active role in determining how crude supplies are refined.

Charges of company misconduct over the past several years have proliferated. The GAO, for example, investigated the oil companies to determine whether they manipulated the Iranian cutoff of oil in 1978–79 for their own benefit. The GAO concluded that the Iranian cutoff was exacerbated by a simultaneous drop in domestic production, but noted that such a drop was normal for that time of year. Furthermore, it found no evidence that the oil companies created the U.S. oil shortage.[36]

Several companies have been charged with improper pricing policies under a variety of government regulations, and they have sometimes made large settlements or agreed to forgo increases.[37] The companies claim the problem is one of interpreting complex and ambiguous government guidelines.[38]

In sum, industry critics are justified in charging the oil companies with manipulation of supply prior to 1973. Since that time, however, the companies have had less opportunity to control supply. That prerogative has largely passed to OPEC. In addition, the effects of pre-1973 manipulation may not have been entirely negative. Supply manipulation is usually criticized for misallocating resources and producing artificially high prices. In the classic case of a monopolized or highly concentrated industry, supply is curtailed below the level of demand that would otherwise prevail. But the oil companies maintain they curtailed supply only to the level of expected demand. They sought to expand rather than contain their markets. If the demand for oil rose, the companies were willing to increase their supply. During this period, the price of oil was also quite stable and low relative to the prices of other goods.

Thus, while supply manipulation did occur, there are arguments supporting the oil companies as well. These concern both the effects of and the decreased possibilities for manipulation after 1973.

Summary

Economic studies of the oil industry tend to argue against reaching quick judgments about allegations of obscene profits, oligopoly, or current supply manipulation. For example, profits increased dramatically during the 1970s. On the other hand, industry profitability over the past thirty years has been no higher than that of other industries. Similarly, the oil industry has been highly concentrated in years past. However, the concentration levels seem to have declined during the postwar period. At the same time, the number of firms operating in the oil industry has increased. The current level of concentration is comparable to that of other manufacturing industries.

Control of supply, long a primary goal of the largest companies, is no longer solely in their hands, due to the current international political context. Supply manipulation unquestionably benefited the companies by keeping prices up. It can also be argued, however, that this did not significantly harm consumers. Without supply control, producers would have been forced into destructive competition in order to protect their investments, with supply and price subject to erratic fluctuations. Additionally, technical characteristics of oil production arguably required a coherent plan for exploitation to maximize the ultimate supply and minimize costs.

In short, the historical evidence is mixed, and recent trends have rendered some charges less relevant than they once were. These analyses do not preclude criticism of oil company practices. Nor do they exonerate the industry executives of venal or even illegal dealings. But they do demonstrate the complexities involved in generalizing about industry profits, competition, and supply control. By the 1960s, the old image of a monopolized, profit-rich oil industry had become a matter of serious debate among economists. In the post-OPEC era, the debate continues. Is the oil companies' public image deserved, or are the companies suffering for the sins of their fathers? To find out, let us turn to the media coverage.

Media Coverage of the Oil Industry

In examining media coverage of the oil companies, this study focused on three areas in which they were frequently criticized: profits, competition, and supply manipulation. We examined all stories dealing primarily with these topics in the *New York Times, Time,* and the three major television networks from 1973 through 1980. This time period was chosen to include the two oil shocks of 1973–74 and 1979.

Many other influences affect these issues, such as price controls, windfall profit taxes, OPEC, import quotas, international treaties, environmental issues, depletion allowances, et cetera. However, we maintained a narrow focus in order to compare media coverage of these three specific issues with the scholarly and expert analyses discussed above.

Coders examined 118 articles from the *New York Times*, and 52 from *Time*, as well as 63 broadcasts at ABC, 102 at CBS, and 65 at NBC—a total of 400 stories. To better reflect the historical context of these reports, most findings are broken out separately for three time periods: the first oil crisis during 1973–74, the interim period from 1975 through 1978, and the second crisis and its aftermath in 1979 and 1980.

Profit

Did the media simply report increasing profits during the oil crises, or did they judge these profits excessive? Did they note the lower profits during the interim years? Was profitability related to inflation or net worth, the performance of other industries, or other periods of history?

Profit Level. All outlets reported heavily on increased profits during the crisis periods (see Table 16). Even though profits fell during the interim period, however, the print media continued to report increased profits. Overall, *Time* reported increased profits in fifteen out of seventeen articles on profits (88 percent), and the *New York Times* did so in thirty-five out of fifty stories, or 70 percent. Most of the remaining pieces were neutral or balanced. Only four stories reported decreased or unchanged profits—two during the interim and two during the second crisis. Even in the years when profits were down, attention focused on earlier increases, as in a 1977 *Time* article: "Few can forget how in their annual reports for 1974, the oil companies showed hefty increases

Table 16—Media Coverage of Oil Industry Profit Reports			
	New York Times	Time	Television
Increased Profit	70%	88%	85%
Decreased/Unchanged	6	6	5
Neutral	20	0	10
Balanced	4	6	0
	100%	100%	100%
Number of Stories	50	18	97

in their profits over the preceding year: Exxon up 28.6%, Gulf up 33%, Mobil up 23.3%."[39]

The networks also reported almost exclusively on increased oil company profits in 85 percent of all broadcasts. However, the networks significantly changed their viewpoints during 1974–77. Only one broadcast during the interim concerned increased profits, compared to four reports of lowered profits, thereby following the actual trends of oil company profits. Note, however, the sharp dropoff in profits reports during those years. In contrast, only one televised report during either oil crisis period dealt with decreased profits, compared to eighty-one broadcasts on profit increases. For example, a 1974 ABC broadcast called one 60 percent profit increase "a jump so big as to prove almost embarrassing."[40]

When all media coverage is combined, reports on increased profits outweighed stories on decreases by a margin of nearly fifteen to one. Stories on increases outnumbered those on decreases even during the 1975 to 1978 period, which saw substantial dropoffs in the industry's profit margin.

Profit Evaluation. Were profits deemed justified, partially justified, or unjustified? Supportive explanations of oil company profits ranged from expert analysis to company executives' denials. Thus, a *New York Times* story justified profits with reference to financial analysts' findings: "But, despite the widely held opinion that the big oil companies' profits are too great, the findings of financial specialists . . . almost uniformly indicate otherwise . . . ."[41]

On ABC, a Texaco spokesman justified high profits by citing the high cost of replacing current stocks: "Oil prices must go up further in the future because it is becoming much more costly to replace the crude oil and reserves that we have . . . ."[42] And CBS aired a different industry argument: "Gulf President B.R. Dorsey said that even higher profits may be needed to encourage the search for new oil sources."[43]

Criticism ranged from charges of profiteering to discussions of how much profit is reasonable. High profits were sometimes linked to accusations of an oil crisis hoax. As one *New York Times* article put it, "the embattled industry appears indecisive and ineffectual in combating charges that they are reaping enormous profits from a crisis of their own making."[44]

The companies' high profits were also contrasted to the average citizen's difficulties in paying higher oil prices. ABC quoted a senator who called the profits, ". . . a travesty when people are paying through the nose for home heating oil and gasoline."[45] And CBS showed Senator Henry Jackson using a phrase that became a famous rallying cry against the industry: "I want to see a reasonable profit, a fair profit, but we can't tolerate obscene profits."[46]

All outlets also carried stories characterizing the profits as partly justified. These combinations of criticism and support often described profits as excessive but explainable, or as legitimate but high enough to require governmental regulation. A 1979 *Time* article shows how explanation could be combined with criticism:

> Oil industry profits for this quarter are expected to rise anywhere from 20% to 40% above last year's. Among the reasons —inventories acquired at last year's prices are becoming more valuable as OPEC pushes up the worldwide cost of crude.
>
> A few companies seem destined to reap an absolute embarrassment of riches . . . Says [Ashland Oil] Chairman Orin Atkins . . . "What is good for Ashland Oil is good for the country." As always, the ultimate victims are the nation's consumers. . . .[47]

The majority of profit reports (59 percent) did not ask whether the amounts were justified or provided arguments on both sides. Among those that did take a position, 23 percent were critical, while 14 percent defended the profit margins, and 4 percent presented them as partly justified. The most negative coverage came during the two oil crisis periods, particularly the first, when critical reports dominated by nearly a two to one margin. The coverage then ebbed and evened out until the second oil shock, when it swung in a negative direction again, although not as sharply as before.

The print media in particular shifted over time toward greater acceptance of oil company profits. This shift was strongest at *Time,* where oil company profits were reported in a balanced or neutral manner during both the first oil crisis and the interim period. The second oil crisis saw *Time* defending oil company profits as fully or partly justified twice as often as it criticized unjustified profits. However, the *New York Times* took the position that profits were unjustified during both crises. The ratio of criticism to support there during the first crisis exceeded three to one. Throughout the interim, the *New York Times* switched to defending industry profits more often than not. But the *Times* returned to criticism of profits with the second crisis.

While the print media gradually softened their criticism of oil company profits, the networks maintained a neutral or balanced stance throughout 1973–80. When the networks did broadcast one-sided reports, they carried an almost equal number representing each position. The only shift over time in broadcasts was toward more neutral reports.

Context of Profits. Simple statements of justification or criticism hardly exhaust the complexities of profit reports. Corporate profitability seemed less extreme when examined in the contexts described above (net worth and return on investment, impact of inflation, comparison with other industries, and historical context). These contexts, among others, give perspective to the figures being reported. Were they included along with the profit reports? Did the media utilize some of the analytical tools of the trade for the economic reports? Or did they simply report raw facts without contextual tools that would make them more meaningful?

First, we coded whether news reports linked profits with net worth or return on investment. These factors tend to moderate a high profit report, because a firm can enjoy increased profits while having an equal or lower profit rate due to changes in net worth or investment. However, the print media took these factors into account in less than one-third of their reports on profits (31 percent). On television, net worth or return on investment were mentioned in only 11 percent of the broadcasts covering profits. The few times this context was considered by the media, it did lessen the perception of high profits, as in this *New York Times* report during the 1979 period of high profits: "But the oil companies insist that, even under the current favorable market conditions, industry profits are not excessive. In the second quarter . . . the return on the $99 billion of invested capital of stockholders was 19.4 percent."[48]

Another important contextual factor is inflation. After accounting for inflation, real profit decreased significantly during the 1970s. Nevertheless, inflation was almost never tied to profit reports. Of all media outlets examined, only the *New York Times* and CBS ever reported any linkage between oil company profits and inflation. Both carried one such story during each crisis. That produced a total of four stories tying inflation to oil company profits out of a possible 164 stories.

One also gains a broader perspective when an industry's profits are compared with those of other industries during the same time period. Overall, oil industry profits did not prove excessively high in comparison with other U.S. industries during the 1970s. This was brought out frequently when the media did provide profit comparisons. However, reporting on this issue was relatively rare. It figured in only 12 broadcasts and 23 articles throughout the period studied, or 20 percent of all relevant stories.

All outlets presented comparative perspectives most frequently during the second oil crisis. But the *New York Times* split with the others over how the oil companies stacked up relative to other industries. During the first oil shock, the *Times* emphasized that oil company profits were equal to or lower than those of other industries. Thereafter, though, the *Times* presented petroleum profits as higher than the norm. A 1979 article is typical: "Global revenues of these eight companies alone, each of them among the largest corporations in the world, exceeded $203 billion last year, dwarfing those of the Big Three American auto manufacturers . . . or the steel industry. . . ."[49]

At the networks and *Time,* this shift was reversed. They treated oil profits as higher than the industrial average early on, then portrayed the companies' profit levels as no better than average after 1974. One 1979 *Time* story concluded,

Are the companies earning excessive profits? Not really. True, they take advantage of overly generous tax credits on their foreign earnings. What is more, their profits rise automatically whenever prices are kicked up by OPEC. With all that, oil firms last year earned only 4.5% on their revenues, vs. 5.25% earned by all U.S. industry.[50]

Finally, we coded whether profit reports were placed in historical (pre-1970) context. When profits are examined over time, oil industry profitability does not appear so excessive. However, only 8 percent of the television reports on profits provided any historical context. That includes only two broadcasts during the last six years of the study. The print media did not do much better. They provided historical contexts in only one in six articles on profits, mostly in the *New York Times*.

Thus, the mitigating contexts of high oil company profits were addressed rarely. These factors were considered most often during the second oil crisis. Just over half of all industry comparisons and historical analyses were observed during the second oil crisis, while only about 30 percent of such reports were made during the first crisis. There was also a slight rise in the number of stories tying inflation and net worth/return on investment to profit. Therefore, there may be a linkage between depth of reporting and a more balanced perspective, since media criticism diminished after the first oil crisis. This may also reflect the life cycle of media coverage of a long-term controversy. Reporters may have balanced their coverage as they gained experience and knowledge of the issue.

Competition

How did the media cover the issues that support or refute accusations of monopolistic or oligopolistic practices? How deeply did they go into important details, and how often did they place the facts in comparative or historical context? To find out, we posed a series of highly specific questions: Did a story portray market entry as easy or difficult? If difficult, who received the blame? Was the oil industry's competitiveness seen as high or low, as increasing or decreasing?

Charges of monopoly or oligopoly are supported by evidence

of industry control over price and supply, both domestic and international. So we asked how industry control over these factors was reported. Some contexts of these stories were also considered. Did the media compare oil company competition to that of other industries? Was competitiveness assessed relative to earlier (pre-1970) periods? Finally, overall assessments of oil company competition were coded. To what extent did the media criticize oil company practices, and to what extent did they defend them?

Market Entry. Ease of market entry is an important determinant of competitiveness. Was market entry for the oil industry reported as easy or difficult from 1973 to 1980?

Of 15 pieces that covered market entry, 12 were from the *New York Times.* Seven articles appeared during the first oil crisis, and all but one identified market entry as difficult. The *Times* maintained its judgment of market entry as difficult in three out of the five remaining articles, thus reporting difficulty in nine out of 12 articles overall. The three remaining stories at other outlets also portrayed market entry as difficult. Therefore, this judgment represents 75 percent of the limited media coverage on market entry.

The paucity of stories on market entry (only 15 out of 274 stories on competitiveness) deprived the public of relevant analytical details that might help assess oil industry competitiveness. This topic was especially ignored by the networks. They ran only one market entry story (on CBS) throughout the study period.

Where the media covered market entry as "difficult," we asked who they blamed—the oil companies, other parties or factors, or no one. Difficulty of market entry is a complex phenomenon. It can be linked to economic conditions, government policies, international politics, and the nature of the industry, as well as anticompetitive practices. However, in all but two of the *New York Times'* twelve articles, blame was assigned to the oil companies. *Time* and CBS also blamed the oil companies in their three reports. So the media blamed only oil company behavior for market entry difficulties 88 percent of the time.

For example, a *Times* report mentioned that, "the major oil concerns had tried to prevent the smaller independents from

getting access to the huge, low-cost Middle East oil reserves."[51]
Similarly, *Time* cited extensive charges by longtime industry critic
John Blair: "Blair discovered a pattern of price fixing and cozy
marketing arrangements by which the big companies divided up
the world for their own gain and tried to ruin any small independent firm that sought to cut prices or intrude on their turf."[52] The
repetition of such charges, whether true or not, was rarely balanced with rebuttals or other perspectives on market entry difficulties.

Competition/Concentration. All media outlets portrayed the oil
industry primarily as uncompetitive or highly concentrated. This
perspective was especially pronounced during the first oil crisis,
though the coverage became more balanced as time passed.

Twenty-eight out of 50 reports (56 percent) during the first oil
crisis pictured competition as decreasing or low. Only one story
(2 percent) reported high competition in 1973–74, with the rest
neutral or balanced. Typical of early negative coverage was a
Times story citing Senator Walter Mondale's allegations of increasing industry concentration. He concluded, in a statement,
"This is a trend which, if allowed to go unchecked, might completely destroy competition within the oil industry."[53]

This view moderated somewhat over time, so that about one-
third of all later reports during the interim lull and the second oil
crisis portrayed competition as low or concentration as high. This
proportionate change, however, was accompanied by a slackening
of coverage. Print articles portraying a competitive environment
increased from none at all during the first crisis to only two in the
interim and three during the second crisis. At the same time,
reports of low or decreasing competition diminished from thirteen
during the first crisis to three in the lull and five during the second
crisis. Typical of these was a 1978 *New York Times* article, which
presented evidence of increasing competitiveness:

> Some of the oil industry's traditional leaders in gasoline sales
> have seen their market share fall off sharply in the last year or
> so, while some of the industry's traditional also-rans have

pushed their way to the top. And simultaneously, the major oil companies as a group have lost business to the smaller integrated oil companies and the independents.[54]

Television also moderated its reporting of anticompetitive practices over time. The networks shifted from heavy coverage stressing a lack of competition during the first crisis to primarily neutral or balanced broadcasts thereafter.

There was far more coverage of competition during the first oil crisis than in later years. Print coverage dropped from 33 articles on competition in the first crisis to 11 during the lull and 14 in the second crisis. Network coverage fell even more dramatically, from 17 broadcasts during the first crisis to 8 during the lull and only 2 during the second crisis. Thus, the anticompetitive perspective early on was followed not by an alternative or more balanced view but by the gradual disappearance of the issue.

Were the media losing interest in the charges of monopoly and oligopoly, or were their analyses shifting to other areas? To find out, we turned to industry control of price and supply. Such practices are primary indicators that antitrust laws are being violated, or are about to be violated. We coded all stories dealing with industry control over prices, domestic supply, and international supply.

Price Control. When opinions were expressed in media coverage, industry control over prices was asserted more often than refuted. This was especially true during the first oil crisis, when this charge was upheld over twice as often as it was rebutted. Coverage shifted to defend the industry's lack of control over price during 1975–78, but tilted back again toward supporting charges of price control during the second oil shock. In all, 28 percent of the stories accused the industry of controlling prices, and 21 percent denied this, with the remainder neutral or balanced.

This overall picture masks significant variation from one outlet to another. In particular, the three television networks' perceptions varied sharply. ABC reported both views equally throughout 1973–80, CBS shifted to reporting industry control during the second oil crisis, and NBC emphasized industry control of prices at all times. The shift at CBS culminated in stories like the following, in which there was no doubt of industry price control: "In another study released today, DOE says the top 15 companies were guilty of massive overcharges in the 3 years after the 1973 Arab oil embargo."[55] Yet television news did maintain a high percentage of neutral or balanced reports. In fact, these constituted solid majorities during both crisis periods.

There were similar differences between the print media. The *New York Times* portrayed the oil industry as controlling prices more often than not during both oil crises, but to a diminishing degree. Reports of industry control predominated by a four to one ratio during the first crisis, but by only a slight plurality during the second. By contrast, *Time* maintained steady coverage emphasizing no industry control over prices throughout 1973–80. In fact, *Time* reported industry control in only one story out of thirty-three. *Time* couched almost two-thirds of its articles in neutral or balanced terms. Overall, this topic illustrates the degree to which national media outlets can present quite different perspectives on a controversy.

Domestic Supply Control. Coverage of industry control of domestic supply followed a similar pattern over time. All media outlets affirmed industry control over domestic supply most frequently during the first oil crisis. Industry control arguments decreased during the mid-1970s, then increased again in the second oil crisis. Overall, these stories alleged industry control over domestic oil supplies four times more often than they exonerated the industry.

The *New York Times* published 57 articles touching on this topic, almost half of all *Times* articles coded. By contrast, *Time* covered it in only 11 articles. During the first crisis, the *Times* indicted the oil industry seven times as often as it vindicated industry practices. An early *Times* article demonstrates the argument of domestic supply control by industry: "The regional unit of the Federal Energy Office here is investigating what its director yesterday termed the suspicious sale of millions of gallons of heating oil by wholesalers that he called 'the dirty dozen.' "[56] Thereafter, the paper's coverage was almost evenly divided between the two positions. For example, this piece presents control over domestic supply as a matter of opinion:

> If shortages occur, the public will blame the industry and Government; the industry will blame the Administration and Congress; the Administration will blame the industry and Congress, while Congress will blame the industry and the Administration. Ascribing the blame is a difficult and possibly a worthless exercise. . . .[57]

Time, on the other hand, kept mainly to neutral or balanced articles throughout 1973–80. The heaviest criticism came from television, which tempered its charges only slightly as time went on. During the first crisis, charges of domestic supply manipulation outnumbered rebuttals by a ten to one margin. During the 1975–78 lull, the margin dropped to two to one. The second crisis brought another surge of criticism, raising the anti-industry margin back up to four to one.

International Supply Control. Industry control over international supply was a different story. The print media provided a nearly equal number of articles on each viewpoint during the first oil crisis, and thereafter shifted dramatically toward the industry's position. During the second crisis, every article accusing the companies of such control was outweighed by eight articles exonerating the industry. Thus, a 1974 *New York Times* article indicated a significant degree of industry control over international supply:

> To this day the OPEC countries do not sell directly to the Ashlands and Citgos and the European and Japanese refiners in any significant volume. Thus such refiners cannot shop around in the OPEC for the best prices; they have to go to Exxon, Shell, Texaco.[58]

By 1979, the *Times* was far more likely to attribute supply control to OPEC rather than the oil companies: "It is already apparent [that OPEC] has managed to keep the oil market tight despite having almost doubled world prices in less than a year.

And now, they say, there are signs that OPEC may succeed in coordinating production cutbacks next year. . . ."[59] Television was, if anything, even less sympathetic to such accusations. Throughout the entire period only two of eighteen broadcasts supported charges of industry control.

Thus, media coverage of industry control over price and supply came in two distinct phases. The first crisis brought forth criticism of the oil companies on all fronts, with little credence given the defenses they offered. During the second crisis, criticism of domestic supply control was somewhat muted, and the coverage supported the oil companies' position on international supply. This turnabout was probably linked to increased media awareness of OPEC's role in controlling price and supply. Unlike some other disputes over monopolistic practices, coverage of these variables decreased only slightly over time.

So the issue of "oilogopoly" was still alive during the second crisis, although in a different form. No longer were the media concerned with the industry's internal dynamics. Who controlled what was a more important concern during the second oil crisis.

Contexts of Competition. Two key pieces of contextual information—competition relative to other industries and in historical perspective—provide broader perspectives that sometimes place industry practices in a more favorable light. However, only 5 articles or broadcasts out of 274 compared the oil industry's competitiveness with that of other industries. Four of these placed petroleum in the low to moderate competition range, and none portrayed the industry as highly competitive.

Only slightly more attention was given to the historical context of oil company competition—a total of eleven stories across all media, including eight by the *New York Times.* All but two of these appeared during the first oil crisis. Thus, once again, important contextual information was left virtually unaddressed by the media. And once again, television coverage was even more sketchy than print.

"Oilogopoly?" Finally, we coded all stories dealing with the industry's competitiveness for their general perspective on this topic. Stories were placed in the anticompetition camp if they asserted that the oil industry was engaging in monopolistic or oligopolistic practices or moving in that direction; portrayed the industry as noncompetitive, or becoming increasingly so; or otherwise charged that small producers were being driven out of business. Stories were classified as procompetitive if they described the industry as nonmonopolistic or nonoligopolistic, or becoming less so; denied that the companies were engaging in such practices; or otherwise portrayed the industry as currently or increasingly competitive. As usual, balanced or neutral categories were also included (see Table 17).

Both print and broadcast media gave far more coverage to the charges of monopoly, although they became more balanced over time. The most striking shift occurred at the *New York Times.* During the first crisis, the *Times* presented the noncompetitive case over three times as often as the competitive view. For example, a 1973 article cited a Federal Trade Commission study which concluded that, "the major oil companies have behaved in a manner similar to a classical monopolist: they have attempted to increase profits by restricting output."[60]

During the mid 1970s, however, both sides were equally represented. By the second crisis, the *Times* made a complete turnaround, portraying the industry as competitive twice as often as the converse. For example, the following article refutes the image of a powerful monopolistic oil industry: "Before the embargo and

Table 17—Media's Overall Assessment of Oil Industry Competition

	New York Times	Time	Television
Monopolistic	32%	3%	18%
Nonmonopolistic	21	8	3
Neutral	24	26	59
Balanced	23	64	20
	100%	101%*	100%
Number of Stories	96	39	140

*Reflects rounding error

1973 price explosion, the Seven Sisters pumped and marketed most exporters' oil at fixed prices under long-term contracts. Today, they control barely 42 percent. . . . [The Sisters] find their role diminished to that of hired hands."[61]

Compared to this turnabout, *Time* was a model of consistency, running mainly balanced stories throughout the study. Television's coverage was more one-sided, although the networks, too, gradually discovered the competitive side of the argument. A majority of all broadcasts were neutral. When a point of view was presented, however, the anticompetitive perspective tended to dominate. During the first oil shock, televised charges of monopolistic practices outnumbered rebuttals by a fifteen to one margin.

As the crisis receded, while the print media were offering balanced coverage, the critics still prevailed over the airwaves by a six to one ratio. During the second crisis, when the *Times* was favoring the proponents of industry competitiveness, television continued to offer the opponents a two to one edge. Overall, TV news presented portrayals of monopoly or oligopoly about six times as often as pictures of competition. For example, in 1974 CBS interviewed an "oil industry analyst," who charged that, "We're being ripped off by the oil companies with the blessings of the federal government. . . ."[62]

Combining print and broadcast reports revealed three general trends in media portrayals of oil industry competition. First, the majority of all news reports were neutral or balanced on this issue. Second, when one viewpoint did prevail, it was much more likely to be the anticompetitive perspective. Finally, there was a significant shift on this issue over time toward the proponents of a competitive industry. During the first crisis, the monopoly view predominated by almost a five to one margin. For the next few years, the competitive view ran a much closer second. By the second crisis, it finally came out on top.

Supply Manipulation

Supply manipulation implies a callous indifference to the public interest. It includes accusations that oil companies suppressed production, withheld supplies, exported oil despite domestic shortages, and even helped create an oil crisis as a hoax for their own ends.

How did the media cover such charges (see Table 18)? Print and television outlets devoted an equal number of stories to them —77 apiece, or 154 overall. The tenor of their coverage was also quite similar, presenting charges about twice as often as rebuttals. Forty-nine percent of print media stories supported supply manipulation charges, compared to 25 percent that rejected the charges, with the rest neutral or balanced.

This disparity was most evident at the *New York Times,* where 56 percent of all articles backed up allegations of manipulation and only 23 percent rebutted them. For example, one *Times* story asked, "are the major oil companies creating a false shortage to raise prices and profits and drive small 'independent' companies . . . to the wall?"[63] The article went on to quote Wisconsin Representative Les Aspin, "There is little doubt that the so-called gasoline shortage in the Midwest is just a big lousy gimmick foisted on consumers to bilk them for billions in increased gasoline prices."

Time was more evenhanded, presenting the promanipulation argument only slightly more often than its opposite, by 36 to 28 percent. For example, one article defended the industry against charges of creating a "phony" oil shortage: "Are the companies creating a phony shortage? No. The crisis is real . . . . Are the companies hoarding gasoline to raise the price? No. They are

Table 18—Media's Assessment of Oil Industry Supply Manipulation

	New York Times	Time	Television
Manipulates Supply	56%	36%	44%
Does Not Manipulate	23	28	16
Neutral	10	0	14
Balanced	11	36	26
	100%	100%	100%
Number of Stories	52	25	77

rebuilding their inventories. . . ."[64] As usual, television was a source of heavy criticism. Whereas accusations of manipulation roughly doubled denials in print, the margin rose to nearly three to one at the networks (44 to 16 percent).

The coverage on this issue was both heaviest and most negative during the first oil crisis. By the mid-1970s, it became more balanced. Over half of all stories on supply manipulation appeared during the initial oil shock of 1973–74. During those years, charges exceeded rebuttals by margins of over five to one at the *New York Times* and nine to one at the networks. Only *Time* provided relatively balanced coverage early on.

After this period, the *Times* maintained a precise 50-50 split in pro- and antimanipulation stories. Television changed more gradually. The promanipulation edge dropped to around three to one during the mid-1970s and almost disappeared altogether during the second crisis.

Even as the media lent a more sympathetic ear to the industry's side, they provided less and less historical information that might help the public understand their shift in perspective. Only one story in seven provided any historical context for the debate on supply manipulation, and most of these appeared during the first oil shock. Once again, television proved the most superficial news source. Only 5 percent of all broadcasts (4 out of 77) supplied any historical background for viewers.

As on most questions related to profit and competition, media coverage on supply manipulation was heavily critical of the oil industry during the first oil shock but somewhat more balanced thereafter. Overall, the critics prevailed over the industry's defenders. Only one outlet, *Time* magazine, gave about equal coverage to both positions. Finally, the media paid little (and, in this case, dwindling) attention to contextual information that might have provided a better longer-range perspective on the hotly contested events of the moment.

Who's to Blame?

Finally, we sought a broader perspective on how the media covered the oil companies' role in the energy crisis. Coders noted every instance in which someone was deemed responsible for problems associated with the oil crises. In the 400 stories coded, there were 473 instances where responsibility was clearly assessed for a problem under discussion. They comprised five categories of culprits: the oil companies, the U.S. government, OPEC or other oil-producing countries, consumers, and all others (ranging from environmentalists to state governments to the weather).

Where did responsibility for the oil crises and their attendant problems lie? Most often, the media laid the blame at the oil industry's door (see Table 19). The answer was the same at all outlets except *Time*, which found the federal government just as culpable as the oil companies. Each received 32 percent of all mentions, compared to 24 percent for the oil-producing countries.[65] Elsewhere it was no contest; the companies shouldered over 40 percent of the blame in the pages of the *New York Times*, double the proportion assigned to both OPEC and the government.

At the networks the spread was even greater. Television fixed the blame on the oil companies exactly half the time. The government finished a distant second at 20 percent, and OPEC trailed behind with 15 percent. The three networks moved closely in tandem; the share of responsibility they assigned the oil companies varied only 3 percent, from 48 percent at ABC to 51 percent at NBC. For example, a CBS story concluded, "A large part of the blame for declining heating oil supplies rests with the major oil

Table 19—Blame Assigned for Causing Energy Problems			
	New York Times	Time	Television
Oil Companies	41%	32%	50%
OPEC	21	24	15
U.S. Government	20	32	20
Consumers	6	6	3
Others	12	5	13
	100%	99%*	101%*
Number of Stories	90	48	133

*rounding error

companies . . . for the past three months the oil companies have produced two gallons of more profitable gasoline for every one gallon of heating oil, despite Federal Emergency Preparedness Agency pleas for more oil."[66]

Trends over time followed previous patterns, with one exception. Four of the five media outlets blamed the companies somewhat less as time went on, although they remained the principal target. For example, the proportion of responsibility the *Times* assigned to the industry dropped by 9 percent from the first to the second crisis; OPEC picked up the slack. The exception to this trend was at CBS. There the blame affixed to the oil companies jumped 25 percent from the first to the second crisis. CBS pointed to the oil industry over two-thirds of the time it assigned responsibility during the second crisis. This was the most striking instance in the study of one network diverging from the others. Even at ABC and NBC, however, the oil industry remained the main repository of responsibility throughout the study.

Conclusion: Major Media vs. Big Oil

This study began by surveying economic analyses of oil industry profitability, concentration and competition, and price and supply practices. It then analyzed media coverage of the same topics during the energy crisis years of 1973 through 1980. A brief review of the findings follows.

Profits. The media featured heavy coverage of soaring oil industry profits during both oil shocks. The amount of coverage fell sharply during the four-year interim, when profits were down. Even during that period of lower profit margins, the print media continued to publish reports mainly stressing the large amounts of money oil companies were making. Overall, reports of profit increases outnumbered decreases by almost fifteen to one.

The media often cast a jaundiced eye on oil industry profits. During the first oil crisis, the level of profits was presented as unjustified twice as often as it was justified. After that, the two views were given about equal weight, until the second crisis brought another upsurge of criticism. The *New York Times* led the criticism, while *Time* magazine was least critical.

This largely negative portrayal of industry profits was also notable for what it failed to include. There was little coverage of several factors that provide contexts for ameliorating the apparent magnitude of profits. Despite heightened public concern over inflation during the 1970s, the effects of inflation on oil company profits rarely were addressed. Nor were profit margins usually linked to a firm's net worth or return on investment, a common tool economists use in assessing profitability. Finally, oil company profits rarely were compared to those of other industries or previous time periods.

Competition. Media treatment of industry competition followed a similar pattern of initial harsh criticism moderating over time, with historical or comparative perspective lacking. Market entry was portrayed as difficult and perceived as the fault of the major companies rather than due to any structural factors. This issue was rarely broached outside the pages of the *New York Times,* or after 1974. The industry was portrayed as noncompetitive or becoming less so, especially during the first oil crisis. Thereafter, coverage of this issue, too, diminished rapidly, especially at the networks.

Charges of price and supply control elicited more continuous coverage throughout the 1970s. During the first oil crisis, the media supported charges of industry price-fixing by a two to one ratio. They supported allegations of domestic supply controls by a margin exceeding eight to one. Only charges of international supply control were rejected from the outset, by a smaller margin.

The coverage became less critical of the industry on all these issues with the passage of time. However, it exonerated the oil companies only from the charge of control over international supplies, as OPEC's primacy in this sphere was noted increasingly. Yet the media remained critical of industry attempts to control domestic oil supplies. For the entire period studied this charge got about four times the coverage given to industry rebuttals. In light of these findings on specific issues, it is not surprising that overall media assessments of oil industry competition came down on the side of the "oiligopoly," by a margin of over two to one. During the first oil crisis few stories portrayed the industry as competitive.

During the second crisis, the print media stressed competitive factors over anticompetitive elements, and the margin enjoyed by the anticompetitive perspective on television narrowed sharply. Despite this shift, the massive early coverage ensured the overall primacy of the anticompetitive view, as did the lack of comparative or historical context in most articles and broadcasts.

Supply Manipulation. The media consistently covered charges that the oil industry tried to manipulate supplies to enhance their profits at the public's expense. Overall, these allegations received about twice the coverage of rebuttals. *Time* provided the most balanced coverage, while the *New York Times* and the networks provided almost equally sharp criticism. The largest number of stories ran during the first oil shock, when negative pieces prevailed over positive ones by margins of five to one at the *Times* and nine to one over the airwaves. During the second crisis, by contrast, coverage at all outlets was relatively balanced.

Blame. Assessments of blame fell right into line with the findings on more specific issues. The oil industry received most of the blame that was meted out, especially during the first energy crisis. *Time* parceled out equal measures of blame to industry and government. At the networks and the *New York Times,* the companies were held responsible for problems more often than anyone else.

These findings are consistent across many controversial topics. The media were primarily critical of the oil companies in areas ranging from profits and anticompetitive practices to allegations that they created the energy crisis, exacerbated it, or callously turned it to their advantage.

The criticisms generally were sharpest during the first crisis period of 1973–74, then moderated during the second oil shock of 1979. On most issues the *New York Times* led the criticism, followed by the television networks. *Time* featured the least negative coverage.

On several issues, this negative coverage brought the media's portrayal of the oil companies into conflict with the technical literature on industry profitability and competitiveness. For example, heavy coverage of soaring profits during 1974 and 1979 was never balanced by pieces on much lower profits during other years, or petroleum's moderate long-term profitability relative to other industries. In fact, stories often focused on high profits even during years when profits had decreased. Similarly, the media's emphasis on industry concentration and lack of competition gave short shrift to the economic literature questioning the image of a highly concentrated industry and showing increased opportunities for market entry.

Media coverage of these issues was hindered by a persistent failure to provide a broader context on controversies of the moment, in the form of comparative data, historical perspective, or explanations of the complicated analytical concepts discussed here. It was also weakened by a paucity of expert testimony that might have provided such perspectives. Out of nearly 1,500 sources cited in the stories coded, only 24, or 1.6 percent, were independent researchers based at universities or think tanks.

This is especially important in light of Barbara Hobbie's surveys. She found that journalists not only were significantly more critical of the oil industry than academic experts; they also portrayed economic opinion as more divided than it actually was. Thus, the coverage seemed to reflect journalists' perspectives more than those of economists.[67]

Journalists attempting to deal with this complex and controversial story were confronted with a welter of contradictory assertions coming from government, industry, and angry consumers. Faced with daily deadlines, and lacking independent expert opinion, it would not be surprising if they tended to fall back on populist mistrust of "big oil" dating back to the early years of the century. This interpretation is supported by the consistency of critical coverage across various topics, despite the sometimes very different perspectives available in the scholarly literature.

The equally consistent shift to more balanced coverage and increased supportive contextual information over time suggests that reporters may have gradually become more attuned to the complexities of these topics, and thereby more able to present both sides of the issues. If so, this study may do more than demonstrate journalists' tendencies to project their own assumptions into the news. It may also show their willingness to alter those assumptions in the face of new information and changing circumstances.

AND THAT'S THE WAY IT IS . . .

"Would I be a journalist everyone could trust if
every time politicians or, God help us,
sociologists told us how to do our job I said, 'Oh
yes, master, we'll do just as you say'?"

—Dan Rather, quoted in the *Washington Post*

DAN RATHER'S irritation is understandable. The news media
often bring cries of outrage from critics who have little else in
common. Conservatives decry the media's liberal bias and try to
combat it by buying CBS. Liberals call for opening up the news to
the underrepresented perspectives of women and minorities. Radicals want the news to concentrate on what *should* be happening,
instead of the "conservative" standard of what *is* happening.[1]
Journalists and academics join the fray with a seemingly continuous series of conferences and symposia that seek to improve the
profession and its public image. To paraphrase Marx, the critics
have attempted to change the media. The point, however, is to
understand it.

Our goal has been to understand the relationship between
journalists' perspectives and their product, in the context of the
media's changing role in American society. To accomplish this we
have combined the approaches of social theory and social science,
the methods of survey research and content analysis, and the

perspectives of political sociology and social psychology. What are the results?

The demographics are clear. The media elite are a homogeneous and cosmopolitan group, who were raised at some distance from the social and cultural traditions of small-town middle America. Drawn mainly from big cities in the northeast and north central states, their parents tended to be well off, highly educated members of the upper middle class. Most have moved away from any religious heritage, and very few are regular churchgoers. In short, the typical leading journalist is the very model of the modern eastern urbanite.

The dominant perspective of this group is equally apparent. Today's leading journalists are politically liberal and alienated from traditional norms and institutions. Most place themselves to the left of center and regularly vote the Democratic ticket. Yet theirs is not the New Deal liberalism of the underprivileged, but the contemporary social liberalism of the urban sophisticate. They favor a strong welfare state within a capitalist framework. They differ most from the general public, however, on the divisive social issues that have emerged since the 1960s—abortion, gay rights, affirmative action, et cetera. Many are alienated from the "system" and quite critical of America's world role. They would like to strip traditional powerbrokers of their influence and empower black leaders, consumer groups, intellectuals, and . . . the media.

These characteristics will likely become more pronounced in the future. Journalists from the post-Watergate generation place themselves well to the left of their older colleagues. Moreover, students at the prestigious Columbia School of Journalism take a quantum leap beyond their elders in criticizing America's economic and political institutions, while sharing their rejection of traditional social and cultural norms. They also profess admiration for liberal public figures and media organs, but disapprove of conservative newsmakers and news outlets.

None of this proves that media coverage is biased. The whole notion of bias has become a straw man that obscures the far less obvious (and less nefarious) processes that mediate between journalists' perspectives and their product. Psychological tests show

how their outlooks can unconsciously operate to shape their conceptions of the news. First, in selecting sources they consider reliable on nuclear energy, welfare reform, consumer protection, and the environment, their choices accord with their own perspectives on business and government.

Second, to a statistically significant degree, leading journalists tend to perceive elements of social controversies in terms that correspond to their own attitudes. The journalists and a business control group were shown specially constructed news stories dealing with topics like affirmative action, bribery in international business practices, and the income gap between blacks and whites. After reading the same stories, the journalists were more likely to recall a rising racial income gap and the businessmen to remember a declining one; the media elite differentially perceived threats to affirmative action where the business group observed reverse discrimination; the newspeople more often stressed business immorality while the executives emphasized unfair standards. The two groups were asked to summarize the stories, not to evaluate the issues involved. But the results show how unconscious evaluation can sometimes help determine perception. Remembering is choosing to remember, though the choice takes us unawares.

This process is not only confined to the political realm. Selective perceptions of controversial cues are emblematic of the many ways we each construct reality for ourselves, projecting yesterday's judgments onto today's events. To show how journalists spontaneously attribute certain characteristics to various social groups and relationships, we probed their apperceptions, the unconscious fantasies they bring to their understanding of the social world. Their responses to the Thematic Apperception Test may show how leading journalists sometimes fill in the gaps between what they know and what they assume when confronting a new situation. When their TAT stories contained socially relevant themes, figures of authority tended to evoke fantasies about the abuse of power in the form of greedy businessmen, deceitful lawyers, conniving politicians, intimidating policemen, and sadistic military superiors. Conversely, socially relevant stories tended to portray the average man as the victim of malevolent higher-ups or an uncaring social system. Once again, these themes and images differed significantly from those produced by corporate executives who saw the same pictures.

In sum, the media elite's conscious opinions seem to be partly reflected in the ways they subconsciously structure social reality. These findings show how pure journalistic objectivity is unattainable, since even the conscious effort to be objective takes place within a mental picture of the world already conditioned, to some degree, by one's beliefs about it. The main question is, are journalists' attitudes and preconceptions consistent with the portrait of social reality that they paint for their audience?

Our study addressed major media coverage of three long-running and controversial stories—nuclear power, busing for racial integration, and the oil industry's role in the energy crisis. After summarizing technical or scholarly knowledge on each topic, we examined its long-term national media coverage. In each instance the coverage diverged from the expert assessments in the direction of the media elite's own perspectives. If journalists' sympathies can sometimes override expert evidence, they presumably also influence coverage on the many topics where such evidence is either missing or irrelevant to the story.

Even according to an arbitrary standard requiring that each side receive equal coverage, the results were consistently one-sided. The media gave greater weight to the anti-nuclear than the pro-nuclear side. They gave greater credence to the advocates of busing than its opponents. They were more sympathetic to the critics of the oil industry than its supporters. In every instance the coverage followed neither the middle path nor the expert evidence. Instead, it veered in the direction one would expect on the basis of the attitude surveys and psychological tests. This is never a case of taking an entirely different path, in the manner of advocacy journalism. But when the road forks, and the signposts are unclear, journalists tend to follow their instincts, those inner road maps that mark out routes of ingrained expectation.

How do these findings comport with the common observation that journalists are non-ideological? The thinking of American journalists tends toward the concrete rather than the abstract and centers on personalities rather than ideas. Moreover, they tend to prize such virtues as pragmatism and adaptability. These traits seem the antithesis of the ideologue. Thus, Stephen Hess concludes from his survey that Washington reporters are mainly apolitical.[2]

Certainly many journalists are anti-ideological in the sense that they mistrust people guided primarily by closed systems of thought. But one need not be an ideologue to uphold, consciously or unconsciously, some set of values. Everyone partakes somewhat of ideology in the broader sense of reference points that guide efforts to assign meaning and value to the social world. Journalists sometimes believe their work immune to such influences, because of their preference for the immediate and concrete. But by rejecting the inevitable limitations of any closed system of thought, they do not transcend the influence of values altogether.

An aversion to abstractions and philosophical issues may leave only unquestioned assumptions that are experienced as instinct. Many journalists who fancy themselves tough-minded pragmatists are instead captives of conventional wisdom, carriers of intellectual currents whose validity is taken for granted. As sociologist Barbara Phillips has written, "Daily journalism discourages its practitioners from recognizing that taken-for-granted assumptions and personal predilections cast their unreflective shadows on reportage . . . . The upshot of journalists' nontheoretic way to knowledge is that they cannot transmit 'philosophic insight' to the public because they themselves do not approach the world from a reflective, theoretical mental attitude."[3]

This is not only a matter of ideology, even in the broad sense of value systems or paradigms. Journalists' personality traits may also affect their approach to the news. Relative to the control group of business executives, the media elite scored high on TAT measures of the need for power, fear of power, and narcissism; their scores were comparatively low on the need for achievement and (to a slight degree) the capacity for personal intimacy. In the absence of baseline scores from a national random sample, we cannot be certain of this group's psychological distinctiveness. As a speculative exercise, however, this motivational profile might add to an understanding of some widely noted features of contemporary national journalism. For example, such tendencies could help explain propensities toward negativism, an adversarial posture, and the identification of one's professional interests with the public interest. More broadly, the ideological currents of contemporary journalism may be more fully understood in conjunction with their emotional or motivational wellsprings.

Both mind-set and motivation are probably the products of larger social and intellectual currents that journalists do not create but carry and amplify. Thus, various liberal themes, negativism, and bad news bias may all express a cosmopolitan cultural milieu and modernist sensibility that values change, stimulation, and liberation from the bonds of authority and tradition. If the news highlights these themes, this is not the product of ideological commitment, in the narrow sense; rather, it reflects a cast of mind that, recalling Walter Lippmann's image, "is like the beam of a searchlight that moves restlessly about, bringing one episode and then another out of darkness into vision."[4]

Washington Post editor Meg Greenfield recently followed the course of that beam as a juror in the Pulitzer Prize competition. She reported on the difference between the America of her everyday experience and that described by her profession:

> "Out there"—wherever that is—people may be smiling and humming . . . but the world according to journalism is, on the contrary, a surpassingly bleak place. A Martian reading about it might in fact suppose America to be composed entirely of abused minorities living in squalid and sadistically-run state mental hospitals, except for a small elite of venal businessmen and county commissioners who are profiting from the unfortunates' misery.[5]

Greenfield argues that political liberalism is not the agent of "the vast discrepancy between the sunny surface preoccupations of American middle-class life and the depiction of a society beset by crime and pain."[6] Disavowing any "crude political motivation," she attributes it instead to the "endemically anti-authority" outlook of journalists. And whence comes the mistrust of authority? She chalks it up to professional experience.

Yet experience may structure the journalist's perspective less than the perspective structures the experience. Our data on both the media elite and journalism students suggest that this anti-authority outlook reflects a pre-existing temperament that brings young people to this profession. This temperament seems reinforced more often than created by professional experience.

Genuine attitude conversion undoubtedly occurs. But what journalists perceive as the lessons of experience may also reflect the hidden influence of group norms. All learning takes place within paradigms that structure the learning experience. So, discovering new realities may mean reinterpreting one's own experiences to conform to the dominant paradigm. As media critic Edward J. Epstein writes of television news staffers:

> Producers who tend to read the same newspapers . . . and news magazines, commute to the same area of [New York] City and discuss with friends the same agenda of problems can be expected to share a similar perspective on the critical themes of the day.[7]

None of this invalidates Greenfield's central point: Liberalism, in the sense of a narrow political agenda, is not all that is at work here. It is one element of a broader cast of mind among journalists. Probably just as important, for example, is the desire to exert moral power, as patrons of outsiders and victims with whom they identify, against traditional restrictions and institutional authority. Thus, after Robert Kennedy's assassination, *Los Angeles Times* publisher Otis Chandler lamented, "There's no one who represents us anymore." Asked whom he meant by "us," he replied, "The black and the young and the poor."[8]

The usual cast of villains will certainly include venal businessmen and bloodthirsty generals, but it can also encompass unfeeling government bureaucrats and corrupt labor leaders. All are seen as part of an establishment that is morally obtuse at best, and an enemy of humane and enlightened values at worst. Somehow, the mavericks and whistleblowers protect America's greatness from the failings of its leaders. In this vision of social reality, the liberal agenda should prevail over its conservative counterpart, but the difference may only be evident over the long term, and many stories will fall into neither camp.

For example, Michael Robinson attempted to classify one hundred days of network news feature stories as either liberal or conservative.[9] He found that only one in four contained political "spin." However, the remaining imbalance was mainly liberal, by margins of two to one at ABC and four to one at NBC; CBS was evenly balanced. Such studies, though useful, are limited by both the brief time frame and the necessity to classify coverage according to ideological categories. Political engagement is most likely to take hold among journalists when its partisan character is least evident to them. As Robinson has noted, on "blatantly partisan topics . . . such as Democrats vs. Republicans or liberals vs. conservatives . . . [journalists] will be most likely to have their 'guard up.' . . . But, in other instances, their understanding will be lacking and a relationship between [their personal] background and story slant will appear."[10]

To discover when and how this happens in specific instances should be a major focus of news content research. The studies reported in Chapters Six through Eight provide some answers, but the task must be ongoing. To be sure, there is no lack of current opinion on the nature of journalists' values and their relation to news coverage. But most scholarly research has been limited by the lack of either empirical procedures or theoretical context. Some studies have told us what journalists think, others have focused on what they say or write, and still others have tried to make sense of what it all means. Without a research design that puts the three elements together, the result is inevitable disagreement and partly overlapping, partly competing, explanations.

What has been missing is an integrated approach that examines the changing relationship between newspeople and the news product by using the tools of social science to test hypotheses generated by social theory. To carry out this research agenda, we have placed data from opinion polls, psychological tests, and content analyses in the service of the sociology of knowledge. These data suggest that (1) subjective elements are inherent in news coverage; (2) recent changes in American society and the journalistic profession have magnified these elements and shaped their direction; (3) as a result, the current intellectual and emotional milieu of the national media is expressed in news coverage of long-term social controversies.

This is not advocacy journalism; still less is it partisan proselytizing. It is an irony of the whole bias debate that the American media's very aspiration to objectivity has sensitized critics to even minor deviations from this norm. Indeed, both the aspiration and the criticism reflect the American political tradition's truncated ideological spectrum, and its claim to a single overarching vision of social reality. Even as today's journalists assert their right to greater interpretive freedom, they find it difficult to admit to the partiality all interpretation entails. But if all perspectives cast both light and shadow on reality, the danger lies in identifying a partial viewpoint with the common good and the whole truth. As one old-fashioned newsman noted in 1911, "truth must be stalked from a point of view."[11]

This issue has been given new urgency by the rise of a national news network and, with it, the creation of a new media elite—the influential professionals who staff that network. This group shares a distinctive sensibility that informs its reportage, all the more so insofar as it goes unrecognized. Even when self-awareness exists, powerful impediments to significant change in journalists' behavior remain. These barriers range from the pressures of deadlines to the need for defenses against outside critics.[12]

Nevertheless, unless journalists take responsibility for their creative role in shaping the news, they will remain mired in a debate over bias that is as misleading as it is acrimonious. As Ted Koppel recently told a gathering of his peers, "It's easy to be seduced into believing that what we're doing is just fine; after all, we get money, fame, and to a certain degree even influence. But money, fame, and influence without responsibility are the assets of a courtesan. We must accept responsibility for what we do, and we must think occasionally of the future."[13]

ΛPPENDIX

Survey Research Procedures

The Sample. To construct the sample of national media journalists, we began by creating lists of all individuals who had a significant input into the news product at each organization selected. This criterion excluded low-level personnel, such as interns and researchers, as well as executives with purely financial responsibilities.

Lists of all relevant employees, including print reporters and editors, broadcast production staffs and on-camera personnel, and executives with news responsibilities, were then created. Names were drawn from organizational telephone directories, newspaper and magazine mast-heads and bylines, and television newscast credits. The lists were then examined for accuracy by journalists at the various organizations and were revised and updated according to their suggestions.

The completed lists were matched against a computer-generated list of random numbers to produce a random sample. This technique of randomization was selected to permit inferences about the entire population of national media journalists, i.e., the media elite as defined in this book. We decided against stratifying the sample according to organization, job function, or other such criteria, because our primary research interest was to characterize the entire population rather than to compare such subgroups. This approach also obviated any need for mathematical weighting procedures in presenting the findings.

The Research Instrument. This consisted of standard demographic and attitude questionnaires, a test of selective perception and retention, and the Thematic Apperception Test. The demographic and attitude items are discussed in Chapter Two. They were drawn mainly from major polls, a forced-choice value selection test developed by political scientist Ronald Inglehart, and a survey of elites directed by political scientist Sidney Verba and sponsored jointly by Harvard University and the *Washington Post*.

The test of selective perception is discussed in Chapter Three. It consisted of four newspaper stories, which were altered slightly to highlight the issues reported. For example, unfamiliar names of sources were deleted, and some purely local features of nationally relevant stories were eliminated. The goal was to present information about social controversies in news story formats to test for selective recall of that information.

The Thematic Apperception Test consisted of the five pictures reproduced in Chapters Three and Four. Respondents were asked to create fictional stories about the characters shown. The test instructions were taken directly from standard manuals for survey administration of this test. This usage of the TAT is appropriate for making statistical inferences about groups of respondents but not for clinical evaluation of individuals.

The Interview. The research instrument was administered through in-person interviews conducted by professional interviewers. The interviews were supervised and the data collected by Response Analysis, a survey research organization in Princeton, New Jersey.

Prior to the survey, we conducted interviewer training sessions in cooperation with the Response Analysis project directors. The instrument was pretested among journalists at a daily newspaper and a television news department in Philadelphia. The instrument and interview procedures were then revised on the basis of interviewer and respondent comments.

For the survey, respondents were first contacted through letters requesting an interview. Interviewers then followed up by telephone to arrange an appointment. The interviews averaged about one hour in length. They were structured to provide similar stimuli (such as interviewer instructions) to all respondents. The general procedure was to hand the respondent a card containing each item, record the response (e.g., agree or disagree) on the interview protocol, and then take back the card. In order to avoid item placement bias, the attitude items were presented in random order by shuffling the cards prior to each interview.

The TAT was administered early in the interview, so that responses were not contaminated by subjects' varying reactions to the rest of the instrument. Respondents could either write their stories or dictate them into a tape recorder. Most chose the former option; for those who chose dictation, the interviewer left the room until the respondent was finished.

At the conclusion of the interview, the protocol and TAT stories were placed in an envelope and sealed. Interviewers were instructed to answer frequently encountered questions with standard responses. They referred all other questions or concerns by respondents to the study directors.

Data Preparation. The interview protocols were returned to Response Analysis, where the data were collated and computerized. Responses to the psychological tests were duplicated, assigned identification numbers, and returned to us for coding. As described in the text, this material was subjected to blind scoring by teams of trained coders. The resulting codes were then returned to Response Analysis for data entry. When the data entry was complete, we received the results in the form of a computer tape and codebook.

The subcontracting of data collection and preparation ensured that we could not, however unintentionally, bias the results through our participation in these phases of the project. To permit independent assessment of the research instrument and data analysis, tapes and codebooks have been placed on file with the Roper Center for Public Opinion Research at the University of Connecticut. Some of the data have been deleted or combined to protect the anonymity of respondents.

Item Wording. The complete wording of the attitude items listed in Table 2 follows. Respondents were asked to choose either "strongly agree," "somewhat agree," "somewhat disagree," or "strongly disagree" in response to each item.

1. Big corporations should be taken out of private ownership and run in the public interest.

2. Under a fair economic system, people with more ability should earn higher salaries.

3. The American private enterprise system is generally fair to working people.

4. Less government regulation of business would be good for the country.

5. The government should work to reduce substantially the income gap between the rich and the poor.

6. It is not the proper role of government to ensure that everyone has a job.

7. The structure of our society causes most people to feel alienated.

8. The United States needs a complete restructuring of its basic institutions.

9. All political systems are basically repressive, because they concentrate power and authority in a few hands.

10. The American legal system mainly favors the wealthy.

11. Our environmental problems are not as serious as people have been led to believe.

12. Strong affirmative action measures should be used in job hiring to ensure black representation.

13. The government should not attempt to regulate people's sexual practices.

14. It is a woman's right to decide whether or not to have an abortion.

15. It is wrong for adults of the same sex to have sexual relations.

16. Lesbians and homosexuals should not be allowed to teach in public schools.

17. It is wrong for a married person to have sexual relations with someone other than his or her spouse.

18. American economic exploitation has contributed to Third World poverty.

19. It is immoral for the United States to use so much of the world's resources while so many nations remain impoverished.

20. The main goal of U.S. foreign policy has been to protect U.S. business interests.

21. It is sometimes necessary for the CIA to protect U.S. interests by undermining hostile governments.

NOTES

Preface

1. C. Wright Mills, *The Power Elite* (New York: Oxford University Press, 1956).
2. Descriptions of our survey methods can also be found in S.R. Lichter and S. Rothman, "Scientists' Attitudes Toward Nuclear Energy," *Nature* 305, no. 8 (September 1983), 91–94; S. Rothman, "Ideology, Authoritarianism and Mental Health," *Political Psychology* 5, no. 3 (September 1984), 341–63; and S. Rothman and S.R. Lichter, "Personality, Ideology and Worldview: A Comparison of Media and Business Elites," *British Journal of Political Science* 15, no. 1 (1984), 29–49.
3. See Chapter 5 for further discussion of this point. In addition, media content is most likely to achieve lasting effects on political learning over time. See Elizabeth Noelle-Neumann, "Return to the Concept of Powerful Mass Media," in Radio and TV Culture Research Institute, *Studies of Broadcasting* (Tokyo: Nippon Hoso Kyokai, 1973), 67–112; *The Spiral of Silence: Public Opinion—Our Social Skin* (Chicago: University of Chicago Press, 1984).

Chapter 1

1. Herbert Stein, "Rating Presidents," *Fortune* (August 5, 1985), 115.
2. On the historical dominance of the ideology of liberalism in the United States, see Louis Hartz, *The Liberal Tradition in America* (New York: Harcourt Brace, 1955); Bialer and Sophia Sluzar, eds., *Sources of Contemporary Radicalism* (Boulder, Colorado: Westview Press, 1977), 31–149); S.M. Lipset, "Radicalism or Reformism: The Sources of Working Class Politics," *American Political Science Review* 77 (1983), 1–18, and Stanley Rothman, "Intellectuals and the American Political System," in S.M. Lipset, ed., *Emerging Coalitions in American Society* (San Francisco: Institute for Contemporary Studies, 1978), 325–52. This interpretation of American history is by no means universally accepted but, as Lipset copiously documents, it is an interpretation that many leading students of American and comparative history, including Marxist and neo-Marxist historians, do support.

3. So pervasive is the influence of its tradition that it is widely regarded as the "American ideology." See, for example, Everett
Ladd, Jr., *The American Polity* (New York: W.W. Norton, 1985),
63–67.
4. See the discussions and citations in Stanley Rothman, "The Mass
Media in Post-Industrial America," in S.M. Lipset, ed., *The Third
Century: America as a Post Industrial Society* (Chicago: University
of Chicago Press, 1979), 345–88; George N. Gordon, *The Communications Revolution* (New York: Hastings House Publishers,
1979); and Robert Desmond, *The Information Process* (Iowa City:
The University of Iowa Press, 1978).
5. For discussions of European-American differences, see Rothman,
Mass Media; Stanley Rothman, *European Society and Politics* (Indianapolis: Bobbs Merrill, 1970), 257–76; Arthur Williams, *Broadcasting and Democracy in West Germany* (London: Grenada Publishing, 1976); Anthony Smith, *The Shadow in the Cave* (London:
Allen and Unwin, 1973); Edward Ploman, *Broadcasting in Sweden*
(London: Routledge and Kegan Paul, 1976); and James B. Chris-
toph, "The Press and Politics in Britain and America," *Political
Quarterly* 34 (April–June 1963), 137–50.
6. Michael Schudson, *Discovering the News* (New York: Basic Books,
1978). See also Alexis de Tocqueville, *Democracy in America*, 2
vols. (New York: Alfred A. Knopf, 1948), I, 181–90.
7. In a "Lockean" individualistic society, only individuals were to be
represented by political parties. The representation of group interests was considered illegitimate. For an interesting contrast between American and British attitudes, see Samuel Beer, *British
Politics in the Collectivist Age* (New York: Alfred A. Knopf, 1965).
For comparisons with France and Germany, see Rothman, *European Society and Politics*.
8. Schudson, *Discovering the News*, 6.
9. Ibid., 7.
10. de Tocqueville, *Democracy in America*, 181–90.
11. Schudson, *Discovering the News;* David Halberstam, *The Powers
That Be* (New York: Dell Publishing, 1980); Erik Barnouw,
Tube of Plenty (New York: Oxford University Press, 1975);
Philip French, *The Movie Moguls* (Chicago: Henry A. Regnery,
1971).
12. Quoted in Schudson, *Discovering the News*, 153.
13. Thomas Patterson and Ronald Abeles, "Mass Communication and
the 1976 Presidential Elections," *Items* 29 (June 1975), 1.
14. For a discussion on the effects of television as television which
draws upon some of Marshall McCluhan's work with less

hyperbole, see Joshua Meyrowitz, *No Sense of Place* (New York: Oxford University Press, 1985).

15. Richard Merelman, *Making Something of Ourselves* (Berkeley: University of California Press, 1984).

16. Ibid., 30.

17. Edward J. Epstein, *News from Nowhere* (New York: Random House, 1973), 37.

18. See, for example, Carol H. Weiss, "What America's Leaders Read," *Public Opinion Quarterly* 38 (Spring 1974), 1–21; Michael Robinson and Maura Clancey, "King of the Hill," *Washington Journalism Review* (July-August 1983), 46–49; Leon V. Sigal, *Reporters and Officials* (Lexington, Mass.: D.C. Heath, 1973).

19. Roper Organization, *Evolving Public Attitudes toward Television and Other Mass Media 1959–1980* (New York: Television Information Office, 1981).

20. Lynne Cheney, "Who Watches Public Television?" *Washingtonian,* February 1986, 144.

21. Weiss, "America's Leaders."

22. William Rivers, "The Correspondents After 25 Years," *Columbia Journalism Review* 1 (Spring 1962), 4–10.

23. The statistics are from Daniel Bell, *The Coming of Post-Industrial Society* (New York: Basic Books, 1973).

24. Eric Goldman, *The Tragedy of Lyndon Johnson* (New York: Alfred A. Knopf, 1979).

25. Epstein, *News from Nowhere*, 219–20.

26. David Halberstam, "Starting Out to Be a Famous Reporter," *Esquire,* November 1981, 74.

27. For a discussion, see Halberstam, *The Powers That Be,* 491.

28. S. Robert Lichter and Stanley Rothman, "The Media and National Defense," in R. Pfalzgraff and U. Ra'anan, eds., *National Security Policy: The Decision-Making Process* (New York: Archon, 1984).

29. Peter Braestrup, *Big Story* (Boulder, Colorado: Westview Press, 1977).

30. Harris polls show that the proportion of the public expressing "a great deal of confidence" in the press dropped from 30 percent in 1973 to as low as 16 percent in 1981. See S.M. Lipset and William Schneider, *The Confidence Gap* (New York: Free Press, 1983), 48–49.

31. American Society of Newspaper Editors, *Newspaper Credibility: Building Reader Trust* (New York: ASNE, 1985).

32. Gladys Engel Lang and Kurt Lang, *The Battle for Public Opinion: The President, the Press, and the Polls during Watergate* (New York: Columbia University Press, 1983).

33. David Gergen, "The Message to the Media," *Public Opinion* (April–May 1984).
34. The decline is documented in Lipset and Schneider, *The Confidence Gap*. In the past few years attitudes toward American institutions and leadership groups have stabilized and even become slightly more positive.
35. *The People and The Press* (Los Angeles: Times Mirror, 1986), 4, 57.
36. "Year-Long *Times Mirror*/Gallup Survey Finds Public Trust of Media High But Independence in Doubt," *Times Mirror* News Release, January 15, 1986, 7.
37. Halberstam, *The Powers That Be*, 491.
38. For the former, see the various publications of the Media Institute, for example, *Chemical Risks: Facts, Fears and the Media* (Washington, D.C.: Media Institute, 1985); and *Punch, Counterpunch: 60 Minutes vs. Illinois Power Company* (Washington, D.C.: Media Institute, 1981). For the latter, see *Television: Corporate America's Game* (New York: Union Media Monitoring Project, 1982).
39. For the former, see Joshua Muravchik, "Misreporting Lebanon," *Policy Review* (Winter 1982/83). For the latter, see Edmund Ghareeb, *Split Vision* (Washington, D.C.: Arab-American Affairs Council, 1983). Evidence on both sides appears in William C. Adams, ed., *Television Coverage of the Middle East* (Norwood, N.J.: Ablex, 1981).
40. For the former, see Michael Parenti, *Inventing Reality* (New York: St. Martin's Press, 1986). For the latter, *Soviet Disinformation and the News* (Washington, D.C.: Heritage Foundation, 1985).
41. Sample titles from recent issues are, "The Media: Freedom's Shield or Achilles Heel," *AIM Report* 14 (December 1985); and "You Pay for Red Propaganda," *AIM Report* 15 (January 1986).
42. In addition to Parenti, *Inventing Reality*, see Herbert Schiller, *The Mind Managers* (Boston: Beacon Press, 1973); and Todd Gitlin, *The Whole World is Watching* (Berkeley, CA: University of California Press, 1980).

    For discussions of various radical perspectives on the media see Michael Gurevitch et al., eds., *Culture, Society and the Media* (London: Methuen and Co., Ltd., 1982; Peter Dreier, "Capitalists vs. the Media: An Analysis of an Ideological Mobilization Among Business Leaders," in *Media, Culture and Society* 4 (April 1982), 111–32, and Peter Dreier, "The Position of the Press in the U.S. Power Structure," *Social Problems* 29 (February 1982), 298–310.
43. Albert Hunt, "Media Bias is in the Eye of the Beholder," *Wall Street Journal*, July 23, 1985.

44. Thomas Griffith, "The Benefits of Surveillance," *Time,* December 2, 1985, 83.
45. For introductions into the voluminous literature on the sociology of knowledge, see Karl Mannheim, *Ideology and Utopia* (New York: International Library of Psychology, Philosophy and Scientific Method, 1936); and Peter Berger and Thomas Luckmann, *The Social Construction of Reality* (New York: Doubleday, 1967). An approach that incorporates psychoanalytic insights is found in Fred Weinstein and Gerald Platt, *The Wish to Be Free* (Berkeley: University of California Press, 1969).
46. Hunt, "Media Bias."

Chapter 2

1. The interviews were conducted for us during 1979 and 1980 by Response Analysis, a survey research firm in Princeton, N.J. The public broadcasting sample included public affairs staffers at PBS and three major producing stations (WNET, WETA, WGBH), along with independent producers whose work has appeared on PBS outlets. We originally reported the number of cases as 240. However, we later ascertained that two respondents who completed the interview had declined to answer virtually every question. Therefore, they were dropped from the analysis.
2. Seventy-six percent of those contacted completed the interview. This response rate was high enough to ensure that our findings provide reliable insights into the composition and perspective of this group.

    Many journalists are uneasy about the term *elite,* although they might be more at ease with appellations like *successful* or *leading* journalists. We use this term in descriptive fashion to refer to the members of the most important media organizations in America. By this definition, a reporter at the *New York Times* qualifies, while the editors and publishers of the *Miami Herald* or the *Boston Globe* do not, although they undoubtedly could be included under another definition. We have already discussed the rationale for our approach, which flows from theoretical concerns about the changing role of the national media in American society.
3. The business sample included top- and middle-level executives from three *Fortune* 500 industrial firms, and one firm each drawn from *Fortune* lists of the fifty leading American retail outlets, banks, and public utilities. In each case, we developed a randomly based sample of top and middle-management personnel from official company lists. The response rate among this group was 95 percent. We can identify the media outlets sampled because person-

nel were interviewed as individuals. We approached the business firms as organizations, however, and a requirement for their cooperation in each case was a promise of anonymity. Our statements about the nature of our samples and response rates can be verified by Response Analysis, the independent survey research organization that conducted the interviews for us.

4. Dom Bonafede, "The Washington Press—Competing for Power with the Federal Government," *National Journal,* April 17, 1982.

5. *Washington Post,* April 4, 1984.

6. Jacob Weissberg, "The Buckrakers," *New Republic,* January 27, 1986, 16–18.

7. Jody Powell, *Washington Post,* May 31, 1983.

8. James Deakin, *Straight Stuff* (New York: William Morrow and Co., 1984), 340–41.

9. *Washington Post,* May 7, 1984.

10. Deakin, *Straight Stuff,* 340–41.

11. Cited in Deakin, *Straight Stuff,* 345.

12. Ben Bagdikian, "Professional Personnel and Organizational Structures in the Mass Media," in W. P. Davison and F.T.C. Yu, eds., Mass Communications Research (New York: Praeger, 1974), 135.

13. Cited in Deakin, *Straight Stuff,* 345.

14. Henry Fairlie, "How Journalists Get Rich," *Washingtonian,* August 1983, 81–86.

15. Jack Germond and Jules Witcover, "Never Eat the Rubber Chicken," *Washingtonian,* January 1983, 58, 62, 63.

16. *Washington Post,* August 3, 1983.

17. Fairlie, "How Journalists Get Rich," 86.

18. Bagdikian, "Professional Personnel," 81.

19. Charlotte Hays and Jonathan Rowe, "Reporters: The New Washington Elite," *Washington Monthly,* July-August 1985, 21.

20. Ibid., 22.

21. *Washington Post,* February 28, 1984.

22. This distinction was originally applied to network and wire service journalists in Michael Robinson and Margaret Sheehan, *Over the Wire and On TV* (New York: Russell Sage Foundation, 1983).

23. Joseph Kraft, "The Imperial Media," *Commentary,* May 1981, 39, 42.

24. No more than 2 percent ever voted for third-party candidates.

25. Everett Ladd, Jr., "The New Lines Are Drawn," *Public Opinion,* July/August 1978, 48–53.

26. Stanley Rothman and S. Robert Lichter, "Personality, Ideology and Worldview: A Study of Two Elites," *British Journal of Political Science* 15 (Fall 1984), 1–21.

Notes

27. Kraft, "The Imperial Media," 42.
28. Ronald Inglehart, *The Silent Revolution* (Princeton, N.J.: Princeton University Press, 1977).
29. Barry Sussman, "Media Leaders Want Less Influence," *Washington Post*, September 29, 1976.
30. The Gallup poll results are reproduced in *Public Opinion*, April–May 1985, 35.
31. *Washington Post*, September 29, 1976.
32. Stephen Hess, *The Washington Reporters* (Washington, D.C.: Brookings Institution, 1981).
33. J.W.C. Johnstone, E.J. Slawski, and W.W. Bowman, *The Newspeople* (Urbana, Ill.: University of Illinois Press, 1976).
34. Fred J. Evans, "The Conflict Surveyed," *Business Forum* 9 (Spring 1984), 18.
35. G. Cleveland Wilhoit, David Weaver, and Richard Gray, *The American Journalist* (Bloomington, Ind.: Indiana University Press, 1985).
36. *Los Angeles Times*, August 12, 1985.
37. William Schneider and I.A. Lewis, "Views on the News," *Public Opinion*, August/September 1985, 7.
38. Ibid., 8.
39. Ibid., 7.
40. *Los Angeles Times*, August 12, 1985.
41. Schneider and Lewis, "Views on the News," 8.
42. Leo Rosten, *The Washington Correspondents* (New York: Harcourt, Brace, 1937), 191.
43. Ibid., 352.
44. William Rivers, "The Correspondents after 25 Years," *Columbia Journalism Review* 1 (Spring 1962), 5.
45. Ibid.
46. Ibid.
47. Hess, *The Washington Reporters*, 5.
48. Quoted in Robinson and Sheehan, *Over the Wire and On TV*, 277.
49. Ben Bagdikian, "Professional Personnel," 134.
50. Tom Teepen, "Press' Liberalism Is Force-Fed," *Atlanta Constitution*, May 22, 1985.
51. The response rate was 60 percent. The sample excluded Bagehot and Mid-career Fellows.
52. To help ascertain whether the students' liberalism was attributable to their youth, we compared them to a random sample of forty students at New York University's Graduate School of Business. This provides a comparison analogous to that of media and business elites, while eliminating the influence of generational effects.

The two student groups are also roughly matched for background characteristics: both share differentially northeastern, urban, upper-status, and Jewish backgrounds. Despite these similarities, the journalism students prove the more liberal. On most issues the differences are roughly as great between the two student groups as those we found between their adult counterparts. Thus, the attitudes of aspiring journalists and businessmen already diverge sharply. This supports the hypothesis that journalists tend to acquire their liberal outlooks more at home than on the job.

53. Daniel P. Moynihan, "The Presidency and the Press," *Commentary*, March 1971, 43.
54. Richard Harwood, *Washington Post*, April 12, 1971.
55. *New York Times*, June 8, 1984.
56. Timothy Crouse, *The Boys on the Bus* (New York: Ballantine Books, 1974), 244.
57. David Halberstam, "Starting Out to Be a Famous Reporter," *Esquire*, November 1981, 74.
58. Deakin, *Straight Stuff*, 328.
59. Stephen Hess, "Washington Reporters," *Society*, May/June 1981, 57.

Chapter 3

1. Walter Cronkite, quoted in *Playboy*, June 1973, 26.
2. For a provocative and original attempt to understand both journalism and politics in terms of the imaginative reconstruction of reality, see Dan Nimmo and James Combs, *Mediated Political Realities* (New York: Longman, 1983). Our own analysis is compatible with much of their theoretical framework, without necessarily requiring such complete subjectivism.
3. The survey was conducted before the Reagan administration dramatically altered the role and activities of formerly activist agencies like the EPA and OSHA.
4. This topic was not included in the original interviews. We decided to add it later because of the directions the research had taken. Several months after interviewing leading journalists and businessmen, we began a separate survey of scientists' attitudes toward nuclear energy. This survey is described in detail in Chapter Six.

The purpose was to compare media coverage of nuclear power with expert opinion on the same subject. By learning about journalists' attitudes as well, we could determine whether their coverage more closely resembled the experts' views or their own. That required returning to the same journalists who were originally interviewed and asking them additional questions about nuclear energy.

Sixty-five percent of the original sample responded. Their attitudes are discussed in Chapter Six. Here we summarize only their listing of sources they consider reliable. Because no comparable data were gathered for businessmen, attention shifts to the journalists' choice of pro-nuclear vs. anti-nuclear services.

5. Joseph Kraft, "Reagan Beats the Press," *Washington Post,* August 2, 1983.

6. The notion that people tend to process new information partly in terms of pre-existing attitudes and sympathies is well documented, although the underlying psychological principles are still debated, as is the extent to which cognitive consistency governs behavior. See Leon Festinger, *A Theory of Cognitive Dissonance* (Stanford: Stanford University Press, 1957); David Sears and Jonathan Freedman, "Selective Exposure to Information: A Critical Review," *Public Opinion Quarterly* 31 (1967), 194–213; Roger Brown, *Social Psychology* (New York: Free Press, 1965), 549–609; W.P. Davison, J. Boylan, and F.T.C. Yu, *Mass Media: Systems and Effects* (New York: Holt, Rinehart and Winston, 1976), 131–58.

7. Scores on this index ranged from -2 to $+6$. The result was a moderate linear relationship (gamma $= .46$, tau $= .33$, p $< .001$), in which different cut-points for the high and low categories produced very similar tabular differences between the two groups. In the table shown, net scores of two or more were placed in the high category, and net negative scores and scores of zero were placed in the low category.

8. Bill Kovach, "Values Behind the News," (symposium held at American University, Washington, D.C., December 6, 1983).

9. Sigal, *Reporters and Officials,* 5.

10. Warren Breed, "Social Control in the Newsroom." *Social Forces* 33 (May 1955), 326–35.

11. See also D.L. Altheide and R.P. Snow, *Media Logic* (New York: Sage, 1979); Epstein, *News from Nowhere*; Bernard Roshco, *Newsmaking* (Chicago: University of Chicago Press, 1975); Gaye Tuchman, *Making News* (New York: Free Press, 1978); Herbert Gans, *Deciding What's News* (New York: Pantheon Books, 1979). Gans does not hold strictly to this approach but presents it as more persuasive than attitude-centered theories.

12. See, for example, Gans, *Deciding What's News,* 78; Epstein, *News from Nowhere,* 7–8.

13. Wilhoit et al., in *The American Journalist,* report differences of only 2 to 3 percent between executives and staffers who placed themselves on the political Left. A decade earlier, Johnston et al., in *The Newspeople,* found that executives at prominent organiza-

tions were substantially more likely to describe themselves as *Left*-leaning (by 73 to 53 percent). At nonprominent organizations they found the reverse, with only 25 percent of the executives choosing a Left orientation, compared to 41 percent of the staffers. The pollsters for the *Los Angeles Times* survey note that editors-in-chief were more conservative than reporters, although no figures are presented (Schneider and Lewis, "Views on the News," 8).

14. Epstein, *News from Nowhere,* 272.
15. *Ibid.,* 233.
16. Roshco, *Newsmaking,* 105.
17. Gans, *Deciding What's News,* 201.
18. Herbert Gans, "Are American Journalists Dangerously Liberal?" *Columbia Journalism Review* (November/December 1985), 32–33.
19. Gans, *Deciding What's News,* 41.
20. Associated Press Managing Editors Association, *Journalists and Readers: Bridging the Credibility Gap* (San Francisco: APME, 1985), 28.
21. Gans, *Deciding What's News,* 48.
22. Theodore H. White, "America's Two Cultures," *Columbia Journalism Review* (Winter 1969), 9–10.
23. Rosten, *The Washington Correspondents,* 149–50.

Chapter 4
1. *Washington Post,* November 5, 1984, section C.
2. Deakin, *Straight Stuff,* 329.
3. Henry Murray, *Explorations in Personality* (New York: Oxford University Press, 1938), xii.
4. *Ibid.,* 545.
5. David McClelland, *Assessing Human Motivation* (New York: General Learning Press, 1971), 12.
6. Ibid.
7. David Winter, *The Power Motive* (New York: Free Press, 1973), 117–18.
8. *Ibid.,* 117–18.
9. McClelland argues that power motivation can be either personalized or sublimated to larger social purposes. The behavioral patterns of sublimated and unsublimated high power scorers are also somewhat different, in ways that seem to conform to theory. At first, McClelland tried to measure sublimated power by differentiating between TAT stories in which power or influence were sought for personal ends ("He wants to be elected President because he wants to be top dog.") and for social purposes ("He wants to be elected president so he can help the poor."). He found few

behavioral differences between respondents who emphasized social as against personal gain. He discovered that use of the word *not* in TAT stories seems to reflect the sublimation of power needs. Individuals who score high both on *n* Power and *nots* do tend to sublimate power to social organizational goals. On the other hand, high power, low *not* scorers tend to exploit others for personal gain. His research procedures and findings are described in David McClelland, *Power: The Inner Experience* (New York: John Wiley and Sons, 1975).

Following these procedures, we also compared unsublimated or personalized power scores of journalists and businessmen. Once again, the journalists produced significantly higher scores (p < .001).

10. David Winter and Abigail Stewart, "The Power Motive," in Harvey London and John Exner, eds., *Dimensions of Personality* (New York: John Wiley and Sons, 1978), 421–22.

11. W.W. Meissner, *The Paranoid Process* (New York: Jason Aronson, 1978). See Winter, *The Power Motive,* 144–48, for empirical evidence on the association of paranoia with fear of power.

12. See, for example, David McClelland and David Winter, *Motivating Economic Achievement* (New York: Free Press, 1969); D. Winter, D. McClelland, and A. Stewart, *Competence in College* (San Francisco: Jossey-Bass, 1981); and John Atkinson, ed., *Motives in Fantasy, Action and Society* (New York: Van Nostrand, 1958).

13. David McClelland, *The Achieving Society* (New York: Van Nostrand, 1961). McClelland's effort to develop broad generalizations about whole societies by using these methods has aroused considerable controversy. The scoring systems which he, Winter, and others have developed, however, have generally been well received by the profession. Most commentators agree that the methods used to develop and validate the scoring systems have been rigorous and empirically sound.

14. Daniel McAdams, "Themes of Intimacy in Behavior and Thought," *Journal of Personality and Social Psychology* 40, no. 3 (1981), 573–87; "Studies in Intimacy Motivation" in Abigail Stewart, ed., *Motivation and Society* (New York: Jossey-Bass, 1981).

15. Otto Kernberg, *Borderline Conditions and Pathological Narcissism* (New York: Jason Aronson, 1975).

16. Jennifer Cole, "Narcissistic Character Traits in Left Activists" (Ph.D. diss., University of Michigan, 1979). Unlike the other TAT scoring systems we have discussed, this was derived clinically rather than experimentally. Although it has met the scientific test of reliability, evidence of its validity is still lacking. It is therefore

a speculative test whose findings are only suggestive. In a previous use of this system, however, we found in two separate studies that male political radicals outscored nonradicals in narcissistic pathologies. The radicals also recalled having more negative relationships with their parents than did nonradicals. These findings supported our hypothesis that one source of their radicalism was injured or "bruised" narcissism early in life. See Stanley Rothman and Robert Lichter, *Roots of Radicalism* (New York: Oxford Press, 1982), 252–57, 345–46.

17. Two other measures of narcissistic traits, which Cole terms "low boundaries" and "heterogeneity," cropped up only rarely and did not significantly differentiate the two groups. These measures are intended to tap emotional fluidity found more often in adolescents than successful adults. Even if these responses are included, however, the resulting overall measure of narcissism produces group differences significant at the .001 level.

18. It might be argued that journalists, as professional writers, would naturally tend toward more flamboyant imagery. It is not creativity, however, but self-reference that is critical to this scoring system. Moreover, this "occupational" argument cuts both ways. One could also argue that journalistic training subdues personal expressions of creativity in favor of a more prosaic orientation toward factual accounts of reality.

19. Longitudinal studies in both the United States and England show that the TAT scores of college students predict their subsequent career choices. This eliminates the possibility that the motives develop as responses to different occupational roles. These findings are reported in Winter, *Power Motive*, 107–9.

20. Rosaline Hirschowitz and Victor Nell, "The Relationship Between Need for Power and the Life Style of South African Journalists," *Journal of Social Psychology* 121:2 (December 1983), 297–304. In this study the journalists worked at newspapers in major cities, and the controls were matched for age, sex, language, and socio-economic status.

21. Daniel Bell, *The Cultural Contradictions of Capitalism* (New York: Basic Books, 1976), Ch. 1; Bell, *The Coming of Post-Industrial Society*, 477–80.

22. Rothman and Lichter, "Personality, Ideology, and Worldview."

23. Max Weber, " 'Objectivity' in Social Science," in Edward Shils and Henry Finch (trans.), *Max Weber on the Methodology of the Social Sciences* (Glencoe, Ill.: Free Press, 1949), 90–103.

24. Hess, *The Washington Reporters*, 124.

25. *Time*, April 11, 1983, 79.

26. Robinson and Sheehan, *Over the Wire and On T.V.*, 147–48.
27. *Washington Post*, November, 11, 1984, section A.
28. Deakin, *Straight Stuff*, 328.
29. Maura Clancey and Michael Robinson, "General Election Coverage: Part I," in Michael Robinson and Austin Ranney, eds., *The Mass Media in Campaign '84* (Washington D.C.: American Enterprise Institute, 1985), 32.
30. David Paletz and Robert Entman, *Media Power Politics* (New York: Free Press, 1981), 16–17.
31. *Washington Post*, July 15, 1984.
32. Sigal, *Reporters and Officials*, 3.
33. Epstein, *News from Nowhere*.
34. Leo Rosten, *The Washington Correspondents*, 243–44.
35. Quoted in Philip Hilts, "And That's the Way It Was," *Washington Post Magazine*, March 15, 1981, 36.
36. Quoted in Crouse, *The Boys on the Bus*, 71.
37. Ibid., 72.
38. Quoted in Charles Peters, *How Washington Really Works* (Reading, Mass: Addison-Wesley, 1983), 22–23.
39. Tom Shales, *Washington Post*, June 5, 1984, section C, 1–2.
40. Clancey and Robinson, "General Election Coverage: Part I."
41. Ibid., 33.
42. Steven Wiseman, "The President and the Press," *New York Times Magazine*, October 14, 1984, 34.
43. Ibid., 36.
44. Rosten, *The Washington Correspondents*, 247–48.
45. Fred Friendly, *TV Guide*, August 1, 1981, 25.
46. Tony Schwartz, "Bill Moyers—the Trick is to Make TV Work for You," *New York Times*, January 3, 1982, 21,27.
47. Harold Lasswell, "Psychopathology and Politics," in the Political Writings of H.B. Lasswell (Glencoe, Ill.: Free Press, 1951).
48. Louis Banks, "Memo to the Press, They Hate you Out There," *Atlantic*, April 1978, 35.
49. Friendly, *TV Guide*, 25.
50. Quoted in *Washington Post*, April 18, 1981.
51. *Washington Post*, October 30, 1983.
52. Deakin, *Straight Stuff*, 352–53.
53. *Time*, December 12, 1983, 76–77.
54. *Washington Post*, January 2, 1985.
55. Kraft, "The Imperial Media," 39–40.
56. Clifton Daniel, "Presidents I Have Known," *New York Times Magazine*, June 3, 1984, 50.
57. Crouse, *The Boys on the Bus*, 5.

58. Kraft, "The Imperial Media," 37–38.
59. *Washington Post,* June 5, 1984.
60. Ibid.
61. "Journalism Under Fire," *Time,* December 12, 1983, 78.
62. *Washington Post,* October 22, 1984.
63. Ibid.
64. *Washington Post,* September 29, 1984, June 30, 1984, February 12, 1984.
65. Robinson and Sheehan, *Over the Wire and On T.V.,* 212.
66. Ibid., 302.
67. Ibid., 91.
68. Hess, *The Washington Reporter,* 126.
69. Rosten, *The Washington Correspondents,* 242.
70. Ibid., 243.
71. Crouse, *The Boys on the Bus,* 371–74.
72. Ibid., 393.
73. Rosten, *The Washington Correspondents,* 241.
74. Ibid.
75. "Can the Press Tell the Truth?" *Harper's,* January 1985, 51.
76. *Playboy,* January 1985, 268.
77. Hess, *The Washington Reporter,* 89.
78. "Can the Press Tell the Truth?" *Harper's,* January 1985, 39, 50.

Chapter 5
1. Quoted in Epstein, *News From Nowhere,* 14–15.
2. Ibid.
3. Quoted in *Playboy,* March 1985, 167.
4. *New York Times,* December 12, 1984.
5. *Washington Post,* December 12, 1984.
6. *New York Times,* September 30, 1984.
7. *Washington Post,* September 30, 1984.
8. *Washington Post,* November 13, 1984.
9. *New York Times,* November 12, 1984.
10. Donald Shaw, "News Bias and the Telegraph," *Journalism Quarterly* 44 (Spring 1967), 3–12, 31.
11. Lewis Lapham, "Gilding the News," *Harper's,* July 1981, 33.
12. Cited in Halberstam, *The Powers That Be,* 36.
13. "Reporting 'Background': You Can Interpret and Still Retain Objectivity," *Nieman Reports* 4 (April 1950), 29.
14. *Washington Post,* December 10, 1983.
15. *New York Times,* February 7, 1984.
16. *New York Times,* October 2, 1984.
17. *Washington Post,* March 4, 1985.

18. *Washington Post,* September 8, 1983.
19. *Washington Post,* March 27, 1982.
20. *Washington Post,* February 10, 1984.
21. *Washington Post,* July 14, 1985.
22. *New York Times,* May 22, 1984.
23. *New York Times,* March 7, 1984.
24. *Wall Street Journal,* June 18, 1984.
25. Ibid.
26. *New York Times,* July 13, 1984.
27. *New York Times,* June 20, 1984.
28. *Washington Post,* June 25, 1984.
29. *New York Times,* June 20, 1984.
30. *Washington Post,* June 19, 1984.
31. Lapham, "Gilding the News," 35.
32. The Roper Organization, *Evolving Public Attitudes toward Television.*
33. William C. Adams, "Visual Analysis of Newscasts," in W.C. Adams and Fay Schreibman, eds., *Television Network News: Issues in Content Research* (Washington, D.C.: George Washington University, 1978), 155–76.
34. Epstein, *News from Nowhere,* 153.
35. Paul Weaver, "Newspaper News and Television News," in Douglass Cater, ed., *Television as a Social Force* (New York: Praeger, 1975), 92.
36. Robinson and Sheehan, *Over the Wire and On T.V.,* 216.
37. H.M. Kepplinger, "Visual Biases in Television Campaign Coverage," *Communication Research* 9 (July 1982), 432–46.
38. Paul Good, "Why You Can't Always Trust '60 Minutes' Reporting," *Panorama,* September 1980, 39.
39. Quoted from Harry Stein, "How '60 Minutes' Makes News," *New York Times Magazine,* May 6, 1979, 76.
40. Ibid., 78.
41. Good, "Why You Can't Always Trust '60 Minutes' Reporting," 108.
42. Media Institute, *Punch, Counterpunch,* 33.
43. Fay Schreibman, "Television News Archives," in Adams and Schreibman, *Television Network News,* 91, 109.
44. Public Agenda Foundation study quoted in Ron Nessen, "Should TV News Always Tell All?" *TV Guide,* June 27, 1981, 10.
45. Don Kowett and Sally Bedell, "Anatomy of a Smear," *TV Guide,* May 29, 1982, 15.
46. Burton Benjamin, *CBS Reports' "The Uncounted Enemy: A Vietnam Deception: An Examination,"* Mimeo, July 8, 1982, 57.

Notes

47. The best introduction to this technique is probably found in Ole Holsti, *Content Analysis for the Social Sciences and Humanities* (Reading, Mass.: Addison-Wesley, 1969). See also Adams and Schreibman, *Television Network News*, especially W. C. Adams, "Network News Research in Perspective," 11–46; and Lawrence Lichty and George Bailey, "Reading the Wind: Reflections on Content Analysis of Broadcast News," 111–138.
48. Edith Efron, *The News Twisters* (Los Angeles: Nash Publishing, 1971).
49. R.L. Stevenson, R.A. Eisinger, B.M. Feinberg, and A.B. Kotok, "Untwisting *The News Twisters*," *Journalism Quarterly* (Summer 1973), 211–19.
50. C. Richard Hofstetter, *Bias in the News* (Columbus: Ohio State University Press, 1976).
51. Clancey and Robinson, "General Election Coverage: Part I."
52. For example, Robinson and Sheehan's conclusion is strengthened by the fact that at least three other scientific studies independently found a pro-Mondale or anti-Reagan tilt in 1984 campaign coverage. See Dennis Lowry, "Measures of Network TV News Bias in Campaign '84" (paper presented at the annual conference of the Association for Education in Journalism and Mass Communication, Memphis, Tenn., August 3, 1985); John Merriam, "Media Coverage of the Election," *Issues Management Letter*, November 13, 1984; Doris Graber, "Candidate Images: An Audio-Visual Analysis" (paper presented at the annual meeting of the American Political Science Association, Chicago, August 29-September 1, 1985). The Graber study is particularly innovative in its examination of TV news "visuals," an element that further studies would do well to incorporate.
53. Of course, there are many aspects to campaign coverage besides the question of partisanship. Among the best additional examples of the extensive content analysis literature on this topic are William C. Adams, ed., *Television Coverage of the 1980 Campaign* (Norwood, N.J.: Abley, 1983); Doris Graber, *Mass Media and American Politics* (Washington, D.C.: Congressional Quarterly Press, 1984), chapter six; and Thomas Patterson's classic study, *The Mass Media Election* (New York: Praeger, 1980).
54. Kurt Lang and Gladys Engel Lang, "The Unique Perspective of Television and Its Effect," *American Sociological Review* 18 (February 1953), 3–12.
55. David Altheide, *Creating Reality* (Beverly Hills, Cal.: Sage Publications, 1976).
56. Ben Bagdikian, "Professional Personnel," 33

Notes

Chapter 6

1. This and the following quotations are from "The Fire Unleashed," ABC-TV, June 6, 1985.
2. Unpublished Cambridge Reports study, July 1985.
3. W.L. Rankin, B.D. Melber, T.D. Overcast, and S.M. Nealey, *Nuclear Power and the Public* (Seattle, Wash.: Battelle Human Affairs Research Centers, 1981).
4. Roger Kasperson et al., "Public Opinion and Nuclear Energy," *Science, Technology, and Human Values,* Spring 1980, 11–23.
5. W.L. Rankin, S.M. Nealey and D.E. Montano, *Analysis of Print Coverage of Nuclear Power Issues* (Seattle, Wash.: Battelle, 1978); W.L. Rankin and S.M. Nealey, *A Comparative Analysis of Network Television News Coverage of Nuclear Power,* Coal and Solar Stories (Seattle, Wash.: Battelle, 1979).
6. Media Institute, *Television Evening News Covers Nuclear Energy* (Washington, D.C.: The Media Institute, 1979).
7. Joseph F. Coates, "What Is a Public Policy Issue? An Advisory Essay," *Interdisciplinary Science Reviews* 4 (March 1979), 29.
8. Alvin M. Weinberg, "Can Technology Replace Social Engineering?" in Albert H. Teich, ed., *Technology and Man's Future* (New York: St. Martin's Press, 1972), 27–35.
9. Nuclear Energy Policy Study Group, *Nuclear Power Issues and Choices* (Cambridge, Mass.: Ballinger, 1977), 399–401.
10. William Proxmire, "Congress Must Act on Proliferation," *Bulletin of the Atomic Scientists* 41 (March 1985), 32–34.
11. Jerrold H. Krenz, *Energy: From Opulence to Sufficiency* (New York: Praeger, 1980), 164–65.
12. Eliot Marshall, "Reactor Safety and the Research Budget," *Science* 214 (November 13, 1981), 766.
13. John Kemeny, "Saving American Democracy: The Lessons of Three Mile Island," *Technology Review* (June/July 1980), 81; Dorothy Nelkin, "Some Social and Political Dimensions of Nuclear Power: Examples from Three Mile Island," *American Political Science Review* 75 (March 1981), 134.
14. Colin Norman, "Assessing the Effects of a Nuclear Accident," *Science* 228 (April 5, 1985), 31–33.
15. Having taken the light water reactor (LWR) path, the federal government and nuclear industry alike have tended to ignore the second U.S. reactor type—the high-temperature, gas-cooled reactor (HTGR), one of which operates at Fort St. Vrain, Colorado. Troubles with the LWR, however, have given increased attention to the HTGR, primarily because of its safety advantages. These are twofold: less radioactivity is inserted into the cooling system, and it

tolerates much higher temperatures in the core. But the debate has expanded even beyond the domestic HTGR. A recent study by the Institute for Energy Analysis suggested a more aggressive posture toward a smaller, German-American modular high temperature reactor and the Swedish Process Inherent Ultimately Safe (PIUS) technology. Both these options are said to possess "inherently safe" characteristics that "rely not upon the intervention of humans or of electromechanical devices but on immutable principles of physics and chemistry." A.M. Weinberg and I. Spicwak, "Inherently Safe Reactors and a Second Nuclear Era," *Science* 224, June 29, 1984, 1398–1402.

16. Gerald Garvey, *Nuclear Power and Social Planning* (Lexington, Mass.: D.C. Heath, 1977), 76–77.

17. Ralph Nader and John Abbotts, *The Menace of Atomic Energy* (New York: W. W. Norton, 1977), 64–65.

18. Nuclear Energy Policy Study Group, *Nuclear Power Issues*, 283–86.

19. Marc H. Ross and Robert Williams, *Our Energy: Regaining Control* (New York: McGraw-Hill, 1981), 67.

20. John P. Holdren, "Energy Hazards: What to Measure, What to Compare," *Technology Review* 85 (April 1982), 37.

21. Julia Bickerstaffe and David Pearce, "Can There Be a Consensus on Nuclear Power?" *Social Studies of Science* 10 (August 1980), 317.

22. Nader and Abbotts, *The Menace of Atomic Energy*, 62–63.

23. Arthur C. Upton, "The Biological Effects of Low-Level Ionizing Radiation," *Scientific American* 246 (February 1982), 41–49.

24. Sam H. Schurr, Joel Darmstadter, William Ramsay, Harry Perry, and Milton Russell, *Energy in America's Future* (Baltimore: Johns Hopkins University Press, 1979), 353.

25. J. M. Harrison, "Disposal of Radioactive Wastes," *Science* 226 (October 5, 1984), 11–14.

26. Ford Foundation, *Energy: The Next Twenty Years* (Cambridge, Mass.: Ballinger, 1979), 441–42.

27. U.S. Department of Energy, *The National Energy Policy Plan* (Washington: U.S. Department of Energy, 1983).

28. Mark Crawford, "The Electricity Industry's Dilemma," *Science* 229 (July 19, 1985); 248–50; Russ Manning, "The Future of Nuclear Power," *Environment* 27 (May 1985); 12–17, 31–37.

29. Holdren, *Energy Hazards*; Robert W. Crandall and Lester B. Lave, eds., *The Scientific Basis of Health and Safety Regulation* (Washington, D.C.: The Brookings Institution, 1981).

30. Dorothy Nelkin and Michael Pollak, "Problems and Procedures in the Regulation of Technological Risks," in Carol H. Weiss and

Allan H. Barton, eds., *Making Bureaucracies Work* (Beverly Hills, Cal.: Sage, 1980), 259–78.

31. Bruce A. Bishop, Mac McKee and Roger D. Hansen, *Public Consultation in Public Policy Information: A State-of-the-Art Report* (Washington, D.C.: U.S. Energy Research and Development Administration, 1978).

32. Dorothy Nelkin, *Technological Decisions and Democracy* (Beverly Hills, Cal.: Sage, 1977).

33. Allan Mazur, *The Dynamics of Technical Controversy* (Washington, D.C.: Communications Press, 1981).

34. Our results are presented in detail in S. Rothman and S. R. Lichter, "The Nuclear Energy Debate: Scientists, the Media, and the Public," *Public Opinion,* August/September 1982, 47–52; S. R. Lichter and S. Rothman, "Scientists' Attitudes Toward Nuclear Energy," *Nature,* September 8, 1983, 91–94; R. L. Cohen and S. R. Lichter, "Nuclear Energy: The Decision Makers Speak," *Regulation,* March/April 1983, 32–37.

35. Robert Cohen, "The Perception and Evaluation of Public Opinion by Decision-Makers: Civilian Nuclear Power in the United States" (Ph.D. diss., Columbia University, 1982).

36. Sharon Dunwoody, "The Science Writing Inner Club: A Communication Link Between Science and the Lay Public," *Science, Technology and Human Values* (Winter 1980), 14–22. Based on this analysis, we added science journalists at such outlets as the Associated Press and United Press International, *Christian Science Monitor, Los Angeles Times,* and *Boston Globe.*

37. Our sources, in this and our other two studies, were the *Reader's Guide* for magazine articles, the *New York Times Index* for its stories, and the Vanderbilt Television News Archive for broadcast material. We examined all 266 articles from the newsweeklies as well as 606 *Times* articles and 657 television stories.

38. The standard was actually somewhat more strenuous. We used a statistic called Scott's pi, which corrects for the likelihood that coders will sometimes agree by chance. Coders were assigned to pairs, and each pair was tested prior to coding each media format (newspaper, magazine, television). They were allowed to begin coding only after they attained an agreement rating on pi exceeding .80. This is considerably more difficult than attaining an 80 percent level of agreement, the widely used minimum.

39. CBS, January 26, 1971 (all television references are to the evening newscast).

40. "How Safe the Atom," *Time,* August 18, 1972, 78.

41. "All About Radiation," *Newsweek,* April 9, 1979, 40.

42. "No Truce in the New A-War," *Newsweek,* June 21, 1976, 61.

43. NBC, June 13, 1981.

44. "Trying to Contain the Genie," *Time,* June 22, 1981, 40.

45. "Too Hot for the Usual Burial," *Time,* January 10, 1983, 19.

46. NBC, April 28, 1982.

47. The coding system was initially applied to the *New York Times,* whose stories could be reliably assigned to either the problem or issue category. However, the highly interpretive character of television and magazine stories (as well as the latter's greater length) often produced a combination of technological and political elements. Therefore, a combination category was added to accommodate the actual structures of the stories. This means that results for the *Times* and the other media are not precisely comparable on this dimension. Luckily, the results were so consistent that this minor change had no effect on the overall pattern. When comparing coverage of technical and political answers, we refer to the "pure" categories, ignoring the combination stories.

48. "Radioactive Water Spills," *New York Times,* February 25, 1977, 19.

49. "The Irrational Fight Against Nuclear Power," *Time,* September 25, 1978, 71–72.

50. "The Nuclear Speed-Up," *Newsweek,* December 10, 1973, 137.

51. CBS News, June 9, 1982.

52. "In the Shadow of the Towers," *Newsweek,* April 9, 1979, 39.

53. "No Truce in the New A-War," 61.

54. "Meet the Nukeniks," *Newsweek,* May 14, 1979, 39.

55. "Question Around the World: When Can We Get A-Power?" *U.S. News and World Report,* September 30, 1974, 51.

56. "A New Hurdle in Way of Atom Power," *U.S. News,* April 15, 1974, 69–71.

57. "U.S. Dilemma," *New York Times,* October 11, 1976, A1.

58. "Who's Going Nuclear?" *Newsweek,* July 7, 1975, 26.

59. CBS News, February 7, 1979.

60. "The Peaceful Atom: Friend or Foe?" *Time,* January 19, 1970, 43.

61. "A City That Loves the Atom," *U.S. News,* August 25, 1980, 55.

62. "Atom Plant Safety—The Big Questions," *Newsweek,* April 9, 1979, 33.

63. CBS News, October 8, 1974.

64. *New York Times,* June 2, 1976.

65. "The Irrational Fight Against Nuclear Power," 71.

66. "Beyond 'The China Syndrome'," *Newsweek,* April 16, 1979, 31.

67. Sources included any reference to a group or individual used to provide information. This meant both indirect and direct

quotations, as well as any other reference that attributed information to groups or individuals other than journalists. We chose this broad definition both because the form of citation is largely a matter of journalistic convention, and also because this enabled us to gain the broadest grasp of where journalists turn for help in constructing a story.

68. This figure assumes that the total number is double that produced by our 50 percent sample of television broadcasts. It also excludes those with a government, industry, or interest group affiliation.

69. "Notes on People," *New York Times,* September 16, 1976.

70. NBC, July 8, 1973.

71. "New Nuclear Power Fears," *Newsweek,* April 19, 1982, 101.

72. Rothman and Lichter, "The Nuclear Energy Debate," 47–52.

73. "$380 Million and Counting," *Newsweek,* October 10, 1983, 30.

74. NBC, June 13, 1981.

75. "Growing Debate Over Dangers of Radiation," *U.S. News,* May 14, 1979, 25.

76. "All About Radiation," 40.

77. See the citations and discussion in Mark Mills, "Errors and Misrepresentations in ABC's 'The Fire Unleashed' " (Washington, D.C.: Science Concepts, 1985), 3–4, 14.

78. One last reminder that it doesn't have to be this way is provided by the *New York Times.* Of the seven media outlets we examined, America's newspaper of record provided coverage most in keeping with (and perhaps informed by) the perspectives of the expert communities. Yet the *Times* may also illustrate the interplay of professional norms and personal attitudes in shaping the news. For example, the relative lack of "spin" at the *Times* probably reflects its adherence to the traditions of objective journalism, and its resistance to the more interpretive styles we found elsewhere. But this very even-handedness, in citing roughly equal numbers of pro- and anti-nuclear experts, conveyed the false impression that the experts were split evenly on both sides of the nuclear debate.

Chapter 7

1. William Raspberry, "The Easy Answer: Busing," *Washington Post,* April 10, 1985, A23.

2. Millikin v. Bradley, 418 U.S. 717 (1974).

3. Columbus Board of Education v. Penick, 443 U.S. 449 (1979); Dayton Board of Education v. Brinkman, 443 U.S. 526 (1979).

4. U.S. Commission on Civil Rights, *Statement on Metropolitan School Desegregation* (Washington, D.C.: 1977), 6–7.

5. J. S. Coleman, S. D. Kelly, and J. A. Moore, *Trends in School*

Desegregation, 1968–73 (An Urban Institute Paper, UI 722–03–01, August 1975).

6. Lee Christine Rossell, "Assessing the Unintended Impact of Public Policy: School Desegregation and Resegregation" (unpublished manuscript, Boston University, Department of Political Science, 1978).

7. Diane Ravitch, "The 'White Flight' Controversy," *The Public Interest* 15 (Spring 1978), 135–36.

8. David Armor, "White Flight and the Future of School Desegregation," in W. Stephan and J. R. Feagin, eds., *School Desegregation* (New York: Plenum Press, 1980). The literature on white flight is voluminous. See also, for example, C. Clotfield, "School Desegregation, 'Tipping,' and Private School Enrollment," *Journal of Human Resources* (1976), 29–50; Luther Munford, "Desegregation and Private Schools," *Social Policy* 6, no. 4, (January/February 1976), 42–45; C. Rossell, D. Ravitch, D. J. Armor, "A Response to the 'White Flight' Controversy," *The Public Interest* 53 (Fall 1978), 109–15.

9. Armor, "White Flight," 36; see also J. C. Weidman, "Resistance of White Adults to the Busing of Small Children," *Journal of Research and Development in Education* (Fall 1975), 124–29.

10. D. Sears, C. P. Hensler, and L. K. Spears, "Whites' Opposition to 'Busing': Self-Interest or Symbolic Politics," *American Political Science Review* 73, no. 2 (June 1979), 369–83.

11. J. C. Weidman, "Resistance of White Adults,"; J. Kelley, "The Politics of School Busing," *The Public Opinion Quarterly* 38, no. 1 (Spring 1974), 23.

12. See Armor, "White Flight," for a detailed critique of the symbolic racism argument.

13. Department of Health, Education and Welfare, *Violent Schools—Safe Schools: The Safe Schools Study, Report to the Congress* (Washington: U.S. Government Printing Office, December 1977). See also M.J. Hindelang and M.J. McDermott, *Criminal Victimization in Urban Schools* (Albany, N.Y.: Criminal Justice Research Center, 1977).

14. J. Toby, "Crime in American Public Schools," *The Public Interest* 58 (Winter 1980), 21; J. Toby, "Violence in School," in N. Moms, ed., *Crime and Justice: An Annual Review of Research*, vol. 4 (Chicago: University of Chicago Press, 1983).

15. M. J. McClendon, "Racism, Rational Choice and White Opposition to Racial Change," *Public Opinion Quarterly* 49, no. 2 (Summer 1985), 214–33.

16. *Brown v. Board of Education, supra,* at 494–5 n. 11. See also K. B.

Clark and M. P. Clark, "Racial Identification and Preference in Negro Children," in T. M. Newcomb and E. L. Hartley, eds., *Readings in Social Psychology* (New York: Holt, Rinehart and Winston, 1947); H. Proshansky and P. Newton, "The Nature and Meaning of Negro Self-Identity," in M. Deutsch et. al., eds., *Social Class, Race and Psychological Development* (New York: Holt, Rinehart, and Winston, 1968); J. Porter, *Black Child, White Child* (Cambridge: Harvard University Press, 1971).

17. S. A. Stouffer et. al., *The American Soldier*, vol. 2 (Princeton: Princeton University Press, 1949).

18. M. Deutsch and M. E. Collins, *Interracial Housing: A Psychological Evaluation of a Social Experiment* (Minneapolis, University of Minnesota Press, 1951).

19. U. S. Commission on Civil Rights, *Racial Isolation in the Public Schools*, vol. I (Washington, D.C., Government Printing Office, 1967), 114.

20. Ibid., 202–4.

21. D. J. Armor, "The Evidence Against Busing," *The Public Interest* 20 (Summer 1972), 90–126.

22. Thomas F. Pettigrew, Elizabeth Useem, Clarence Normand, and Marshall Smith, "Busing: A Review of the 'Evidence,' " *The Public Interest* 30 (Winter 1973), 88. See also Armor's reply, "The Double Double Standard: A Reply," *The Public Interest* 30 (Winter 1973), 119.

23. C. Jencks, *Inequality: A Reassessment of the Effects of Family and Schooling in America* (New York: Basic Books, 1972), 255, 258.

24. H. J. Walberg, "Student Achievement and Perception of Class Learning Environments," (Boston: METCO, 1969); David J. Armor and W. J. Genova, "METCO Student Attitudes and Aspirations: A Three-Year Evaluation," (Boston: METCO, 1970); P. M. Carrigan, "School Desegregation via Compulsory Pupil Transfer: Effects on Elementary School Children," final report for project No. 6–1320, Contract No. OEC c-3–6–061320--659, U.S. Office of Education (Washington, D.C.: U.S. Office of Education, 1969). Robert Crain and Rita Mahard, "Desegregation and Black Achievement: A Review of the Evidence," *Law and Contemporary Problems* 42 (1980); Ronald A. Krol, "A Meta Analysis of the Effects of Desegregation on Academic Achievement," *The Urban Review* no. 4 (1980).

25. N. St. John, *School Desegregation: Outcomes for Children* (New York: John Wiley and Sons, 1975).

26. Ibid., 59.

27. Ibid., 85.

28. W. Stephan, "School Desegregation: An Evaluation of Predictions Made in *Brown v. Board of Education,*" *Psychological Bulletin* 85, no. 2 (March 1978), 221.

29. J. B. McConahay, "Reducing Racial Prejudice in Desegregated Schools," in W. D. Hawley, *Effective School Desegregation* (Beverly Hills: Sage, 1981), 18–36.

30. Ibid., 38–39. See also M. Patchen, *Black-White Contact in Schools: Its Social and Academic Effects* (West Lafayette, Indiana: Purdue University Press, 1982), 69.

31. *Boston Globe,* June 28, 1979; National Assessment of Educational Progress, "Science Achievement: Racial and Regional Trends, 1969–73," March 17, 1975.

32. J. S. Coleman, "Remarks on the Topic 'Court Ordered School Busing' " (speech before the General Court of Massachusetts, March 30, 1976).

33. The slightly lower level of support at the *Post* may reflect our inability to code the earliest years of *Post* coverage, when media perspectives on busing tended to be most favorable.

34. Again, this may reflect the fact that stories early in the decade focused most heavily on concerns for equal education, while the white flight debate heated up during the mid-1970s.

35. *Washington Post,* March 2, 1972.

36. *Time,* September 17, 1979, 76.

37. CBS, October 29, 1975.

38. "The Busing Dilemma," *Time,* September 22, 1975, 14.

39. CBS, February 16, 1972.

40. "A Lesson in the South," *Time,* November 4, 1974, 88.

41. *New York Times,* September 8, 1977.

42. *New York Times,* September 18, 1976.

43. "If Not Busing, What?" *Time,* April 24, 1972, 61.

44. "The Busing Dilemma," 13.

45. *New York Times,* September 18, 1976.

46. "Coleman: Some Second Thoughts," *Time,* September 15, 1975, 41.

47. "Forced Busing and White Flight," *Time,* September 25, 1978, 78.

48. *Washington Post,* March 4, 1973.

49. CBS, May 16, 1974.

50. *New York Times,* July 8, 1974.

51. *Washington Post,* March 18, 1976.

52. "Boston: Preparing for the Worst," *Time,* September 15, 1975, 41.

53. *Time,* September 12, 1977, 71.

54. *Washington Post,* May 31, 1976.

55. CBS, March 13, 1972.

56. "A Tale of Four Cities," *Time,* September 17, 1979, 78.

57. *Time,* December 23, 1974, 65.
58. *Washington Post,* n.d. #88.
59. "Desegregation Grades," *Time,* September 6, 1976, 64.
60. "Seeing your Enemy," *Time,* April 3, 1972, 46.
61. CBS, February 16, 1972.
62. *New York Times,* July 8, 1974.
63. Official political activity referred to any busing action taken by an elected or appointed individual or group at the local, state, or federal level. This included speeches, policy announcements, legislative debates, and voting. Grassroots activities were defined as those undertaken by citizens seeking to influence political decision-making, short of disruptive protest. This included voting, letter-writing, local organizing, and signing petitions. Nonviolent protest encompassed all disruptive activities by individuals or groups attempting to influence political decision-making without violating laws relating to persons or property. These included marches, demonstrations, and school boycotts. Violent protest included destruction of property, as well as attacks on students or other individuals.
64. School routine referred to activities associated with the normal school day for students, teachers, and school officials. These included classroom attendance, riding a school bus, and extracurricular activities, such as sports or cheerleading. Disruptive incidents referred to violent or destructive acts within the school, related to race or busing. These included physical assaults or destruction of property by students. Police security activities involved the use of police, national guard, or any other security forces in response to violent or disruptive activity in or around schools. This included stationing guards on school property, having them ride buses to protect students, et cetera.
65. *Time,* September 29, 1975, 48.
66. CBS, September 12, 1975.
67. *Washington Post,* May 31, 1976.
68. The later ranking of these activities should be interpreted cautiously, because there was a sharp drop-off in all media coverage after 1975, giving relatively few stories to rank for this period.
69. After surveying poll results throughout the 1970s, Sears and his colleagues found that only about 15 percent of whites typically supported busing for desegregation. The figures varied somewhat over time and according to different question wordings. The authors concluded, however, that "the overwhelming majority of whites oppose busing, no matter how they are asked about it." (Sears et al., "Whites' Opposition to Busing," 371). By contrast,

they found that blacks "are about evenly divided about it." (Ibid., 372.) The most recent surveys suggest that these conclusions are still valid. See, for example, Linda Lichter, "Who Speaks for Black America?," *Public Opinion,* August-September 1985, 43; National Opinion Research Corporation General Social Survey, Spring 1983.

Chapter 8

1. Lipset and Schneider, *The Confidence Gap.*
2. Anthony Sampson, *The Seven Sisters: The Great Oil Companies and the World They Shaped* (New York: Bantam Books, 1976), 313.
3. Ibid.
4. Ibid., 318.
5. A second distortion occurs in the calculation of depreciation allowances. Firms are permitted a tax write-off on the historical purchase price of capital equipment to provide for replacement. In periods of high inflation, however, this depreciation allowance is inadequate to cover actual inflated replacement costs.

   A third distortion is the underestimation of net worth or net assets. The profit rate is typically calculated by dividing the firm's net income by its net assets. Income, however, reflects the current inflated value of the dollar, while assets are carried on the books at their historical or original value. This makes the denominator in the income/asset ratio artificially low, resulting in an exaggeration of the profit rate.
6. U.S. Department of Commerce, *Survey of Current Business,* various issues, cited by Walter Mead, "Private Enterprise, Regulation and Government Enterprise," in Campbell Watkins and Michael Walker, eds., *Oil in the Seventies: Essays on Energy Policy* (Vancouver, B.C.: The Fraser Institute, 1977), 162. See also the discussion of price trends in M.A. Adelman, *The World Oil Market* (Baltimore: Johns Hopkins University Press, 1972), 160–90. Adelman's analysis is quite complex although he too finds the price trend was clearly downward from 1957–69.
7. First National City Bank, *Economic Newsletter,* April 1979, 5.
8. George Terborgh, cited by Harold Williams, "When Profits Are Illusions," *Across The Board* 15 (June 1978); 71–72.
9. A second consideration is the effect on net worth. Due to the magnitude of company income and the effects of OPEC price increases, the distortion in the net income/net worth ratio may be quite significant.
10. First National City Bank, *Economic Newsletter,* 5.
11. Other industries included, for example, drugs, clothing, chemicals,

building heating and plumbing equipment, lumber, glass products, and automotive parts.

12. U.S. Congress, Senate Committee on Finance, *Oil Company Profitability* (Washington, D.C.: U.S. Government Printing Office, 1974), 5–11.

13. For example, they are able to utilize depletion and drilling cost allowances to their advantage, as well as increase crude prices while maintaining unchanged prices downstream at the refined products level. John Blair, *The Control of Oil* (New York: Pantheon Books, 1976), 237.

14. Shyam Sunder, *Oil Industry Profits* (Washington, D.C.: American Enterprise Institute, 1977).

15. Edward J. Mitchell, *U.S. Energy Policy: A Primer* (Washington, D.C.: American Enterprise Institute, 1974), 91. See also Sunder, *Oil Industry Profits,* 41–49. For example, a firm with a high proportion of debt to equity financing will show a higher return on equity than a firm with a lower debt to equity ratio. The particular accounting method used to calculate depreciation allowances and the time pattern of a firm's cash flow will also affect the rate of return. Since each company has several accounting options, there will inevitably be differences in the interpretation of the data. Additionally, accounting measures of profitability cannot account for risk differentials between firms. A high-risk industry will exhibit a higher than normal rate of return to compensate investors for that risk. The oil industry is typically viewed as a high-risk industry due to the uncertainty and expense of the exploration phase of production. Other segments of the industry have a lower degree of risk. In addition, a high risk may be mitigated by tax write-offs for unsuccessful exploration efforts. A second risk component for investors is the industry's future prospects.

16. Sunder, *Oil Industry Profits,* 70.

17. Mitchell, *U.S. Energy Policy,* 93–95.

18. Blair, *The Control of Oil.*

19. U.S. Congress, Committee on Banking and Currency, Ad Hoc Committee on the Domestic and International Effect of Energy and Other Natural Resource Pricing, *Oil Imports and Energy Security: An Analysis of the Current Situation and Future Prospects,* cited by Walter Mead in Watkins and Walker, *Oil in the Seventies,* 134.

20. Neil Jacoby, *Multinational Oil: A Study in Industrial Dynamics* (Studies of the Modern Corporation, Graduate School of Business, Columbia University, New York: Macmillan Publishing Co., 1974), xxiii.

21. Blair, *The Control of Oil,* 77.

22. Blair bases his argument on ". . . the inability of the Iranian government to market oil seized from a concessionaire [in 1952], the failure of the Iraqi government to induce independents to take concessions . . . and the ending of a competitive threat from Italy and the subsequent subordination of the Italian government to the majors." See Blair, *The Control of Oil*, 77–78. In the case of the Iranian government's failure to market its nationalized oil, it is important to note that prospective buyers were threatened with legal action by the companies subjected to the seizure. They contended that the oil was their property until the Iranian government compensated them for the seizure.

    Similarly, the reluctance of independents to bid on Iraqi concessions can be traced to the legal dispute concerning the nationalizations. The U.S. State Department advised U.S. companies to stay out of Iraq until the legal questions were settled. Finally, the "ending of the competitive threat from Italy" was also due in part to unsound business decisions. See Blair, *The Control of Oil*, 93.

23. Jacoby, *Multinational Oil*, 124.

24. Neil Jacoby, "Vertical Dismemberment of Large Oil Companies—A Disastrous Solution to a Non-Problem," *New York Times*, cited by Barbara Hobbie, *Oil Company Divestiture and the Press* (Praeger Special Studies, New York: Praeger Publishers, 1977), 20.

25. Neil Jacoby, "International Aspects of Dismemberment," Statement before Subcommittee on Antitrust and Monopoly, in Patricia Maloney Markun, ed., *The Future of American Oil: The Experts Testify* (Washington, D.C.: American Petroleum Institute, 1976), 84. Hastings Wyman, Jr., compiler.

26. Jacoby, *Multinational Oil*, 172–211. It should be noted that critics have observed concentration occurring from vertical integration, the use of joint ventures, communities of interest, cooperative action, or government decisions that strengthen control.

27. Edward Mitchell, ed., *Vertical Integration in the Oil Industry*, (Washington D.C.: American Enterprise Institute, 1976), 41, 26.

28. See Richard Mancke, "Competition in the Oil Industry," in Markun, *The Future of American Oil*, 97–132; Adelman, *The World Oil Market*; Edward W. Erickson, "The Energy Crisis and the Oil Industry," in Markun, *The Future of American Oil*, 27–38; Walter Mead, in Watkins and Walker, *Oil in the Seventies*, 136; and Charles Doran, *Myth, Oil and Politics* (New York: The Free Press, Macmillan Publishing Co., 1977), 76.

29. Walter Adams and Joel Dirlam, Statement before the Energy Subcommittee, Joint Economic Committee, U.S. Congress, December 8, 1975, 2, cited by Hobbie, *Oil Company Divestiture*, 20. See also

Notes

Walter F. Measday, "The Case for Vertical Divestiture," in George Reigeluth and Douglas Thompson, eds., *Capitalism and Competition: Oil Industry Divestiture and the Public Interest* (Baltimore, Md.: Johns Hopkins University, Center for Metropolitan Planning and Research, 1976), 13.

30. Hobbie, *Oil Company Divestiture*, 121–44.
31. Ibid., 132.
32. This discussion was derived from Adelman, *The World Oil Market.*
33. Blair, *The Control of Oil*, 60–62, and Senate Small Business Committee, *The International Petroleum Cartel*, Staff Report of the FTC, 82nd Congress, 2nd Session, 1952, 244–65.
34. In 1972, the Seven Sisters produced 77.1 percent of all OPEC oil. U.S. Senate, Committee on Foreign Relations, Subcommittee on Multinational Corporations, 1974, part 4, 68, cited by Sampson, *The Seven Sisters*, 241.
35. Ibid., 297–301.
36. *New York Times,* September 16, 1979.
37. *Newsweek,* February 25, 1980, 60.
38. *New York Times,* April 25, 1980.
39. *Time,* October 24, 1977, 27.
40. ABC, January 23, 1974.
41. *New York Times,* June 3, 1979.
42. ABC, April 23, 1974.
43. CBS, April 22, 1974.
44. *New York Times,* July 1, 1979.
45. ABC, October 23, 1974.
46. CBS, April 23, 1974.
47. *Time,* March 19, 1979, 72.
48. *New York Times,* July 30, 1979.
49. *New York Times,* July 1, 1979.
50. *Time,* May 7, 1979, 70.
51. *New York Times,* March 29, 1978.
52. *Time,* February 28, 1977, 47.
53. *New York Times,* May 16, 1974.
54. *New York Times,* May 22, 1978.
55. CBS, August 14, 1979.
56. *New York Times,* January 17, 1974.
57. *New York Times,* June 19, 1975.
58. *New York Times,* October 30, 1974.
59. *New York Times,* October 24, 1979.
60. *New York Times,* July 18, 1973.
61. *New York Times,* December 30, 1974.
62. CBS, January 11, 1974.

334

63. *New York Times,* June 8, 1973.
64. *Time,* May 7, 1979, 70.
65. We will use OPEC as shorthand for this broader category, since this organization or its members were nearly always the focus of relevant stories.
66. CBS, January 11, 1973.
67. In her own content analysis, Hobbie found that *Time, Newsweek,* and the *New York Times Magazine* all gave at least twice as much coverage to anti-oil arguments and sources as to their pro-oil counterparts. She concluded that major periodicals "provided uneven coverage, often lacking in impartial information and perspective. The most visible sources and audible arguments were often seized upon uncritically. Nearly completely ignored was the testimony of experts who had made intensive studies of the oil industry." Hobbie, *Oil Company Divestiture,* 118.

Chapter 9
1. Gans, *Deciding What's News,* 306.
2. Hess, *The Washington Reporters,* 89.
3. E. Barbara Phillips, "Approaches to Objectivity," in Paul Hirsch, Peter McMay, and Gerald Kline, eds., *Strategies for Communications Research* (Beverly Hills, Cal.: Sage, 1977), 67–68, 71.
4. Walter Lippmann, *Public Opinion* (New York: Harcourt, Brace, 1922), 364.
5. Meg Greenfield, "Why We're Still Muckraking," *Washington Post,* March 20, 1985, 15.
6. Ibid.
7. Epstein, *News from Nowhere,* 206.
8. Cited in Richard John Neuhaus, "David Halberstam Tells Stories About Important People," *Worldview,* July/August 1979, 46–47.
9. Michael Robinson, "Jesse Helms Takes Stock," *Washington Journalism Review,* April 1985, 14–17.
10. Michael Robinson, "Future Television News Research," in Adams and Schreibman, *Television Network News,* 202.
11. Will Irwin, quoted in Roshco, *Newsmaking,* 45.
12. Gaye Tuchman, " 'Objectivity' as Strategic Ritual," *American Journal of Sociology* 77 (January 1972), 660–70.
13. Quoted in *Harper's,* January 1986, 19.

INDEX

337

Index

Gergen, David, 17
Germond, Jack, 26
Goffman, John, 61
Goldman, Eric, 13
Good, Paul, 151
Gray and Company, 27
Greenfield, Meg, 298–99

Halberstam, David, 17, 52, 122
Hart, Gary, 60, 124, 156
Harvard University, 38, 39
Harwood, Richard, 51
Hayden, Tom, 60, 61
Helms, Jesse, 18
Herburgh, Theodore, 235
Hersh, Seymour, 121
Hess, Stephen, 40, 43–44, 53,
  109, 127, 129, 297
Hewitt, Don, 150
Hobbie, Barbara, 264, 291
Hofstetter, Richard, 157
Hoover Institution, 56
Humphrey, Hubert, 157

Illinois Power Company ("60
  Minutes" program), 150–51
Indiana University, 40
Inglehart, Ronald, 35–36
International issues, journalists'
  opinions on, 32, 41, 49

Jackson, Henry, 273
Jackson, Jesse, 56, 156
Jacoby, Neil, 262, 263
Jencks, Christopher, 228
Jennings, Peter, 166
Johnson, Haynes, 110, 121
Johnson, Lyndon, 15, 17, 160
Jordan, Barbara, 56
Journalists: achievement needs
  of, 98–101, 109–17, 127–28;
  adversarial orientation of,
  114–17; demographics of, 21–27,
  46, 294; ideological
  self-perceptions of, 28–33, 42,
  45, 48; income levels of, 23–24;
  on media bias, 33–35, 40,
  54–55; needs for stimulation

and variety, 127–29; nuclear
energy attitudes of, 179–81,
183–84; observer/participant
conflicts of, 138–44; personality
traits of, 95–108, 120–21,
123–26, 128–29, 295–96,
297–98; personal relationship
needs of, 102–6, 126–27;
political affiliations and
opinions of, 28–33, 35–40, 43,
45; power needs of, 98–101,
109–17; preconceptions and
perceptions of news by, 63–71;
professionalization and
prominence of, 12–19, 23–28;
public interest motivation of,
117–20; responses to criticism
by, 120–23; self-image of,
51–53; social and political
outlooks of, 72–87, 294; on
social power, 37–38; sources
and experts used by, 55–63,
139, 209–14, 290–91, 296;
students' attitudes compared
to, 45–51; voting records of,
28–30, 39, 40, 41, 42, 48

Kaiser, Robert, 112
Kaltenborn, H.V., 139
Kendall, Henry, 61
Kennedy, Edward, 49, 60, 124
Kennedy, John, 159–60
Kennedy, Robert, 299
Kirkpatrick, Jeanne, 50
Kohut, Andrew, 17
Koppel, Ted, 301
Kraft, Joseph, 28, 33–34, 62, 123,
  124

Ladd, Everett, 32
Lang, Gladys, 16–17, 161–62
Lang, Kurt, 16–17, 161–62
Lapham, Lewis, 138, 147
Lasswell, Harold, 119
Life, 7
Lippmann, Walter, 6–7, 129,
  298
Los Angeles Times, 41, 42, 91

Index